THE LIFE OF
CARDINAL MERCIER

Un cher Lieutenant Commander Alyne Suat
en témoignage de gratitude et de cordiale
sympathie. + D. J. Card. Mercier, arch. de Malines

7 Janv 1919.

Mercier just before his visit to America in 1919

THE LIFE OF
CARDINAL MERCIER

By
JOHN A. GADE
Citoyen du Hainaut

ILLUSTRATED

CHARLES SCRIBNER'S SONS
NEW YORK · LONDON
1934

———

Nihil obstat
    Arthur J. Scanlan, S.T.D.
       Censor Librorum

Imprimatur
    ✠ Patrick Cardinal Hayes
       Archbishop, New York
         New York, January 6, 1934

TO

R. S. G.

IN GRATEFUL APPRECIATION OF TWENTY-FIVE YEARS
OF DEVOTION

PREFACE

Is it too early to form a proper estimate of Cardinal
Mercier's personality and work? Several of those who stood
nearest him have felt that a longer perspective of time is
needed for this, and some have expressed the opinion that his
life can be adequately appreciated only by one of his own
belief and profession. I have for some time had the conviction, however, that the great Cardinal's life should be
written while some of those who have known and loved him
are still alive to tell the epic, and that the witness borne to
his great and noble qualities would be all the stronger when
coming from a Protestant. I have been strengthened in my
belief that this work is not inopportune by the recent state-
ment of the man who is possibly the best judge in the matter,
Monseigneur Noël, the Cardinal's distinguished successor as
President of the Institute of Higher Philosophy at Louvain.
He says: "The time has come when Mercier's tall silhouette
should, through pious recollections, assume its full value as
a symbol and an example." In this biography, however, I
have not felt myself bound to pious recollections alone in
building up an impartial but sympathetic picture of the
man, Désiré Joseph Mercier.

I shall have ample reward for my long labor if the essential humanity of the hero of this volume becomes as convincing to the reader as it has been and is to me. Nor do
I wish in displaying his humanity to strip the heroism from
the character of the man—a task which it seems to me would

be impossible even for a biographer who is most sympathetic
with the ideal of "deflation" in biographical writing. André
Maurois says: "The cult of the hero is as old as mankind.
It sets before men examples which are lofty but not inaccessible, astonishing but not incredible, and it is this double
quality which makes it the most convincing of art forms and
most human of religions." It is the task of the biographer
to set the hero down among us and make us understand him
from his own point of view, and to show his relation to his
contemporaries and to ourselves. It is because the life of
this man has seemed to me to touch us all so closely if we
could but know him, not as the enshrined and awesome
Cardinal sternly defying the Church's enemies, but as the
man whose will and character were moulded by kindness and
strengthened by devotion to fine human ideals and sym-
pathies, that I have given myself to this labor of love.

My work would have been impossible without the assistance of Professor Robert P. Utter of the University of
California, who gave me first aid in the organization of the
material and the polishing of the English expression, and
Doctor Henry V. McNeill, a student at Louvain, who has
given me invaluable assistance in gathering documentary
material, and checking facts and impressions during my
labor of composition. I have been favored also with the
generous help of the Cardinal's sister-in-law, Madame Léon
Mercier; the Cardinal's nephew and literary executor, the
Abbé Joseph Mercier; his two old friends and colleagues,
Professor Maurice de Wulf and the Canon Armand Thiery;
Monseigneur Léon Noël, before mentioned; the Canon G.
Simons, Dean of St. Gilles in Brussels; Judge Georges

PREFACE

Heupgen of Mons; Senator, Father Rutten, O.P.; Professor H. Pirenne of the University of Ghent; and the Vicomte C. Terlinden, Professor at Louvain University.

I am indebted, too, for many miscellaneous items, to a number of former students and associates of the Cardinal who have been very generous in giving me the benefit of their intimate knowledge and personal impressions of the man in his earlier as well as in his later years.

I am deeply appreciative of the courteous assistance of Monsieur Victor Tourneur, the Director of the Royal Library at Brussels.

A word should be added concerning the translations, particularly of the public and private utterances of Cardinal Mercier, which I have used in this volume. For the most part I have made my own free renderings from the French originals, whose sense I hope I have conveyed clearly, but whose simple eloquence and unaffected force and dignity of style I made no pretense to have done more than suggest.

JOHN A. GADE.

ARGENTEUIL, WATERLOO.

CONTENTS

ILLUSTRATIONS

"Les evénements sinistres de ces deux dernières années ont secoué les âmes . . . le besoin d'idéal est devenu plus impérieux."—CARDINAL MERCIER.

CHAPTER I

IN THE BEGINNING

IN the time of Louis XIV, when Turenne was adding many a rich Flemish city to the kingdom of France, a family of the name of Mercier left the region of Cambrai to go north. It settled in the countryside just to the south of Brussels, where the villages cling thriftily to the hillsides, leaving the scattered plots of arable land in the wet lowlands to the hard-working farmers. The natural fertility of these patches of heavy soil the farmers keep up by the hoarded *fumier* and by ceaseless cultivation, sixteen hours a day in the long days of spring and summer. Here it was that in 1794 a young Irish colonel, Arthur Wellesley, stationed his regiment, the Thirty-third Moira, and here he accomplished nothing but to march up hill and down again after his commander, the Duke of York, whose name is a household word for such tactics in every well-regulated nursery. Twenty-one years later he was on the same ground again, himself a great Duke, and in supreme command. Here again on a June morning when the grain was in full promise of its best, English, Dutch, Hanoverian, and Belgian troops were arrayed against the last flight of the Eagle.

1

THE LIFE OF CARDINAL MERCIER

The Belgians stood to the right of the line, in and around the town of Braine l'Alleud, which exhibits conspicuously a pretentious barrack in ink-colored stucco, known inappropriately to the countryside as *Château du Castegier*.[1] Its garden is as barrack-like as its walls—a central pear tree with a corporal's guard of pollarded lindens on a parade ground of uncomfortable cobbled paths. Its owner at the time of Waterloo and long thereafter was a well-known figure in the region, for he was mayor of the town, but his neighbors did not call him officially *"Monsieur le Bourgmestre,"* nor yet plainly Francois-Joseph Mercier, but affectionately *"le Vieux Maire."* Master he was of a local industry, perhaps a tannery, perhaps a brewery, thriftily managed to enable him to lay up *"des rentes"* where they would do him most good. He was not too thrifty to be hospitable, though; his house was open, and whoso came to talk business or pleasure was sure to be called on to drink his share of a bottle of sound Burgundy. He was a solid citizen, on good terms with his neighbors, established and known in the land, for the family that came north from near Cambrai had by then been on the soil of Braine l'Alleud for two hundred years.

A son of the *Vieux Maire*, Paul-Léon, was incomprehensible to his father, and therefore a puzzle and a disappointment. We see him from the point of view of the thrifty tanner as silly and impractical. He reached out to the arts; he wanted to write; he wanted to paint. The painter Navez, from whom the boy had had lessons, had made him believe

---

[1] The building has now been turned into an old men's home, and the little square on which it faces has been named the *Place Mercier*.

he was a genius, so he wanted to go to Paris and fling the good tannery money into the Seine. He would have to see reason! Doubtless he was made to see it; there is no record that he saw aught else, little of happiness and nothing of success; his best of fortune was his marriage with Barbe Croquet, the daughter of the Toutlifaut farmer.

She was an angel, as all about her knew. After her marriage she was known not as the wife of her husband but as a saint in her own right, "the saintly Madame Barbe." Long after that time her saintship was proclaimed by her illustrious son:

My constant desire, my profound aspiration, was ever to be a better man myself and to lead morally upwards all those over whom I might have some influence. I do not doubt that this thirst for moral ascent was first instilled in me by my Mother. I am happy that a delicate allusion has afforded me the opportunity to utter here the name of her to whom, after God, I owe the best part of myself: My Mother, my sainted Mother! From her example, I learned dimly—unconsciously at first, later on consciously and clearly, that true love consists in forgetfulness of self and in devotion to others. It was in her heart, in the serene virility of her resolutions that I first read this great lesson of life: That man is nothing, that success and adversity are nothing, that God alone matters.

Indeed there was a strain in the family of the stern, tireless, selfless devotion that makes saints and martyrs, and Madame Barbe and her illustrious son were not its only exemplars. Her brother, Adrien, ordained a curé, had gone far and far afield, to the farthest wildernesses of America. He had found the path of his duty in the Oregon trail, and had followed it, literally and figuratively, to its end. The processes of canonization are not the same there as in Rome, but the result seems much the same. Indians and settlers alike called the Curé "the Saint of Oregon," and his seat is among the blessed in the Happy Hunting Ground.

Madame Barbe, too, had a fair field for the exercise of her saintly talents. The babies came one after another to the sum of eight. The first four were girls; the fifth was Désiré Félicien François Joseph, born 22 November, 1851, baptized Désiré, the son long-desired. Then came others, Jeanne, Elise, Léon. As the numbers increased the income diminished. The tannery slipped away, and so did the *rentes*. Two of the children died; the rest were brought up as best their mother could contrive. Paul-Léon died, and the town lost no more than a *Commissionaire-voyer*[2] and an unsuccessful tanner—if the world missed a painter of parts, it never learned the fact. Then for the family Mercier there was no more living in the Château Castegier; it went to the creditors. So Madame Barbe conducted her flock to shabby crowded quarters in the shadow of the village spire, whence Désiré and his little sister Léontine, in their black alpaca pinafores clattered daily down the hill, hand in hand over the village cobbles, to the school of the *Frères de Marie*. There the good Father Oliviers taught the boy the rudiments of Latin, and helped Madame Barbe to teach him lessons believed to be even more important than those of school. Between them, the two must have done their work thoroughly with the whole flock, for three of the little girls became *religieuses* under the names of Sister Margaret, Sister Silesia, and Sister Madeleine, and Léon became no less de-

2 Road inspector.

voted in tending his fellow men in times of illness and pain. As for little Désiré, if the Blessed Mother herself had come down from her throne to tell Father Oliviers what he was to become, the good curé would have found it hard to believe her.

Désiré was endowed with a sheer goodness of temperament, for which his mother, being what she was, probably did not flatter herself but thanked God. For all that, he was an entirely human boy, high-spirited, with a completely lovable personality, and an intelligent, inquisitive mind. He learned much from poverty. No other teacher could have given him his fundamental understanding of the hardship and miseries of humble folk which permanently moulded his soul in sympathy with them, a sympathy which went far to make him what he was. "Suffering," he once said, "accepted and vanquished, will place you in a more advanced position in your career, will give you a serenity which may well prove the most exquisite fruit of your life."

Much, too, he learned from Father Oliviers who was at one with his people, in his origin, and in his sympathy with their cares, their sorrows, and such pleasures as they had. Oliviers had nothing, claimed nothing for himself; his life and his fare were Spartan. His sympathy for his people was not measured by their sympathy for the Church. Whoever or whatever they were, he tucked up his cassock and trudged along the muddy *pavés* to advise and comfort them. For their souls and for the glory of God he intoned masses amid the damp drafts of his ramshackle church. From him, too, Désiré learned to smile, a human smile of pleasure in things of beauty, as when a flock of little red-cheeked girls came scurrying through the drizzle in their white veils to their first communion.

Désiré grew lanky and long-legged, and as his stature increased so also grew his duties. Almost from the beginning he had served Father Oliviers as altar-boy. This service and his studies took most of his time; in what was left he earned what he could, chiefly with his little pushcart, delivering parcels about the village. Often his only recreation during the day was the companionship he had with other children as they accompanied him and helped him on his rounds. No doubt he might have worked into business; no doubt Madame Barbe and Father Oliviers discussed the possibility, the chance that he might lift himself above the grinding edges of poverty, above his father's level, back to that of his grandfather. Or that of Cousin Edouard, who several times had been a minister. Or that of Uncle Simeon; if you wanted to see him, you had to get by first one watch-dog *huissier* and then another to come to his *bureau*, an inner shrine of the Ministry of Finance. An easy life, that, to sit all day at a huge baize table with a big inkstand, and then, to go home to a comforting meal and a pipe on the horsehair of the mahogany sofa. These fine gentlemen wore *redingotes* with little purple ribbons in their button-holes, and silk hats just like *Monsieur le Maire* at the *Pompiers'* drill or the *Fête Nationale*, and on the really great occasions they even wore gold braid. All this, for the boy himself his mother might have chosen, but the saint in her, and the ascetic in Father Oliviers must surely have ended their conferences on the subject of careers with the preference for the little Désiré of the threadbare cassock and the poverty-stricken flock of the village church. **6**

Other influences there were which tended to soften the hard life. There were vacation days without work or lessons when Désiré and Léon went for long rambling walks. They inspected the big lion, looking across the Waterloo fields toward France. They explored the lovely *Forêt de Soignes* where the pale columns of the beeches were as straight and regular as those of Ste. Gudule in Brussels. They wandered in *Monsieur le Baron's* park, with its trees of the wood rejoicing before the Lord, the "twilight bell sounding in the distance, seeming to mourn departing day."[3] They loved the sunshine when they had it, but scarcely less did they love the soft Belgian fog which painted the landscape in shadows on veils of silk, and turned the sun as it neared the horizon into a great ruby with fire in its heart. Désiré so often stood gazing into the distance, pointed so often to the sweep of the lowland views, that the boys nicknamed him "Panorama," the whole view. All this loveliness made itself a part of the mind and heart from which he spoke fifty years later:

And the birds of the fields, who can neither sow nor reap. —Does not our heavenly Father feed them? To the child who grows up in the country, such sights are very familiar. When you see them in the company of your mother, your heart grows tender and opens to confidences.

One day Father Oliviers signalled Madame Barbe eagerly to wait for him after the service. It was a real bit of news he had for her. He had been appointed Vicar of Our-Lady-Beyond-the-Dyle in the Cathedral City of Malines, where, as she knew, the great Archbishop lived. He had thought it

---

[3] *"Squilla di lontano, che paia il giorno pianger, che si muore."*—**Purg.** VIII, 6–7.

7

all out. Désiré, now twelve years old, might go with him to enter the College of St. Rombaut. After that he would go to the *Petit Séminaire*, then the *Grand Séminaire*, and then, said Father Oliviers with his benignant smile, then, with the grace of God and the help of Our Lady, Désiré would be ordained a servant of Jesus Christ. To Madame Barbe it seemed to open a view to her dearest wish, but seen through poverty such views are stripped of illusory colors. Where was the money to come from to keep the boy at Malines for twelve years of study? His contemporaries would be plowing fields of their own before that time had passed. Father Oliviers reminded her that large benefits may be the sum of small economies. It would not be easy; economies must be built into sacrifices, but it would be worth it. Perhaps an aunt or uncle would help, and God certainly would. Then there were the *bourses*, and the kind teachers who knew many ways to smooth rough paths. The weight of Désiré's own wish turned the scale, if the decision had been in doubt; so one day in the autumn of 1863, just before his twelfth birthday, he and Father Oliviers, with the blessings of all the village, mounted the diligence for Malines. It was Désiré's first departure on the road by which he was so often to return as a man for rest and happy memories. Now his look was forward, to school away from home, to him, as always to boys, a new world.

New as it was to him, the College of St. Rombaut which he entered as a day pupil is one of the oldest of the so-called "free" schools of classical studies established in Belgium, though it had not long been housed where he found it. After the agitation of the school question it was quartered in the building he was to know so well, of sandstone, its three gables fronting on the cattle market. Its sandstone is gray-green like that of the cathedral just around the corner, and there are shades of purple in the old glazing of its leaded windows. Close by, in the home of the Demoiselles Rydam, Father Oliviers found lodging incredibly cheap for Désiré. Here he soon learned the Flemish *patois* of the district from which most of his schoolmates came. Always the elegant scholar, later, when he was master of many languages ancient and modern, he had pride and amusement in his ability to speak Flemish in the accents of the street urchins. Mercier shared the hospitality of the Demoiselles Rydam with a lad of his own age named Scheuremanns. They lived together in the attic, and whenever either brought home a prize, usually a book of moral virtue, the Demoiselles would celebrate by baking a tart for dessert. The boy who shared these celebrations and the attic with Mercier is now a mild canon bent with age, who shuffles around the corridors of the episcopal palace, and still remembers how good was the Demoiselles' pastry, and how little difference it made which of the two boys brought home the prize, for they received equally generous portions of the festive tart.

The old canon remembers, too, that the boys were real boys, and that Mercier was one of them. They were natural, healthy specimens of their kind, normal in preferring recess to study. Mercier had a fine sense of fun, was fond of jokes and pranks, radiant in good humor, and of gay and buoyant spirit. We wonder how he could have sustained such *esprit* when we look at the record of the hours of toil he must have gone through to balance the scrimping and saving at home, to learn the astonishing amount he indubitably did learn then of French and ancient literature, especially Tacitus. Either he had before he went to St. Rombaut, or acquired as he entered its door, the faculty of concentration for which he was afterward conspicuous. Perhaps he brought with him, perhaps he learned at the school, the principle he stated so clearly in the later years, that the master faculty in life is not the intelligence, but the will. But how could a boy of twelve learn these stern lessons and remain a boy? Probably by the sheer resiliency of boyhood. The instruction in moral precept was catechismal:

Q. What shall your watchword be?
A. First, Order at all times and in all places; Second, Obedience to the masters; Third, Self-respect; Fourth, Silence in the Chapel, in the classroom and in the ranks; Fifth, Good behavior in public; and last, Christian Charity.

Here is a load of virtue that would break an angel's back. But it could not oppress the human boy; he throws it off and springs back to normal or a bit beyond. Mercier was human; a saint, perhaps, but the greater part of his saintliness was humanity.

Like every normal boy, he counted the days from one vacation to the next. The love of books was no rival in his heart to his mother's warm embrace, and the comfortable home meals with the sisters and brother around the modestly spread table, the day-long rambles in the familiar countryside. These days afield were not always confined to meadow and stream, but often included beer and skittles. The boys of the neighborhood, he the gayest among them, would walk together to some nearby village to bowl or play piquet or billiards for a rabbit or a brace of pigeons as prize, finishing with beer and lively talk at the *estaminet*. As time went on this group organized a club which became an important factor in the life of the region, The Catholic Association of St. Francis Xavier. Catholic it was in more senses than one; it took in without prejudice all classes of the five thousand or so who dwelt in Braine l'Alleud and thereabouts, farmers, workers in the textile mills, brickyards, and starch works, employers, clergy, students, old or young, they would march together arm in arm to a hall they called their *"local"* lent them rentfree by its kindly proprietor. Of these days he said later to his students:

One of the pleasantest recollections of my schooldays is that of the joyous vacation days spent with the workmen of Braine l'Alleud, competing with them for rabbits, and then afterwards eating the prizes in each other's company.

Such association was part of Mercier's identification with the classes with whom he worked, whom he was to benefit; without it he could not have been what he was or have done what he did. He became a Prince of the Church, but his outward rank was never so much a part of him as was the soil of the fields from which he sprang. And he learned of men from the book in which that knowledge is most plainly to be read. "The workingman thinks aloud," he once said; "his simple language ignores artifice. No one helps you better to read the secrets of the soul."

We see shaping influences, too, in his teachers of the academy at Malines. The headmaster was Father Pieraerts, who had probably never heard Lord Melbourne's cynical advice, "You had better try to do no good, and then you'll get

11

into no scrapes." If he had, he would doubtless have serenely continued to teach his charges that they had better try very hard to do a great deal of good if they hoped to go to heaven. Perhaps Mercier did not need the lesson, but surely Father Pieraerts confirmed it in his spirit. There was M. Robert, too, who taught him to obey; M. La Force, who taught him to work; M. Pieraerts who taught him to dare. If it was from them he learned these lessons, he owed his teachers much; but surely there are students to whom they cannot be taught.

It was in the autumn of 1868 that Mercier was admitted to the *Petit Séminaire*. If any American or British reader finds himself thinking of "seminary" in its genteel Victorian suggestion of "three little girls from school," he will form no guess of the rigors of the seminarian's twelve-hour day beginning at five-thirty and including but one hour of recreation. *Séminaire* is almost necessarily translated *Seminary*, but it is seldom anything other than a school instituted for the training of the Catholic diocesan clergy. These seminaries owe their foundation to a wise decree of the Council of Trent:

Every diocese is bound to support, to rear in piety, and to train in ecclesiastical discipline, a certain number of youths, in a college chosen by the bishops for the purpose. The institutions are to receive boys at least twelve years of age, who can read and write passably, and who by their good disposition, give hope that they will persevere in the service of the Church. Children of the poor are to be preferred.

To this original idea the Continental seminaries have held with remarkable fidelity. Their training is directly professional, and since the priest's profession is not only to know but to be, the seminary seeks to train its students not only in what they ought to know but in what they ought to be also. A liberal education is a necessary part of this training; quite as necessary are the manners and personal habits becoming to the calling. The aim of the *séminaire* is to turn out Christian gentlemen who know their work. The training extends through two schools. The preparatory or *petit séminaire* keeps the student occupied for six years, and then he studies philosophy for two and theology for four years in the *grand séminaire*. In the lower school are taught Christian doctrine, Latin, Greek, a modern language, rhetoric, elocution, history, geography, mathematics, natural sciences, and the Gregorian chant. The upper school has philosophy, theology, Holy Scripture, canon law and liturgy. The great majority of the secular clergy study in these *séminaires*, where the student's life is that of the *pensionnaire*, with no contact with his lay contemporaries except during vacations. Of the Belgian students, the more brilliant, either through means of their own or such as are found for them by the Church, continue their studies at the University of Louvain. Their formal training finished, the young priests are assigned either to parish duty or to a teaching office in one of the many educational institutions maintained by the Church. In Belgium, the upper and lower seminaries differ in that the upper are public establishments, civic bodies, the administration of which is subject to the control of the *Députation Permanente* as well as that of the central government, though their teaching proper is absolutely under ecclesiastical direction. The lower seminaries, on the other hand, are private establishments administered by the bishops, who owe no accounting of their stewardship to any but the Congregation of Studies in Rome, which is very cognizant of the status of each and every one of the seminaries.

The curriculum of the College of St. Rombaut overlaps that of the lower seminary to such an extent that Mercier and those of his classmates who entered with him had to complete only two years of philosophy and four of theology in the two seminaries. When Mercier entered the *Petit Séminaire* at Malines, it had some fifty students in the old buildings, which stood on the foundation walls of the old castle of the Lalaings. There was a new building under construction which had just then brought misfortune. The headmaster, the Canon de Beeser, had gone up the scaffolding to inspect the work, and had fallen to his death, and Mercier's headmaster, Father du Rousseau, had just succeeded him. The old buildings were of mellow crumbling brick and sandstone in the façade of the time of Henry IV, the inner walls inclosing court after court bordered with scarlet geranium and thick-grown holly where successive academic generations of boys run and shout, play handball and leapfrog. Among them move slowly the black-robed priests in conversational pairs, seemingly unconscious of the noisy life about them, actually alert to any infraction of the discipline of the hour. So it looked when Mercier was a student, and so it looked fifty years later when the tall cardinal coming upon it by chance would stoop through the opened panels of the big gate to forget for a moment the sorrows of the present in a glimpse of the past.

Mercier's program here was as crowded with work as is that of the American student with "activities," but a most important element of it was that which the American seldom learns—meditation. His first week in the seminary was given to retreat, devoted mainly to meditation in his cell, broken only by frequent conferences with his spiritual director, by visiting the Blessed Sacrament, and reciting the Office daily. He learned to begin his day with a half-hour's quiet contemplation, a habit which was to stand him in such good stead later in life, and which he was time and again to urge upon his clergy. To him *Cella continuata dulcescit;*[4] there, and there only he found the peace which passeth understanding; there he learned by experience that the best advice he could give his priests was that of the psalmist: "Commune with your own heart in your own chamber, and be still."[5]

After the first week of retreat, *laboremus* was the watchword, and that was nothing new to Mercier, either then or at any other time of his life. The day began at five or five-thirty and went on with meditation, mass with communion, breakfast at seven-thirty, four hours of class and study in the forenoon, four hours more in the afternoon, broken by an hour's walk or other recreation, and more study after supper. Then, when he had visited the Blessed Sacrament, recited the rosary and completed spiritual reading and prayers, he might stretch himself on his hard narrow bed with nine hours work and three of exercises of piety to his credit. On one day a week this rigid program was relaxed enough to allow the students a little more time for a favorite study, a little more exercise, or a visit to some neighboring institution

[4] "Thy cell, if thou continuue it, groweth sweet."   [5] Psalm iv, 4.

which might give them a foretaste of their future service.

Such were the auspices under which Mercier, at the age of seventeen, began his study of philosophy. It is not surprising that his first acquaintance with it left his mind dazed and dissatisfied. The outlines of speculative thought as they were then viewed in France and Belgium were blurred by the overlapping of the multiple systems devised by the philosophers of the time in their attempts to make a complete break with the past. Mercier's mind, like that of most earnest beginners in philosophy, sought clear-cut ideas, orderly exposition, a coherent system with an unshakable point of departure, and above all an intelligible relationship to life. His intelligence, which had found illumination and orderly paths in such realms of learning as it had explored, here found itself baffled, groping in a fog, oppressed with uneasiness and dissatisfaction. Only one light shone clearly for him in this bewildering maze, Father Tongiorgi's *Institutiones Philosophicae*. In it he found what vainly he sought in lectures and other reading, an exposition of philosophy clear enough to give him a rational and coherent spiritualistic system and an answer to current positivism.

The lectures were suspended from time to time at the seminary to allow the students to polish their intellectual weapons in controversial exercises. These were the public debates of the "Academy of Literature and Music" in which he who most ably, and in the best Latin, defended his thesis was proclaimed victor. All the proceedings were conducted in Latin, as, indeed, was the greater part of the curriculum of the seminary. Three times did Mercier win in these discussions, to the delight of even his opponents, for all had learned to love the big lanky fellow, who was joyous even in the lugubrious *Petit Séminaire.*

It seems incredible that he or any one could have been so. If it were merely a school for boys, it would have been incredibly stupid of the wise old Church to herd her fifty boys together and drill their minds and their spirits with so little heed to the flesh. But such was to be their future life, and if a candidate could not endure, it were well to find it out before it was too late. Mercier had been trained in worldly poverty and spiritual wealth till he knew no other way of life. The few still alive who knew him in the days of his adolescence all agree that the sensuous repelled him. Loose talk and manners, even among the rough-and-tumble farm hands and factory workers among whom he spent his vacations, seemed to pain him to such an extent that none of his careless companions who indulged in them once in his presence ever repeated the experiment. And it was not that he lacked virility or passion. Time and again when he was deeply stirred by injustice or wrong, those who observed him saw from his tight-drawn lips what self-control he was exercising. Had he not possessed the passion he did, much of his best work would have lacked the fire that made it successful and supreme.

In October, 1870, Mercier entered the *Grand Séminaire.* Here no more than in the lower school was there for him the slightest political preparation for the great European scenes in which he was to play so great a part. The fact that Europe was being reshaped did not seem to signify much in the cold bare corridors and cramped halls of the Malines theological students. For Victoria the calming tonic of Beaconsfield's flattery had been replaced by Mr. Gladstone's distressing and agitating reforms. Darwin was at work on *The Descent of Man.* Huxley was being drawn away from scientific research to public duty, feeling that the obligations of citizenship were more imperious than those of a teacher of philosophy. Herbert Spencer had declared that in religion the really vital and constant element was the sense of mystery, and that both science and religion must come to recognize as "the most certain of all facts that the power which the universe manifests to us is utterly inscrutable." The future of the Irish church was hanging in the balance. Ibsen had found Scandinavian bigotry and narrow-mindedness both ridiculous and hopeless, and so plainly told his countrymen. King Leopold II was dividing his time between colonial expansion abroad and the blandishments of Cléo de Mérode at home. The Iron Chancellor's dream had come true; his policy had triumphed; the German Empire had been proclaimed. Napoleon minor was waxing his moustaches at Chislehurst, while France was in the dust. Zola was giving the world—which swallowed hard—his first doses of sordid crime and realism to counteract the spun-sugar romances on which, it seemed to him, it had been growing unhealthily fat. The tiger was snarling in the streets of Montmartre; the Commune was spattering the pavements of Paris with the blood which was to them no new tint. Nietzsche, though still an undergraduate, had been appointed to a professorship extraordinary of classical philology at Basel. And Désiré Mercier was beginning the study of theology in the *Grand Séminaire* at Malines.

While Zola was writing *Les Rougon-Macquart,* Mercier

18

assimilated the substance of the Gospels, learned the Epistles of St. Paul by heart, acquired a sound knowledge of the Church Fathers, and an enthusiasm for Montalembert. Yet in the best sense he was nearer to life itself than Zola—Zola discovered life; Mercier knew it all the time. His talent for life and his love of the beauty of nature were so strongly planted and grown before he began his academic training that books served not to make him one-sided, but merely to round him out. He might go as far as he liked in theological and philosophical abstractions, but he could not lose contact with life, for he carried it with him. Nor could logic and philosophy destroy his faith, for he soon learned that faith is the beginning and the end of logic, that the acceptance of the axiom with which logic begins is an act of faith, as is also the acceptance of the unknown where logic ends. His intellectual insight went always hand in hand with a rare and profound imaginative sympathy. Study was apprenticeship for action. His deepest lessons were learned in the cell of the soul, "where silence makes you hear the voice of God." He observed the silences, and none doubted that he heard the voice. His punctuality, industry, devotion at all services were like the examples of early piety in the lives of saints, and no doubt his associates would have scorned him as a prig had not his humor, sincerity, simplicity, and sympathy won all hearts. It was not solely his academic merits that won him the approval of his superiors. He was marked for promotion. The president of the seminary, the Coadjutor Bishop Anthones, gave him first the tonsure, and shortly thereafter the minor orders. He was entrusted first with various small offices in the *Grand Séminaire*, and assisted the archbishop, Cardinal Deschamps, at Pontifical services. Finally he was made a sub-deacon, and it so happened that just at this time, Canon du Rousseau, needing a temporary teacher, called him in that office to the *Petit Séminaire* as one who could teach, inspire, and convert the boys. From January to October of 1873, Mercier served there as instructor. He received higher orders before he left the *Grand Séminaire*, but had not been raised to the priesthood.

It was to finish his preparation for ordination, and to prepare for even higher duties, that he was sent in the autumn of 1873 to the University of Louvain. Adrian of Utrecht had taught at Louvain, and had among his pupils Charles of Hapsburg. Later, Adrian became Pope, and Charles became Emperor. Adrian had a much shorter rule than his pupil, scarcely more than a year and a half. To his old university he bequeathed the house in which he had taught, which, by the addition later of other buildings on the property, became in time the College of Pope Adrian the Sixth. In the time of Napoleon it became a *succursale* of the *Invalides*, and was occupied by wounded soldiers of the Imperial armies. Now tourists gaze at it respectfully as the building where Cardinal Mercier lived and taught for four years.

Mercier's reputation had preceded him, for the affiliation was, naturally, close between Louvain and Malines. The great majority of the students either lived in the free rooms furnished them by the university in various places throughout Louvain, or came into town from their homes, for their day's work. When Mercier arrived, there were only two dormitories, the "Pope's College," where lived some of the lay students, and the "College of the Holy Ghost," which Mercier entered. As the young student of theology matured he was offered the position of *"sous-régent"* in the *"Collège du Pape."* This post corresponded to that of an "advisor" in our American universities. It became his delicate task to act as the spiritual guide of students intending to enter the various professions.

The following spring, in a mood of high spiritual exaltation, the young Abbé went to Brussels, and on April 4, 1874, the Papal Nuncio, Mgr. Cattani, assisted by the future Cardinal Vanutelli, ordained Mercier as a priest. As soon as possible he went to Braine l'Alleud, and on Easter Sunday he celebrated Mass for the first time in the little church where he had learned his catechism, where as altar boy he had swung the censer. Father Oliviers had come from Malines for the occasion. His mother could not go to see her dear hope fulfilled; she had suffered a stroke of paralysis; nothing short of that would have prevented her. But we may be sure the others were all there, the sisters who had come with Father Oliviers, the intimates of Mercier's childhood, those who had been the village boys and girls, now grown and wearing their best clothes. *"Ad Deum, qui letificat juventutem,"* he wrote in his diary; to God, who had blessed his youth, he dedicated his life.

His studies he dedicated to St. Thomas Aquinas. He was seeking anew what he at first seemed to find in Tongiorgi, unshakable ground under his feet and a system that would arm him for a successful attack on the forces of the time that were arrayed against his beliefs, materialism, positivism, pragmatism, Bergsonian mysticism. In the philosophy of St. Thomas he believed he had found the fundamental principle of an epistemology and metaphysics capable of refuting positivism. Long before external events had contrived to guide his interests in that direction, his faith in the soundness of that philosophy was already firm. But he expressed this belief most clearly in later years:

I am convinced that he who has the courage to pursue his philosophy to the end and to its logical conclusions, will agree with me that in the analysis of the very foundations of speculative science and ethical philosophy, no other man has ever thought or written with the powers of St. Thomas Aquinas.

This conviction was perhaps the best fruit of his studies. The staunchness of it kept his courage high, and gave freshness and energy to his presentation of his system of the other sciences co-ordinated under the leadership of philosophy, which won the sympathy and adherence of his pupils and inspired them with enthusiasm for their work. His own progress was measured step by step with theirs. In July, 1877, he became *Licencié en Théologie,* and defended his examination thesis with such brilliancy that his old friend in Malines, Canon du Rousseau, once more requested his services, recommending him to Cardinal Deschamps for a vacant position in the Faculty of Philosophy at the Seminary. Thus at the age of twenty-six Mercier once more returned to his familiar haunts in the cathedral town, looking forward to a long career in his congenial pursuits there. Once more promotion came quickly. Canon du Rousseau was promoted to the Bishopric of Tournai, and Mercier to his former master's professorship and the spiritual care of his students.

Some understanding of the elements which contributed to

Mercier's success with his pupils we may gain from one and another of his expressions of practical advice to them and to others.

Don't be superficial. Try to think logically and classify in your head in an orderly manner what you know you can retain.

Youth has always been the age, not only of initiative, but of audacity, surrounded by an atmosphere not only favorable to enthusiasm, but at times to digressions. At twenty, imaginative dreams and youthful ardor have not as yet met the shock of reality. The will suspects neither internal nor external obstacles, but is impatient for success, which is always slow in arriving.

So few men have the courage to question themselves in order to ascertain what they are really capable of becoming, and so few then have the will to become it.

Don't look back in the hope of gaining complaisant self-respect from the road you have traversed. March on! Proceed!

It is easy to read in these expressions phrases that have come into fashion—and perhaps out again—since his time, "the will to succeed," "the habit of success." But he did not try to erect them into an educational system that will work regardless of who works it. The principle is as old as life, but none can make it work save he who discovers it for himself. Mercier was one of these, and for five years at Malines it turned his students into his disciples.

Votre effort suprême doit tendre à développer votre personnalité, à réaliser le type particulier de perfection qui est le vôtre et qui ne doit ressembler à aucun autre.
                                                    —CARDINAL MERCIER.

CHAPTER II

DIVINE PHILOSOPHY

IN 1878, very near to the time when Mercier was appointed to his professorship at Louvain, Gioacchino Pecci, then nearly seventy years of age, was elected to the Papal throne of Rome as Leo XIII. In appearance he was the emaciated ascetic, with a skeleton-like figure, a parchment-like skin, but with glowing eyes suggesting the penetrating solicitous mind, the "depth of thought, tenderness of heart and winning simplicity" which Cardinal Newman saw in him, qualities by which he raised the Papacy to a prestige it had scarcely known since the Middle Ages. His earlier practice in the application of these qualities to administrative problems was in Belgium. At the age of thirty-three he had been sent to Brussels as Papal Nuncio. There he and that cultivated Nestor, Leopold I, had taken one another's measure and realized one another's worth. There he had needed all his patience and all his diplomatic skill to reduce the friction between the Jesuits and the Catholic University of Louvain over educational policies. Now he needed

24

them as never before, for he had the whole of Christendom on his shoulders.

And Christendom, as he viewed it, was suffering from a mind diseased to which he felt it his duty to minister. The rising tide of science was depriving traditional teaching of the very ground under its feet; there seemed scarce a rock left to cling to. Philosophic thought was to Leo a Babel of confusion, the realm of learning mere anarchy: philosophic processes were nothing but questioning, speculation, and doubt. Philosophy had lost its old authority to marshal all human thought in orderly ranks under its banner, a compact little group that the Church could keep well in hand. Science was scattering it in alarming disorder. Disturbing numbers were straggling after Kant and other harmful Germans. Cardinal Newman, no less than Leo himself, was convinced that he was living in an age of general and widespread unbelief, and to many another the Church seemed already defeated in fields of thought which it had scarcely felt itself called upon to defend. Moreover, at this time when need was greatest, strength was least to command. As a scholar Leo was offended by the low state of learning among his clergy, and as a reformer he was saddened by their low spiritual tone.

To find a remedy for all this, Leo looked, naturally enough, backward down the centuries toward the period of the Church's greatest strength, the Middle Ages. Then truth had flowed forth from the Church in a clear united current. How in the ages since had it become muddied and divided? Truth is eternal, and if the unchanging Church had it then, there it still must be. If in the Middle Ages the truths, first of Aristotle and Plato, then of the great scholastics, sounded in harmony with the dogmas of the Church, the defilement must come from the later thinkers. Men must have forgotten the veritable fountain-heads of true knowledge. The need was to hark back through modern philosophy, back through the decadence of the fourteenth and fifteenth centuries to the golden age of scholasticism in the thirteenth. Indeed, there were giants on the earth in those days, Albertus Magnus and Thomas Aquinas, surely the best and greatest of all Dominicans, their thought shaped by all the best in both pagan and Christian tradition. Both understood that faith and reason alike must lead to the One Eternal Truth; the methods of the two great thinkers differed though, and that of St. Thomas perhaps included the best of the system of the other. The Church could do no better than accept the Angelic Doctor, that Prince of Scholastics, as her great master in theology. The synthetic and orderly genius with which he had summarized, developed, and exposed the theology of the Church placed him far above the earlier writers on systematic theology. And was not his Aristotelian philosophic system equally acceptable? Did it not share the characteristics of his theological syntheses? St. Thomas' philosophy stood without modification in its fundamental tenets, the only system which so stood; it needed only to be known to command respect. Could not now all Catholic thought be unified by a system of philosophy sufficiently vast and compelling to dominate authoritatively, yet without violence, all human knowledge new and old? Leo saw his answer clearly in the work of Thomas Aquinas, who had realized for his own time the synthesis needed for Leo's. He saw a way to restore the full moral force of the Church by an intellectual renaissance wrought from within. And having resolved, he proceeded to action.

The first step was the encyclical of August, 1879, entitled *Aeterni Patris*. It urged the renaissance of Thomism on the Catholic world as a measure of common sense and scientific procedure, contrasting the philosophy of St. Thomas as pure gold with the tawdry tinsel of the modern philosophers, urging the return to his sound principles as a cure for the ills of modern thought. It argued that the marvellous progress in the natural sciences was from the beginning due to the unbroken continuity with which the acquisitions of one generation have been passed on to be perfected by succeeding ones. If philosophy does less than this, it closes the doors on its own progress. Descartes opens a new chapter in the history of thought by closing the one before, by casting aside without reflection the hard-earned treasures of thirty centuries of reflection. To follow such a process is voluntarily to reduce philosophy to the stone age. A look toward the past shows St. Thomas Aquinas standing head and shoulders above his satellites, who in turn stand no less above the moderns. One sees there a faith that completes the power of intelligence, and a philosophy that smooths and fortifies the road to faith. And philosophy not only makes the road to faith but gives to theology the organic structure of a science. Knowledge and understanding of sacred theology are easily and fully attained by one who joins to integrity and love of life a mind rounded and finished by philosophic studies. The duty of religious defense of truths divinely delivered pertains to philosophic pursuits. It is the glory of philosophy to be esteemed the bulwark of faith and the strong defense of religion.

The Church itself, the Encyclical went on, faithful to a constant tradition, had commanded Christian teachers to seek help from philosophy. Those who with the study of philosophy united obedience to their Christian faith were none the less philosophers, for the splendor of the divine truths received into the mind helped the understanding, and in no wise detracted from its dignity and liberty. Faith is opposed neither to reason nor to natural truths. St. Thomas, the master among the scholastic doctors, loved truth for its own sake, and clearly distinguished faith from reason, happily at the same time associating them together. "Nothing is more desirable or closer to my heart," said Leo, "than that you furnish to studious youth a large and copious supply from the crystal spring flowing in a never-ending prolific stream from the fonts of the angelic doctor." Not (he hastened to explain) that he advocated a blind and rabid reactionism, the disinterment of an archeological doctrine to be worshipped and maintained as dogma—far from it! But "every wise thought and every useful discovery, wherever it may come from, should be gladly and gratefully welcomed."

Such was Leo's survey for the modern road he wished to pave to revelation. The contempt of the calumniated learning of the Middle Ages which had begun with the Fifteenth Century Humanists was to give way to an enlightened study of its true teachings. The philosophy of its greatest master was to be restored to favor, to give unity to the teaching of the Catholic schools and command the attention and the respect of non-Catholic philosophers. Thomistic philosophy

28

was to be applied as a touchstone to modern thought to destroy what was unsound therein and save what was best. It was such a correlation of the everlasting principles of thought and being as Newman expressed later in his *Idea of a University:* "The comprehension of the bearings of one science on another, the use of each to each and the location of them all with one another—this belongs, I conceive, to a sort of science of sciences, which is my conception of what is meant by philosophy."

Having announced the plan, Leo proceeded at once to practical measures. In Rome he founded and endowed an academy in the name of St. Thomas Aquinas to undertake the teaching which the encyclical advocated. He caused to be brought forth a magnificent critical edition of St. Thomas's works. Now in Rome at least the right training could be had, and the influence of the Thomistic teaching could flow out to all of Leo's world. And as a gesture to show that truth has naught to fear, that his spirit was truly the disinterested spirit of science, he threw open the doors of the Vatican Library to all qualified scholars, churchmen and laymen, Catholic and Protestant alike. Then, when he looked about for other promising places in which to start cultures of the new leaven, he naturally thought of Belgium, where thirty-five years before he had entered so vigorously into the fray at Louvain.

The University of Louvain had developed a school of thought which might be termed original but not independent. It had reacted against the eighteenth-century empiricism of France, and against Kantian criticism no less. The Rector Magnificus, Laforet, as well as the philosopher, Ubaghs, felt that revelation was best defended against modern attack by the traditionalism of La Mennais and Bautin, or by the antilogism of Gioberti and Rosmini. The Church, however, promptly condemned these false *démarches*. None the less, as Leo's sojourn in Belgium may well have reminded him, Louvain was one of the few complete Catholic universities of the world. It had all the university faculties; surely he remembered that at its meetings which he attended as Papal Nuncio, professors of science, of philosophy, of theology, of law, of medicine, met and exchanged views. Very clearly it was a strategic point of the highest importance for him to occupy in his campaign against modern error. In 1879 he sounded the Belgian bishops as to the possibility of giving a special course in Thomistic philosophy at Louvain, and received an evasive reply. On Christmas Day of 1880 he wrote to them again, asking them not only to found a chair of Thomastic philosophy at Louvain, but also to found an elective course in it open to all students.

Cardinal Deschamps and his brother bishops deliberated long. That the request was unwelcome need be no matter for surprise; no one charged with the delicate balance of a university curriculum can enjoy having a sudden weight thrown jangling into it from without. Already they had at Louvain a Faculty of Philosophy and Letters, and neither they nor the students nor the public wanted another professorship of philosophy and certainly not one devoted wholly to Thomism. Where was the money to come from for a thing no one wanted? Philosophy of any kind harmonized little enough with the prevailing utilitarian tone of the Belgian mind, "divine philosophy" perhaps least of all. Thomism would indeed have little to say to Belgian students: the Belgian public, scholars, scientists, were all busy enough with the present, too busy to kindle to the thought of a return to St. Thomas and the Middle Ages, or to the ideal of pure scholarship, devoid of practical purpose. What did the parents care, or the students either, except that the boys should get ahead as rapidly as possible to the great business of earning a livelihood? They slaved and sacrificed for the education of their boys, not to bring them within reach of the high abstractions of philosophy, but of good solid Belgian francs.

When the Pope first raised the question, the university authorities felt that, if the thing must be done, the best man for it would be Mgr. van Weddingen, almoner of the court, a philosopher of erudition and some reputation. The suggestion that he should undertake the work, however, he dismissed for personal reasons, particularly his wish to prepare a book for publication. Since the Pope did not press the matter at the time, Cardinal Deschamps let it rest. It rested for two years. Then the Pope suddenly informed the Cardinal and the Bishops that he had sent at his own expense an able young Dominican bishop to begin the work he wished done at Louvain. That roused the university to precipitate action. If they must have it, better some one of their own appointment than one thrust upon them. The rector of Louvain, Pieraerts, made a quick decision—the young Abbé Mercier, inexperienced, to be sure, but undoubtedly the best man in Belgium for the work. A telegram stopped Leo's Dominican, who had by then got no farther than Trent on his way north, and Désiré Mercier was sent to Rome to report to and be instructed by the Holy Father. It was in the *grandes vacances* of the year 1882, and the Abbé was not yet thirty-one.

Spiritually and mentally the young teacher was well matured, but of the ways of the world he knew little or nothing; of any world, that is, but the little one of his own which lay between Braine l'Alleud, Malines and Louvain, the radius of Greater New York. Even of this little world, two-thirds was academic, professors and students, and the other third almost as completely out of the main currents, his humble family, and the village workmen and farmers. But his professional equipment for a man of his age was ample to justify the appointment. His intellectual experience was as large as his worldly experience was small. For a man who for no more than five years had been a bachelor of divinity, his knowledge of philosophy and theology might almost justify the term prodigious. Inevitably, of course, he paid for it the price that is always paid for great learning, the renunciation of a world which attaches much importance to itself, especially when it finds itself weighed against such things as philosophy and theology. But to Mercier things temporal were of trivial importance; things intellectual and spiritual were pearls of price. Small wonder, then, that at thirty he knew his Latin as well as he knew his French, that he quoted Aristotle, Socrates, and Plato easily in Greek, knew Huxley, Spencer, and Darwin in English, Kant, Schopenhauer, and Fichte in German, and Balmes in Spanish. It would have been hard to trip him on a quotation from St. Thomas or St. Augustine. Somewhat of this learning Leo had heard, somewhat, too, of the young Abbé's genius for teaching, his compelling influence upon youth;

enough, no doubt, to cause him to accept the hasty appointment and the recall of his own emissary as an act of Providence which had put the one usable tool in his hand at the exact moment of his need for it.

Slow of speech but energetic of gesture, Leo questioned at length in his grave, serious manner the gaunt young giant who smiled so winningly and was so eager to serve.

"Do you love St. Thomas?"

"Very much, Your Holiness," answered the Abbé with convincing warmth. "I believe I can answer that I have loved him in my past teaching. I can certainly answer with confidence that I love him now and will do so in the future."

Before leaving Rome, Mercier, upon the advice of Leo, spent long hours in conference with the masters of Thomism there and in Naples, with Zigliara, Liberatore, Prisco, and Mgr. Talamo. At length he completed his program for the new curriculum, and submitted it to Leo, who approved it with very few alterations. After Mercier had left Rome, Leo's comment touched characteristically on the essentials of the man: "I like that good Mercier," he remarked, "he is a most intelligent fellow; a pious man, and a man of great will power. What a sympathetic character!" It was not altogether Providence that enabled Leo to take up, as he so often did, the only tool on his work-bench capable of doing what he had dreamed and planned.

Mercier left the Holy City with a great vision and a great resolve. Could it be really true that the Pope had confided to him, Désiré Mercier, the execution of their common dream, the rehabilitation of Thomistic philosophy? His own Louvain might perhaps become the cradle of a great neo-scholastic movement. But his heart was sore within him at the thought of leaving his beloved seminarists. Louvain, now because it was newly his own, was for that very reason less so than Malines, within whose bare walls lay so much of his life of a time when life means most. His pupils there one and all had turned to him with their youthful enthusiasms and aspirations. He had in reality been their father, teaching them charity and abnegation, and leading them to the foot of the Throne. He had tried so hard to discover them to themselves and then to lead them to higher levels. Now he would have to desert them and take up life anew amid strife and dissension. It was not easy.

But before that he had still another task to do. His new work was to be a correlation of all that was new and true and all that was old and unshakable, of the new science and the old philosophy. The old philosophy was familiar ground to him, but he must have first-hand knowledge of some of the essentials of the new science. He felt the need of more advanced study of physics, chemistry, biology, neurology. He summed up his dissatisfied state of mind in a word to a friend, "Give me masters who can scientifically teach religion, and religiously teach science." To be such a one himself, he must go to the masters of science. There was Charcot, not only arousing local enthusiasm but attracting international attention by his clinical demonstrations at the *Salpetrière* in Paris and his published theories on neurotic cases, the most advanced work of the time in diagnosis and treatment of nervous diseases. On his return from Rome, Mercier did no more than to report to his Belgian superiors and say good-bye to his pupils and his family before he was off again, this time for Paris, the ill-ventilated clinic, and nearby lodgings in a *pension de famille* in the *Rue Notre Dame des Champs*.

He grew a big black beard, and changed his cassock for the highly proper though sober frock coat of the gay nineties. Who would ever have taken this for the ascetic Abbé? But instantly on his return to his room from lecture hall or street, the student would transform himself into the priest. The metamorphosis excited the attention of the agents of the *Sureté Publique*. Who was this lightning-change artist? What mischief was he up to? He frequented no suspicious resorts; he never so much as took a glass at the corner café. On the contrary, his habit was to stride into churches and pray, pray for hours at a stretch, then read in libraries, or study till early morning. None of this, they decided, was likely to work harm to Parisian society. They left him to his own devices. His time was short; he worked hard to make the most of it. He worked intensively on such subjects as the part played by the retentive and productive imagination, the peculiarities of instinct, the dual physiological and psychological aspects of internal phenomena. He mastered what he could of Charcot's teaching in the time at his command, then hurried back to the work that he was not to lay down for nearly twenty-five years.

It was on July 29, 1882, that Mercier was appointed Professor of Thomistic Philosophy at Louvain. At that time the last embers of the Gothic fires were still alive in the city, enough at least to tell the observer what a lovely place it must have been in the mid-fourteenth century, when Wenceslas, Duke of Brabant, made his famous *Joyeuse Entrée* into his capital, then busy with the looms of its many weavers. The university was founded by Duke John in 1423. A bull of Pope Martin V declared that "the University was founded so that those who will abandon themselves to the study of the sciences and of wisdom may perfect themselves for their own good and for that of others." It was extinguished during the French Revolution, in 1797, and not revived again until 1834, but except for this period of darkness its light has shone high and steadily for more than five centuries. Not long before Mercier took up his work there, the university had acquired by legislative act complete independent legal status. To the Church of Rome, the university owes much of its endowment and large funds for maintenance. To the university, the Church owes much that is beyond money, for during most of its life it has been the only Catholic university with a full complement of faculties. To Belgium its importance is no less. It is today as it has always been perhaps the only Belgian university with an international reputation, and unquestionably the most representative and best-known university of Belgium. It has a subsidy from the government, but it is not wholly controlled and supported by the government as are the universities of Ghent and Liège, and of the three it is the only one where the Flemings and the Walloons intermingle freely. This makes it a strong influence for national unity, which gives it its peculiar value to the government and to the nation.

Louvain was genuinely a university town in Mercier's time, with much of color and movement in its narrow cobbled streets. Of its forty thousand inhabitants, most of those who were not teachers and students were small tradespeople. In the days of its highest popularity, the university had had as many as six thousand students; in Mercier's years there it had some two thousand; more recently it has had twice that number. Of these, a very few were foreigners; by far the larger part came from all parts of Belgium, principally from "believing" families, and generally from the middle class, the *petite bourgeoisie*. In Louvain, as in all university towns, there was the everlasting dissension between town and gown, which flared up and died down again with small effusion of blood and vast effusion of language. Since the seventeenth century, when the industry of the weavers had declined, the university had dwelt in the beautiful old halls of their guild, and such residence colleges as had sprung up about them. Laboratories and lecture rooms were badly equipped, ventilation was poor, comforts which modern universities deem requisites were non-existent. But a disinterested zeal for things of the spirit had enabled its professorial corps to transcend material handicaps and take a high position in the life of the mind. The material world offered them little. The professor's salary was nominally four thousand francs a year, but from it was subtracted twelve hundred for the lodgings and other benefits provided by the university. Mercier's salary in American terms was some five hundred and sixty dollars to live on and to give from. Of necessity the social life of both teachers and students was on the most modest scale imaginable. A walk in the Heverlée woods during *l'heure de promenade*, an evening pipe, good and stimulating conversation in other professors' rooms for such teachers as sought it, and for the boys a game of cards or a stroll when lessons were done was nearly the extent of it. There

37

were meetings of the provincial guilds uniting those coming from the same Belgian provinces, and there were meetings of the musical and literary societies, but exercise and sport as known in American universities scarcely existed, and the introduction of them in the nineties met with the greatest resistance from the students. More important to Mercier than social relaxation or recreation was the library, which he had learned to know well in his student days. Among its precious incunabulæ were copies of St. Augustine's *De Verae Vitae Cognitione Libellus* and *Singularitate Clericorum*, and Cicero's *Officia*. There was many a fine commentary on that stout Stagirite, Aristotle, and other precious volumes made in Louvain itself in the earliest days of the printing art. There were manuscripts written by Thomas à Kempis and Denis le Chartreux. Mercier had handled them as if they were reliquaries.

Mercier was thirty-one years of age in the summer of 1882 when he returned to Louvain, young enough to approach the new work with buoyant energy and hope, mature enough to face squarely the obstacles to its success. He would have to build his structure from the very foundations, and carry every stone himself. He must find students for himself. Neither theological students nor laymen would flock to a course of three or four years superimposed on the work already before them. Theological students considered that they had finished their philosophical studies in the seminaries; lay students did not demand them except for an elementary course in philosophy preparatory to the study of law. He would have to find money for courses which nobody seemed to want, courses in an unpopular subject to

be given at unpopular hours, for, in order not to interfere
with the established curriculum, he had to schedule his lectures for early morning hours. He would have to write his
own text-books. He would have to perfect his own knowledge of science. All these were to him the details of organization of his single-handed attack on the philosophic and
intellectual tendencies of the time; he viewed them not as
lions in the path, but as obstacles to be surmounted. Of his
equipment in the mediæval side of his studies he felt well
enough assured. If Thomism as taught in the seminaries
was proving too weak to withstand attacks on it by modern
thinkers, the weakness surely was not that of St. Thomas,
but of the teachers who did not understand their master.
More often than not, he felt, their teaching represented less
the thought of St. Thomas than that of successive com-
mentators, who, in résumés of résumés had reduced his doctrine to a series of meaningless simplistic formulæ. It was
in the name of scientific rigor that the Pope insisted, and
Mercier no less, that Thomism should return to St. Thomas.

Mercier soon made his voice heard outside the classroom.
In the *Revue Catholique des Idées et des Faits* he published
a series of articles on "Mechanical Determinism and Liberty." Perhaps it was to do honor to the author of these
articles, perhaps to lend authority to the voice of youth that
on July 26, 1882, the university authorities conferred upon
Mercier the degree of Doctor of Philosophy and Theology.
On August 12, he was made Honorary Canon of Malines.
The numbers in his courses increased. His course in Thomistic philosophy was prescribed for all the theological students. The lay students began to enter, at first probably

attracted largely by curiosity, but then held by the energy
and sympathy of the lecturer. In his opening lecture he
announced his principle:

Although we have given our course the name of the Great
Scholastic, we do not hold that Thomistic philosophy is
either an ideal which we cannot surpass or a barrier limit-
ing mental activity. We do, however, believe, upon examination, that it is as wise as it is modest to take it as a point of
departure and support. This has been said in reply to those
among our adversaries and our friends, who believe it at
times interesting to ask if we intend to make the human
mind return to the Middle Ages or to identify philosophy
with the thought of a philosopher.

And again he stressed the principle of living growth in
philosophic study:

Philosophic thought is never completed. It remains as
living as the spirit which conceived it. It is no mummy
wrapped up in a tomb in front of which we merely have to
mount guard. It is an organism which is ever young, always active, which personal effort must maintain and sus-
tain in order to insure its perpetual growth.[1]

Great teachers, like all great men, are born, not made.
Certainly Mercier was born with the gift of teaching in his
soul. He was a teacher in the profoundest sense of the
word, for his greatest happiness lay in developing not only
the minds of his pupils, but their souls as well. In this
sense, as a leader and inspirer, he was a teacher all his life,
not merely while at Malines and Louvain.

His ability as a teacher in the narrower sense of the word,
an imparter of intellectual knowledge, was very great. There

[1] *Le Bilan Philosophique du XIX Siècle.*

was no subject that he touched upon, however complex and abstruse, that the youthful canon did not make simple and understandable. He thrilled his hearers by the earnestness and assurance of his manner, and by the logical development of his ideas. His enthusiasm and informal manner broke down the customary barriers between teacher and pupil. It was a quality in him perhaps best described by the Italian term *simpatico*. His lectures were a brilliant display of intellectual powers, while his manner of delivery revealed the human warmth and light that ever glowed through his logical precision. He talked in a language every one understood; students of law, of medicine, and of the various branches of the sciences were astonished to hear him speaking their own technical languages, and formulating the most recent scientific discoveries in the time-honored phrases of St. Thomas. He had the genius to speak of St. Thomas in terms of modern science, and of the latest scientific innovations in terms of the mediæval scholar. This was because he had a clear perception of the vital issues, so that he was not confused by the errors of the contemporary philosophers, but with a sure hand cleared away the obscuring falsehoods, revealing in their naked simplicity the great Thomistic truths. Through his constant study of Aristotle and St. Thomas he retained his contact with and mastery of what were to him the living, fundamental realities. No matter how far he penetrated into thin-spun metaphysical speculations, his logical consistency prevented him from losing sight of his starting point, which was always human experience. Philosophy was not to him a collection of obscure musings, but a systemized and rational view of reality. He therefore remained consistent both with his premises and with the fundamental teachings of his masters from whom he learned. He never escaped a difficult problem by obscuring the issue. Nor was he one to crawl in the ruts of habit or of tradition. In this way he combined a freshness and spontaneity of thought with intellectual rigor and adherence to the principles of St. Thomas. One of his pupils, M. Deploige, in his toast at the banquet given after Mercier's Episcopal consecration, said of him,

His lectures were never conventional, never studied, never stilted. What he said was always free and spontaneous, drawn from his truest and most intimate spiritual experiences, and from his sincerest thought. That was the way he guided and taught you.

He could make all his happy-go-lucky boys feel

How charming is divine philosophy!
Not harsh and crabbed, as dull fools suppose,
But musical as is Apollo's lute.

One of these boys, now a distinguished scholar, describes Mercier's teaching quality and methods:

Like a shrewd teacher, thoroughly versed in his subject, he managed to elucidate the most complex theories by simple comparisons and familiar examples. To clarity and simplicity of exposition, he added precise diction, commanding the attention of every one and making the hardest subject seem easy. Gentle, friendly Professor Mercier was just another comrade among younger ones. His students adored him. The authority he enjoyed from his recognized scholarship, his perspicacity, and his tact more than offset anything lacking in him on the score of age.

Another of his pupils of this time, who is now a white-haired biblical authority, tells the following anecdote which illustrates Mercier's love and tact in dealing with his pupils:

He had a way with him. How well I remember handing in a thesis with the sinking feeling that my lack of study would at once be noticed by Monseigneur Mercier. I expected the worst a few days later when he beckoned to me after the lecture, to invite me to after-lunch coffee in his study. Once there, his conversation was so fascinating that I forgot my anxiety, and it was not until I prepared to say good-bye that he returned my thesis to me. As he did so, he wrote on the cover: "II Thess. III—10." I rushed to my cubicle to open the Bible by my bed. Turning to the reference, I read: "For even when we were with you, this we commanded you, that if any would not work, neither should he eat." The humor and the kindliness of the criticism has followed me through life.

Young van Cauwelaert, who was acting as his secretary, was an enthusiastic Fleming. He gave vent to his feelings by a none-too-discreet public speech on the inflammable *Flamingant* subject. The matter came to the ear of the Cardinal who in turn instructed Professor Mercier to reprimand his young charge. After reasoning with the lad, who was later to become the eloquent burgomaster of Antwerp, a bony hand finally descended on the boy's shoulder: "I much prefer," said Mercier, "a young man who has a different ideal from my own, to one without an ideal."

Mercier himself was modest about his own powers of leadership. He insisted that the most he could do was to lead the way. The achievements of his followers must be brought about by their own efforts. And these efforts, he knew, must be their very best if they were going to master the obscure profundities of philosophy. He assured them he would do his best to help them over the rugged and unfamiliar paths they must climb. But he could not carry them. With him as guide, they must accomplish their ascent on their own feet or not at all.

It was perhaps this insight into the real quality of leadership that made him more than a mere imparter of knowledge to passive minds. Knowing that successful teaching requires activity on the part of the pupils as well as on the part of the teacher, he undertook to see that his pupils were inspired to sincere and honest mental activity of their own. As soon as he finished his lecture-work for the day, he went home to his quarters in the *rue des Flamands*, where pupil after pupil would follow him, all bursting with questions about difficulties in the lectures and knowing full well that their confusions would soon be cleared. Thus there soon arose a little discussion group called the *Cercle d'Étude*, which met weekly for informal discussions. In this way a means of intercourse was established between pupils and teacher which was not possible in the lecture hall alone. No matter how confused the student nor how naïve the question, Mercier was never anything but patient, kind, and understanding. The shy ones forgot their embarrassment in his encouraging smiles; the alert and forward ones found here an opportunity to exercise their mental powers to their fullest capacity. For the stimulation and guidance of the boys' scholarship Mercier introduced the practice of having each student expound some aspect of his work followed by a critical discussion in which he defended it against the attacks of his classmates. As a result of this happy intimacy,

Mercier came to be known to the boys as *Le Grand Sympathique*, instead of by the imposing title of *Monsieur le Chanoine* or *Monsieur le Professeur*.

More than an intellectual inspirer, he was a moral inspirer as well. He never missed an opportunity to give his boys a helping hand. Prayer had revealed to him, as it had to St. Thomas, other realms besides the intellectual.

> To pray with saints yet press the sinner's hand,
> This was thy aim and this thy constant goal.
> One word will sum thy life up round and whole:
> All longings fail save that to understand.[2]

To Mercier it was quite as important a function of education to establish a proper sense of values in his pupils' minds as to establish the proper principles of discovering truth. He had well learned the lessons of the *Salpetrière*, so that he knew that no two individualities are alike. Well he knew how to adjust his teachings to the various needs and capacities of his pupils. It was his superior insight into the psychology of human nature that enabled him to know so well the human heart, and to become, like his Master and Teacher, an inspiration to his pupils to mold their moral lives in accordance with the sublime truths to which in the classroom he gave them mere intellectual guidance. For he believed with Milton "that depth in philosophy bringeth men's minds about to religion." He was always a fisherman of men, always absorbed in the endeavor to inspire and lead them to the Truth. He yearned to make all these future priests, lawyers, doctors, and scientists who were his pupils,

[2] Gamaliel Bradford in a sonnet to Sainte-Beuve.

into servants of Jesus Christ. No matter what their calling was to be, he hoped that the finding of God would prove to be the supreme event in their lives. His untiring efforts in this direction have borne rich fruit. Many a leading man of Belgium today has been led to the divine illumination through Mercier's devotion to the cause of conversion.

In addition to his advanced course in philosophy, Mercier after a while gave a broader one in the same subject, meant particularly for the boys studying law. He was also appointed *"assesseur du vice-recteur,"* a position somewhat similar to the Oxford proctor, in which he was in charge of the boys' moral behavior.

Of course he had all kinds of boys, brilliant, stupid, colorless, and even a few that had fallen into the ways of dissipation. He was interested in them all in different ways. The keenest minds he hoped to inspire to open new paths that would lead to the enrichment of human knowledge; he hoped to kindle in their hearts the fire of disinterested scholarship that would be kept burning from generation to generation. On the other hand, to bring the strayed sheep back to the fold was just as important to him. One of the youths whom Mercier had reclaimed from his ways of error, confided forty years later, when he had become a distinguished national leader, how he had been brought to his senses one evening in the teacher's study. Clutching the boy by the shoulders with bony hands, his glowing eyes piercing the soul of the youth, Mercier vividly pictured how the boy was breaking his mother's heart. The impression was deep and lasting. The boy gave over his wild ways and began his serious life work. Sometimes, when among those who he feared might be wasting their energies by sowing wild oats, he would say, "Imagine that Christ stood in your midst, and said to each one of you, '*Voco te*,' 'I call you.' What would you reply to Him?"

His sympathy was so all-embracing that it was not confined to members of the church. Even where he could not convert, he was a ready sympathizer, an understanding helper, and a warm friend. Gerard Herry, in the *Annales Politiques et Littéraires* of February, 1926, tells the following anecdote which illustrates his ready sympathy with all men, no matter what their religion:

Mercier went to call one day on Meunier, the great painter and sculptor, who had recently been lecturing on Fine Arts at the university, despite the fact that he was not a practising Catholic and that he was a man of most original ideas. Meunier was surprised to see who his caller was, but soon found that the cleric Mercier was really an artist as well, keenly appreciative of Meunier's sketches and paintings, an enthusiastic talker about art. The two had a long discussion about æsthetics and philosophy. Mercier realized that this man was portraying the nobility of labor, was doing just what he himself hoped to do with words, and that in every work of art that Meunier created there was a definite moral good. And Meunier in his turn realized that the long-skirted clerical garb of Mercier's did not prevent him from entering into Meunier's own vision of things. Finally, just as Mercier was reluctantly about to leave, he remembered his mission. He told Meunier that he had almost forgotten to tell what he had come for.

"*Enfin!*" said Meunier in astonishment.

So Mercier disclosed the reason for his coming. It was because the son of one of his very devout Catholic friends wished to marry Meunier's daughter, and Mercier had felt such a union could only end unhappily on account of the religious differences. But now he had changed his mind. It was the spirit not the form that mattered. Perhaps he remembered the counsel of St. Augustine, that many people who seem to be outside the Church are really in it. In his visit with Meunier he had been able to penetrate beneath mere external appearances and to see the essential moral value of the man beneath his atheism.

"You see," said Mercier, "I almost made a great mistake. I don't care what you think you believe or don't believe. Now that I know you, I salute in you a Christian, as truly so, in the real meaning of the word, as the professing Catholic. *Au revoir! A bientôt!* I leave you to plead your daughter's cause."

Not only did Mercier give the young couple his blessing, but he paid many a subsequent visit to the great sculptor's atelier.

Besides his rare qualities as a teacher and inspirer of men, he possessed the generosity of great scientists and thinkers, for he gave lavishly of his whole lifework. This was what he gave to his Louvain pupils, his whole self. During the Great War, an American was sitting in Mercier's study. With his usual graciousness Mercier talked about the members of the Relief Commission who had given food and work and devotion. The young American ventured that he and his countrymen were, after all, only doing their duty, and they felt distressed that they and their countrymen were not as yet fighting. The Cardinal suddenly became abstracted, as if struck by a profound thought. Then he smiled, and said, wishing to make clear to his guest the truth he felt concerning generosity,

"Yes, we must not only give what we *have*, we must also give what we *are*."

In the midst of all this teaching and apostolic work, Mercier was himself studying as hard as the most studious of his pupils. His mantelpiece bore the inscription, *Labora sicut bonus miles Christi*, "Work like a good soldier of Christ." He followed this advice, becoming himself a student as soon as he stepped down from the lecture platform. He studied neurology under Van Gehuchten, chemistry under Paul Henry, mathematics under Mansion, and biology under Van Beneden. The laboratory work or the lecture over, Mercier would discuss with his teachers at length the relation between science, philosophy, and faith. He would tell them his view of psychology, that it was a living science, which to advance must not separate itself from the biological and anthropological sciences. These scientists marvelled at the priest's audacious genius, for he was years ahead of his time in correlating Aristotelian vitalism with modern biology. Moreover, his correlation of science with philosophy was equally audacious and brilliant, for he insisted that the value of the sciences depended in great part upon philosophy. He realized that the endless modern scientific discoveries, though unknown to his beloved St. Thomas, were perfectly submissive to the Thomistic synthesis. He knew that all science was a loyal search by the varied resources of the mind for the truth which is essen-

tially one. The eminent scientists with whom he worked soon
accepted the priest as a welcome co-worker in their special
fields of experimental science, and recognized that in his own
realm of metaphysical speculation, Canon Mercier towered
above them all.

"Seules les forces intellectuelles et morales d'une nation fécondent sa prospérité."—CARDINAL MERCIER.

CHAPTER III

THE WORLD AND THE SPIRIT

IN the beginning of his work at Louvain, Mercier received the full approval of the Pope. In 1886 he was appointed a member of the Roman Academy of St. Thomas Aquinas. The following year, Leo, acting *motu proprio*, made him a domestic prelate, an office which gave him the title of Monseigneur.

The feeling of his superior officers at Louvain had in it at the outset more of pity than of sympathy. The rector, Pieraerts, was Mercier's old friend; he had no lack of vision or courage, and the spirit of Mercier's teaching was entirely in conformity with that of the university. Still, the project was one which had been thrust upon them, and the university authorities were incredulous of its success. It was natural, no doubt, that they should not at once put all their energy into it. Neither did they regard it with any hostility; rather they seem to have looked upon Mercier at first with commiseration, as one leading a forlorn hope.

A forlorn hope indeed it may have seemed in one or another of its aspects. To oppose a mediæval religious philosophy to the whole impact of modern science and thought might seem about as effective as to try to stop an express train with a feather. Mercier, however, was ready for any

51

forlorn hope so long as there was hope. There was no lack in his spirit of the will to succeed. In 1888, the Pope had written his first letter to the authorities, outlining the scheme of his "Institute." Mercier, too, felt the need for a larger organization to carry on the work he had started. Probably his equipment was as good as any one man could carry, but it became clear to his mind that one man and one course were not enough. There must be a corps of well-equipped specialists in the diverse disciplines, particularly in the sciences, men of sympathy and energy offering courses co-ordinating and interlocking with his and with each other. With such help, Mercier felt, he could overcome all difficulties. After arduous days of teaching, he spent night hours in planning the organization he wished, and at length laid the plan before the Pope. Pope Leo smiled upon the eager young professor's project, and in the summer of 1892 praised him in a brief directed to him personally.

It was not till Mercier had the Pope's approval of his plan that he laid it before a sectional meeting of the Catholic Congress which was being held at Malines. Though the young philosopher's eloquent presentation of his scheme was applauded by many, the bishops shook their heads. Naturally, since he had been so far insubordinate as to submit it directly to Leo, they looked upon it coldly. And it was not unreasonable for them to challenge the undertaking of a whole institute to teach a subject for which there was hardly support enough or students enough to justify a single course given by one professor. The bishops, then, felt that Mercier was inflating himself and his work unwarrantably. They would not promise him students transferred from the diocesan seminaries, or any other form of help. Probably their cordiality toward the project was not increased by the fact that Mercier's proposals were upheld by the Pope, who wrote to the bishops and administrative officers of the university to tell them that he wished an institute established at Louvain according to Mercier's plan and with Mercier at its head.

This strengthened Mercier's hands, but by no means smoothed his path. He was not, however, the man to turn away from opposition. Difficulties never turned him back; rather they lured him on. They made him what he was, for they furnished the heat that tempered the steel that was in him.

Mercier's superior officers in Belgium were the rector and the council of the university, and less directly, the College of Bishops. The rector is appointed by the College of Bishops. He is responsible to them for the government of the university, in which he is aided by the council, which consists of the deans of the faculties of theology, law, philosophy, and letters, and the presidents of certain schools within the university (now including the *Institut Supérieur de Philosophie*). Mercier's old friend Pieraerts, who was rector at the time of Mercier's first connection with the university, had died, and Mgr. Abbeloos had succeeded him. Mercier's first relations with him were friendly enough, but it soon began to appear that Abbeloos's personality was what is sometimes called "difficult"; that is, it was not easy for those whose opinions differed from his to keep on easy terms with him. Mercier, naturally, felt himself pretty directly under the orders and supervision of the Pope in beginning and carrying on his work at Louvain. No less naturally this appeared to Abbeloos a dangerous division of authority, tending to the erection of a state within a state. It was inevitable that this should lead to a feeling of jealousy on his part; a feeling that the Pope was more interested in Mercier's work than in the prosperity of the university as a whole. Leo's Brief of November, 1889, had founded Mercier's school at Louvain; another in 1894 established it as an integral part of the university under the name of the *Institut Supérieur de Philosophie ou l'École Saint-Thomas d'Aquin*, and named Mercier as its first president.

Mercier began the organization of the institute by obtaining the collaboration of several professors who were teaching various scientific subjects in the university. He soon found, however, that his staff was composed of men of divergent views, not in full agreement among themselves, and by no means at one with him in his project. Particularly unfortunate in this respect was his choice of a colleague in his own subject, philosophy. He found himself trying to work with a man whose ideas did not at all harmonize with his own, and whose classes were most unpopular with the students. Success for the Institute would be difficult enough under the best of circumstances, even with a united staff pulling smoothly and strongly together. With such a group of colleagues as he had, Mercier felt it was impossible, and success at any legitimate cost he must have. There was nothing for it but to return them all to their former duties, and replace them by others who could work smoothly with him. He found such a group among his own former pupils, men whom he had himself started on paths along which they had since made progress toward distinction, who could, each in his own

Painting of Mercier as President of the Institut, hanging in the Institut

Institut Supérieur de Philosophie, Louvain

field, see the path of his own science trending toward unity with the others. These were Deploige in sociology, Nys in cosmology, Maurice de Wulf[1] in the history of mediæval philosophy. Some of these still illuminate Belgian thought and research.[2] M. Thiery, fresh from Germany, organized a laboratory of experimental psychology, a thing of which few universities at that time could boast.

The instructors whom Mercier thus relieved of their duties in the Institute felt in his action the stigma of dismissal; others sympathized with them; all these joined in sympathy with the rector in his feeling of jealousy for what he regarded as Mercier's encroachment on his authority. From them a leaven of mistrust of Mercier spread through the university. He soon began to feel opposition as from a hostile group organized to undermine his position. Their first active move was an adroit one. They gave the Pope to understand that Mercier was neglecting the essential of his plan, the Thomistic philosophy, and was laying his principal emphasis on science, and that he was teaching in French rather than in Latin as was specified in his plan and in the Pope's approval of it. The first charge was undoubtedly unfounded. Not Leo himself had more nearly at heart the plan of synthesizing the Thomistic philosophy with the modern world than had Mercier, who was obviously the last man to favor the modern world at the expense of St. Thomas. As for the second, there seems to be no doubt that Mercier had

---

[1] Maurice de Wulf was Professor of Philosophy at Harvard University from 1929 to 1931. He has devoted himself to restoring around St. Thomas the intellectual milieu of the Middle Ages, and has published a history of that period which has attained international importance.

[2] Among his pupils there were a number of foreigners who were later to become leaders in European philosophic thought, such as Gemali of Turin and Gaspard Descurtin, founder of the Catholic University of Freibourg.

Leo's permission to use French so far as seemed to him
necessary. It must have been as clear to Leo as it was to
Mercier that to use Latin exclusively would be to guarantee
the failure of the Institute. There were none too many students at best; to give instruction in nothing but Latin would
be to confine the course to few beyond the students of theology, for not many of the lay students or the more or less
casual auditors were qualified for such work. Mercier was
always a strong advocate of the use of Latin in scholarship;
he expressed regret that scientists no longer corresponded
with one another in Latin as had Descartes, Leibnitz, and
Newton. In his work in the Institute he used it so far as was
practicable; his reviews and summaries of his lectures were
in Latin, and his references to his sources. He conducted
conference and discussion classes and examinations in Latin.

Before the question of the use of Latin had reached the
status of dissension or dispute, the College of Bishops had
seen the difficulty, and had gone so far in sympathy with
Mercier as to write a collective letter to Rome requesting that
he might be allowed to use French in his teaching to the extent he deemed it necessary. To this the Pope gave either
tacit agreement or private assent. Not so the Congregation
of Studies. By the time Mercier's final draft of the statutes
for the Institute came to them, they seem never to have considered the possibility of using anything but the original
language in the exposition of Thomistic philosophy. This
gave Mercier's opponents their opportunity. They conveyed
to Rome and whispered to the Congregation of Studies that
the use of French in any measure was not with the consent of
the Pope, or not a part of his plan, and that even the consent

of the Council of Bishops was brought about by undue influence on Mercier's part. The result was that Mercier's project was returned to him modified by the Congregation of Studies in two essentials. His list of courses in the sciences was reduced, that of courses in philosophy was increased, and it was prescribed that Latin only should be used in all instruction in philosophy.[3]

To a teacher of philosophy it was not profoundly disturbing to have orders to teach more philosophy; a gradual increase there was part of his own plan. But to the president of the Institute it was profoundly disturbing to have orders which tended directly to its failure. He took such measures as he could at the time to get the Congregation of Studies to alter the decision, and in the hope of success continued the use of French in his classes. To the rector this looked like downright insubordination, and as such he reported it to Rome. The response was a sharp letter of censure from Cardinal Mazella on behalf of the Holy Father. It directed the president of the Institute to submit to the rector, and to distribute copies of the Cardinal's rebuke among his colleagues. Mercier had his choice, to defy, to resign, to submit. His attitude was that of prayer; "Lord, I gladly accept this humiliation if it be to Thy glory."

[3] Monsieur Collinet, who was Professor of Comparative Literature, was even a more bitter enemy than Abbeloos. Though both Mercier and Collinet were so-called "democrats," Mercier's democracy was mediæval in comparison with the twentieth-century democracy of Collinet.—His desire to harm Mercier went so far that he even procured some note-books of Mercier's pupils and sent them to the Congregation of Studies in Rome to prove what fallacies the professor of Thomistic philosophy was teaching.

The feeling against Mercier in Rome was increased by a certain jealousy, for the new school of Thomistic philosophy at Louvain was rapidly eclipsing the Pope's own school in Rome.

But this did not solve the problem; there was still the Institute for him to save if he could from hopeless wreck. There was only one way, to appeal directly to the Pope; all other appeals had proved vain. He decided to steal away to Rome before any one could stop him. He confided only in Nys and his confidential colleagues. A cold gave him an excuse for leaving town, ostensibly to go to Brussels to consult his brother Léon, the physician. His absence, however, roused the suspicion of the rector, who called at the Institute and asked to see the president. When told that Mercier had gone to consult his brother, Abbeloos left a message of sympathy and said he would not fail to inquire further in Brussels. Nys promptly telegraphed to Mercier to warn him of Abbeloos's suspicion. Mercier decided to try to anticipate the discovery of his ruse; he wrote at once to Abbeloos, "I am in Rome, and am myself astonished to be here."

Quick as his move had been, he found that the mistrust of his colleagues had reached the Vatican before him. Leo had obviously been told about his insubordination, and of his absence without leave from the rector. Leo refused to see him, and directed Cardinal Mazella to write to Abbeloos, telling of Mercier's unauthorized journey, and of the Pope's refusal to receive him. The letter also reassured Abbeloos that the president of the Institute was in all matters subordinate in authority to the rector of the university. Meanwhile Abbeloos had issued a public condemnation of Mercier's action, making it worse than it actually was by falsely declaring that Mercier had gone to Rome after explicit orders that he should not do so, and that his use of French in his classes had been contrary to the rector's orders.

Again Mercier had to make atonement for his impetuousness by public humiliation. At the first meeting of his class after his return from Rome he told his students that he had received orders from the rector to lecture in Latin, and as obedience is a virtue which all must practice, he bowed in submission. A gray-haired old canon, who was one of the boys present, told recently of the scene as he remembered it: "A shiver went through all of us pupils—we suffered and sympathized with our beloved teacher, and I remember seeing tears in the eyes of some of us." Canon Simons, who was one of Mercier's first seven pupils at the Seminary Leo XIII,[4] and who now cares for some thirty thousand souls in the poorer quarters of Brussels, related a pathetic incident from this time:

The president of the Institute had been instructed to appear at a meeting which was to be held at Malines in order to settle the much-discussed question. It had been decided, despite all that he had said, to insist upon his using Latin. The experience of subsequent years proved how well justified Mercier was in saying that its use would inevitably compromise the future of the Institute.

Mgr. Mercier had been instructed to appear at half past five. First he went to pray in the Cathedral, and thereupon, having time to spare, he thought of calling upon some colleague or other. But, he mused, would he not compromise him by doing so? Guided by his usual delicacy of feeling, he felt afraid that this might prove the case. So he went instead to the seminary where his first pupils had just returned from their vacation. It was a bleak November day, and the boys were coming back from their afternoon walk. Mercier met one of his old students, spoke to him, and made him join him in the frigid parlor where he wanted to hide away and see no one until the time of the meeting. The coming disaster

4 Opened in 1892.

afflicted him. He was very sad, almost discouraged. How alone he was in his future episcopal city! What could be more touching than this great man, discussed, contradicted, and thwarted, seeing that gigantic work of his menaced, which was to become the highest Catholic intellectual conception of the nineteenth century, and to which he was giving his whole life! What could be more moving than that his only resort was to go and efface himself in a dark parlor beside an old pupil, an entirely powerless confidant in such a disaster!

It was a dark moment, but there were qualities in his character to carry him through and above it, courage, hope, optimism, faith, and the will to succeed. The element of his character that made for greatness was that he had enough of these qualities to carry him above darker moments than this.

In the course of time, Cardinal Mazella gave place in the Congregation of Studies to the enlightened and fair-minded Cardinal Satolli. He found occasion to make a personal inquiry into the state of affairs at Louvain, saw the practical necessity underlying Mercier's contention, and ruled that Mercier should be allowed to lecture in French, while the references would continue to be given in Latin. This time it was the rector who proved insubordinate. His refusal to submit to Satolli's ruling led to his dismissal. Hebbelynck succeeded him, a man of mild character, peaceful to the point of indifference in matters of academic controversy. Under him was established a peace which offered fair hope for Mercier and the development of his project. Indifference would have been the truer wisdom in the beginning, for there was no principle involved in the choice of language as a means of instruction.

The ending of this controversy, however, by no means

smoothed Mercier's path to immediate success. Suddenly an order came to him from Rome debarring him from conferring degrees. It seemed at the moment Leo had suddenly decided to destroy all that he had so enthusiastically ordered built up. It did not quite destroy the Institute, but it very effectually retarded it for a number of years, for Belgian students are no more inclined than are others to put in years of hard work on a course that leads to no recognizable result. That Mercier kept any students whatever at the Institute through that period is liberal testimony to his personal qualities of leadership.

Another difficulty was the question of land. A Monsieur Helleputte—afterwards a cabinet minister—had somehow managed to have the first buildings placed on a lot which was altogether too small, and what had been started had to be torn down again. Helleputte modified his plans, and the reconstructed Institute proper remains today an attractive and serviceable group of buildings. One of the associate professors, Armand Thiery, in addition to his equipment in mathematics, law, and psychology, prided himself on his attainments in architecture also. He had, unfortunately, in the words of his colleagues, "Une brique dans le ventre." He is still busy today, forty years later, erecting and tearing down buildings in all parts of Louvain. He was a man of some wealth, with an income from a lucrative department store belonging to his family. He helped Mercier liberally with money, but what he planned on the spacious isosceles triangle which the institution at length obtained for its buildings turned out to be an architectural hodge-podge. The main buildings of the Institute escaped his touches, but the *Sémi-*

naire Leon XIII suffered. The seminary staircases ascend and twist as if designed for snakes instead of future priests, and the planning of the rooms is little better.

There were serious difficulties, too, about money. In order to attract gifts, word went out at the beginning that Leo had given 150,000 francs to the foundation of the Institute. The plain fact is that he merely gave the equivalent of five per cent of that amount, a yearly grant, that is, of 7500 francs to be drawn from the Peter's Pence contributed by the Belgians. At the time when Abbeloos's opposition was at its height, the rector went so far as to accuse Mercier of having received the capital and wasted it. At this, the loyal Thiery hastened to Rome, and explained to the Holy Father that Mercier had the yearly receipts for the grants, for which Leo had signed the requisitions, though the act might not have lingered in his memory. Leo smiled, and remembered other false impressions that had been conveyed to him from Abbeloos and his faction. So far from gaining by these transactions, Mercier as a matter of course impoverished himself. As to every good cause with which he was connected, he gave more than he could spare from his own meagre funds; so did his brother the physician, and so did many well-to-do Antwerp merchants. None the less, the work repeatedly came to a standstill for lack of money. Of one such occasion Mercier told the following story:

It is quite true—I had nothing. *That* was one of the first requisites for success. There were, however, also other requirements in addition to hundreds of thousands of francs. I passed through days of agony. I well remember one dark day when I anxiously faced a large note of 25,000 francs. No money came in; I worked and begged in vain. One would have said all the sources had gone dry. So I put the Seminarians to praying. Despite this, I had received nothing on the morning of the day when the note fell due. At two o'clock in the afternoon, a respectable-looking unknown man asked to see me, having first made certain that I was the professor whom the Sovereign Pontiff had charged with the building of the Institute. Upon entering my study, the stranger handed me a sealed envelope, and then left at once, unwilling to disclose his identity. Even today I am ignorant of the name of this benefactor who wished that only God should be a witness to his liberality. His anonymous gift amounted to 30,-000 francs.

Faith to move mountains seemed quite as needful to move buildings, to spirit away an old soap factory and a number of dwelling houses, and conjure up in their stead the rather ambitious brick walls of the new buildings. They are Gothic in treatment, similar to so much of the architecture of Holland and the old Hanseatic cities of northern Germany. They stand grouped pleasantly round loggia and courtyard, now beautified by replicas of Meunier's bas-reliefs glorifying Belgian labor, by Père Ephrem's statue of Mercier, and by the beds of roses that bloom between the gravel walks. The president's house and the porter's lodge flanked the entrance grille, not far down the street from the Institute's first modest quarters. The overhanging gabled front and the entire façade and twin chimneys of the president's house were soon hidden by the ivy which grows so luxuriously in the drizzle of the incessant Belgian rain. On the ground floor was the official reception room, on the wall of which at a later day admiring pupils hung Janssen's speaking likeness of the emaciated professor with the burning eyes. In the rear of the house, toward the courtyard and the school, were Mercier's living

63

and working quarters. One mantelpiece bore the inscription, *Labora sicut bonus miles Christi Jesu—Hilarem datorum diliget Deus*—"Labor as a good soldier of Jesus Christ. God loves him who gives himself joyously." The other had the Flemish greeting *Welkom.* St. Thomas in glorious scarlet and gray blessed the chapel from above its altar. So the buildings stood when at last Mercier had obtained the money for them by faith, hope, and the hardest kind of work, and had pushed them to their completion. In the spring of 1894, the Pope gave the Institute its charter, and before Christmas it was inaugurated with formal solemnity.

This marked the end of many difficulties, and the beginning of another, by no means the least. How was the new seminary to be supplied with students? There had been few enough in the former narrow quarters, rented from the Scheut Missionaries, where all had dining-room and study-room in common, where the chapel was bare and simple, and the service scarcely less so, but now spacious halls were to be filled. Mercier could expect but few of the graduate theological students from the higher seminaries, and probably few from the lay universities. Some, however, of the most ambitious of the students in the diocesan seminaries might seek the advanced philosophical training. The Cardinal and the ever faithful du Rousseau from his See at Tournai did send a few, and the other bishops began grumblingly to follow suit. A few foreigners straggled in. But there were not enough. In each of the two successive years there came only four new students. Mercier had done his best by ordinary human measures, and it was not enough. He came to his last resort; he summoned his little flock, and exhorted them all to pray, telling them of the efficacy of prayer in the past, and his faith in it now. So they prayed specifically for the numbers they wished, twenty-five new students for the first year; for the second, thirty-three, the number of our Saviour's years on earth; and for the third year, fifty-six. Each of the three years the miracle came to pass; the exact number for which they prayed entered the Institute. To Mercier, this seemed the fulfilment of the word: "If this be the work of men, it will come to naught, but if it be of God, you cannot overthrow it." His own word was, "It needs courage to throw oneself forward; but it needs not less to hold oneself back." Courage, energy, tenacity, carried them forward, Mercier and his devoted assistants, Deploige, Nys, de Wulf, and Thiery. The poverty of their resources set them on the path to honor. In their new field they were obliged to write new text-books, and for these books their names are now known wherever philosophy is studied.

The dormitory of the Institute's ecclesiastical students had been founded in 1892 and named the *Séminaire Léon XIII*.[5]

In the early days when the seminary was small in numbers, it was strongly united in earnestness of common purpose. Students and teachers lived together on terms of familiar intimacy. At the outset there had been no academic body as a whole. As the body grew larger other measures became necessary, but the old spirit was long maintained. Mercier continued his personal relations with the students. Often he dined with them, and often when he did not, one or another dined with him for the opportunity of special conference or

[5] Mercier was president of the two distinct institutions, the Institute of Philosophy and the *Séminaire Léon XIII*. In later times, they were put under different heads.

advice. Daily he encouraged all who would come to his study to have coffee with him after lunch. Students and instructors studied, played, walked, and talked together. Mercier had much companionship from all of his staff, but especially from Thiery and Deploige, who lived with him. He depended much on the help he got from his talk with them on whatever he was writing, and on the criticism he had from Deploige on the written draft. With them perhaps more than with others he was genial and expansive in talk. With them and with the students also he was at ease in playful as well as serious moods, which may account for the ability attributed to him to exert authority without making it felt as such. With the students he kept a true fatherly relation, trying so far as possible to replace in their hearts their absent parents, making much of birthdays and fêtes, now and then organizing excursions, encouraging athletics, fencing, and the newly introduced football, and going with them on the yearly all-night walk to the shrine of Our Lady of Montague.

The old janitor, Edmond, who remembers Mercier, still tends the standard roses that bloom the summer through in the courtyard of the Institute. Ask him whether the great Cardinal ever joked with him, and he replies, "Yes, whenever he passed, but I did not always understand him, for he sometimes made philosophical jokes." Then, apologetically, "Of course, that was as it should be, here in the courtyard of the Institute."

His lighter moments Mercier shared easily with his colleagues, his students, even his servants. His dark moments he refused to share. Even in the moment of humiliation his reaching out for companionship was not an appeal for sympathy but an involuntary gesture of loneliness. This sweet self-effacement of his gradually removed the obstacles from his path. Rome gave in on the question of degrees and the new rector worked with him in adjusting their relations. He looked back on those days without bitterness, as a happy spirit looks back on hardships overcome. A student of those days later wrote about them and sent his manuscript to Mercier, who commented on it in the spirit of *forsan et haec olim meminisse juvabit.* "In reading your article," he wrote, "I have relived happy days; the happiest of such are perhaps just those which as they pass seem to us the most painful." The verdict of his successors on those days was pronounced at the dedication of Mercier's statue in the court of the institute in 1931, when the present rector, Mgr. Ladeuze, said of him,

Thanks to Mercier, in all parts of the university students now live in a scientific atmosphere. . . . He changed the course of the internal evolution of our institution. Thanks to him, our faculties are no longer superimposed one upon the other. They co-ordinate in an organism whose real object is the cultivation of truth and thus bear complete witness to the true notion of a university. What we owe to him is a method—a wide and comprehensive method—infinitely precious to an institution of higher education.

"Cristes lore, and his apostles twelve
He taughte, but first he folwed it himselve."
　　　　—CHAUCER: *Prologue of Canterbury Tales.*

CHAPTER IV

FRUITS OF CONTEMPLATION AND LABOR

THROUGHOUT all his trials with the fallibility and triviality of human nature, Mercier maintained his high speed of intellectual activity. He was an indefatigable worker, reading and writing at a prodigious rate. He would allow himself hardly any time away from his work of lecturing and writing, so that he saw little of the other professors. The lights in his windows were always distinguished from the rest by being the last to go out, usually burning till far into the early hours of the morning. His mind never seemed to grow weary, never seemed to stop working. His nervous, leaping handwriting galloped over page after page as the night slipped past. This tireless speed of his mind enabled him to write some of his most profound works with astounding rapidity. When his work grew so pressing that he had to employ secretaries, he wore them out with his unflagging activity. He never could realize that other people did not possess the same capacity for work that he did. Such was his capacity that in one night he wrote as an article for the

Revue Néo-Scolastique what later became one of the greatest chapters in his *Criteriology.* He wrote the greater portion of his *Ontologie* while travelling on trains, for even when away on his vacation, his active mind did not stop working. He thought out much of his future writing as he stalked along the countryside, or jotted down endless notes as the railway carriage rattled over the rails. Very often he aptly quoted St. Paul's saying, *"Si quis non vult operari, nec manducet."* (He who refuses to work deserves nothing to eat.)

Besides original writing, he did a large amount of reading. He read both widely and thoroughly. His thoroughness in reading is shown by the way in which he dealt with Herbert Spencer. He had criticized in various articles much of what Spencer was championing. Spencer wrote to him, believing that upon further study Mercier would retract much of what he had said. Mercier would not reply until he had actually re-read the whole of Spencer's voluminous works, which must have taken an incalculable amount of his valuable time, and finally replied, after this conscientious and careful preparation, that he felt sure that his original opinion was correct. How few men would have been as careful and thorough as this in expressing an opinion! Mercier was essentially fair-minded, more than ready to give his opponent a fair showing. But he never let this consideration for others cloud his intellectual sincerity.

He read widely as well as carefully. He went through much of Newman and Vaughan and John Tyndall. The writings of Father Faber, whose sermons were causing a great stir in London in those days, he read with great interest. William James' *Varieties of Religious Experience* excited him tremendously. When he first discovered it he read it straight through, forgetting entirely the late night hours. Dawn found him still buried in his book. Facing his class a few hours later, as fresh as if he had had ten hours of sleep, he began his lecture, "A non-believing American psychologist, Mr. William James, whose loyalty and authority no one can deny, characterized religious sentiment as 'that mysterious force by which the soul of the believer triumphs over suffering.' Let us now, gentlemen, consider this assertion." He quoted James repeatedly, and years later in his great speech on *The Modern Conscience* he again referred to the Harvard professor, expressing a desire to meet him personally. He also read Bossuet, "of the eagle's eye," with almost as much pleasure as he read St. Paul. Bossuet was to Mercier the greatest thinker of modern times, and St. Augustine the most powerful genius of Christian antiquity.

Competent as he was as a writer, he constantly asked for criticism from his younger colleagues or his more brilliant pupils. In his *Origins of Contemporary Psychology* he collaborated with Mgr. Pelzer, who is now *Scrittore* of the Vatican Library and an authority on mediæval history. He was constantly working with the younger professors and insisting on giving them the credit for writing. In a letter to Father Simons, he says,

My dear Friend,

The principal merits of this study on the principles of individualism belong to you because of the solutions which you have given, as well as the stimulus you have given me. You have made me return to the analysis of the problem, despite my personal repugnance and the advice of others differing from yours. I had, owing to an easily understandable feeling of lassitude, left to the reader the interpretation of the *"dimensiones interminatæ."* I have now regained my courage and rewritten more clearly, I believe, the conclusions to which I had come. For that too, I have to thank you. . . .

Concerning this matter, Dean Simons said, forty years later, "And I had done so pitiably little to help the patient worker!"

In 1894 Mercier and his associates founded the *Revue Néo-Scolastique de Philosophie.* It was in this publication that so many of Mercier's articles appeared. He published in other scientific and philosophical magazines throughout Europe, but it was in the *Revue* that there appeared such articles as "The Philosophic Definition of Life," "Scientific Induction," "Speech," "The Notion of Truth," "Modern Science and Thomistic Philosophy," and others. The *Revue* meant a great deal to Mercier, for it was the chief means of sowing far and wide the ideas he was promulgating. There were many obstacles to its progress. When it first appeared, its name and purpose were scoffed at by its opponents. Then it suffered financially. One day when Mercier and de Wulf, who was his right-hand man in the undertaking, were talking the situation over as they were standing at the door of Mercier's study, Mercier suddenly rushed in to his desk, seized a handful of bank notes, and said, pressing the money into de Wulf's hand, "Here, you had better take these for the *Revue*, or I'll be giving them tomorrow to some poor unfortunate!"

Right around the corner was the press, the *Nova et Vetera*, run by the devoted Warny, who was always prepared to keep the establishment open all night if the manuscripts of Mercier arrived late. These manuscripts were always clearly written and had few corrections. But this, Warny knew, meant nothing, for, easy as this first manuscript was for the compositors, the proof sheets were another story. These were voluminously corrected, and additions made which would often increase the article to twice its original size so that the whole set-up of the magazine had to be altered. But Warny bore all this patiently, for he was devoted to the writer.

Mercier was not idle during his vacations. He spent them in travelling about, making the Institute known to various foreign people of influence who might be interested and be able to help build up the attendance by sending students. He always wanted somebody with him, for being both an excellent talker and excellent listener he needed a sympathetic companion with whom to interchange ideas. It was Thiery or de Wulf who usually accompanied him. Almost every year they took some trip and eventually had covered a large part of Europe. England and Ireland, Switzerland, Spain, and Italy were some of the countries they visited. Two years in succession Mercier went to see the land of his Irish students, travelling by stage coach along the Lakes of Killarney. He celebrated Mass at various places for the benefit of the peasants, and at Maynooth College near Dublin he lectured to the students concerning his own beloved Institute. "For the first time," said de Wulf later, "I noticed how completely my friend, though hampered by a foreign tongue, held his audience in the palm of his hand when he had warmed to his subject." The authorities of the college were so impressed that they not only asked his advice as to changes which they were considering, but later asked him to be the head of the enlarged college. Once he was asked to speak in London on behalf of Maynooth College, having been one of three representatives chosen by Mgr. Ryan, the head of the Thurles Seminary, to speak before the English authorities. He practised his English on the Channel boat and the Dover train by conversing with the passengers. The summer he went to Switzerland he took a walking trip. He loved to stretch his long legs whenever he could, and here was a glorious opportunity. He was in ecstasy over the panoramas and the brilliant colors of the flowers. He would continually call his companion's attention to them. "Just look at the blue of the gentian flowering against the pure white of the snow," he would say, and add that it was a glorious thing that the *Bon Dieu* had such a good eye for color.

He went to Spain in 1906 with de Wulf to spend the Holy Week in Seville. As they rolled southward in the "*Express du Sud*" they fell into conversation with a stranger sitting opposite them in the compartment. Later, when the new acquaintance could get de Wulf off by himself, he handed him his visiting card, and said,

"I have met many great and remarkable men in my life, but I have never heard any one talk on weighty topics with the seductive charm of your clerical companion. He has made such a deep impression upon me that I cannot refrain from asking you who he is."

The new acquaintance, so interested in Mercier, was M. de Bétancourt, the well-known diplomat. He became very friendly with the two Belgians, and invited them to be his guests when they reached Seville. He was preceding them there, for they were stopping over in Burgos. In Burgos the streets were heavily guarded because of a recent Carlist uprising. Mercier had been in the evening to pray in the Church of St. Lesmo near his lodgings, and the next morning at five o'clock, thinking he could find his way without any trouble, set out to go there again. But he was not sure of his way, and ran into a suspicious sentry, who challenged him with, "*Alto! La guarda!*" (Halt! The guard!) But Mercier did not understand and kept right on in what he took to be the direction of the church. The guard raised his rifle but withheld from shooting as the figure continued to approach, apparently oblivious to the danger. Mercier was arrested and taken to the gate of the guard house. The commanding officer could make nothing of his story as he told it in broken Spanish, but fortunately the Sacristan of the church where Mercier had been and to which he was bound, had heard something of the commotion, and running forth with his lantern protested that this man was a pious priest who had remained for a long time prostrate before the altar of his church on the previous evening. His identification was finally deemed sufficient, for they released Mercier. When he returned to de Wulf he was white and shaken, and said, "I have looked death in the eye." Unable as he was to make himself understood in Spanish at this time, two weeks later when he left the hospitality of M. de Bétancourt he was using the language with great facility and ease.

Mercier's teaching progressed triumphantly, making the dreariest of philosophical abstractions into living realities pregnant with significance. He never allowed respect for tradition to become slavery, for he insisted many times that philosophy as all else was subject to progressive changes. Thomistic philosophy was a starting point rather than an ideal that could never be surpassed.

He never lectured above his students' heads. He had the surpassing power of being able either to descend to their level or raise them up to his. He began his lectures with one prayer to the Holy Ghost and another to St. Thomas for the sake of his students. Then he would launch into his subject, emphasizing the points he wanted to make by tapping the desk with his pencil which he held between the hunched tips of his long fingers and emphasizing the important points with the pencil as he rocked back and forth on his heels. And the points he would make would be such as these:

Have the ambition to conquer! Be men of initiative, have a horror of routine. Above all, never tremble!

The work is worthy of your undivided attention and generous hearts. I want only those who are willing to devote themselves to science for its own sake.

All knowledge is sterile which does not lead to action and end in charity.

Wisdom is the only money of such good alloy that all others may be changed for it. With it, you can buy everything. With it, you possess courage, temperance, and justice.

The law of the world is the law of progress. Man's reach is constantly upward, towards something better. This being so, the general theory of the universe should be optimism. Are not the noblest souls those who have the highest ideals?

Be gay and enthusiastic. Good humor is not merely a normal frame of mind and a spontaneous feeling, but it depends for a large part on the will. St. Paul said to the Christians of the Church of Philippi, "Rejoice in the Lord alway; and again I say rejoice."

I say to you as the Pope said to the faint-hearted, "*Andiamo avanti!*"—courage and forward march!

Of Mercier's work at the Institute, M. Jacques Maritain, Professor at the Catholic Institute of Paris, said,

In his union of philosophical and spiritual work he saw not simply an accidental encounter, but the working of the basic law of Christian intellectuality. For the philosopher does not work as the contemplative man, merely in spiritual regions that are supernatural; he works, in reality, in the most elevated temporal spheres, he cannot remain indifferent to culture of his own destiny.

Besides the approval of such men as this, he had the goodwill of Pope Pius, the successor of the wise and genial Leo. This put the final stamp of approval upon his work, which Mercier received in the form of the following communication shortly after Pius came to the Papal throne:

We greatly appreciate the services rendered by your Institute. Do not, therefore, fear that the particular interest and marked good will, of which our predecessor has given you so many proofs, will now discontinue.

Being a student, had Mercier had his choice, he would have chosen a life of quiet and saintly contemplation, though not one of complete withdrawal. He would have liked to live as St. Francis, to put the fret of the world behind him and seek union with God in the secluded shades of his Louvain College. He would have found expression and given inspiration through his writing and preaching. He felt what he called the "security of books," and wished he could retreat from his worldly cares into the world of his library in which he found communion with God.

But this was not to be. When he had finally got the Institute running smoothly in 1905, he asked the rector if he could not be relieved of some of his lectures so that he could devote himself to the publication of the things he had been trying to work at for years. This was granted to him, and he made a good start on his *Philosophic Study of Life,* but soon was obliged to lay down his pen again. Had he not been forced to put aside his work again here, he might have become a truly great world figure in philosophy. The renown today of his pupil, de Wulf, shows what Mercier might have attained. His successor, Monseigneur Noël, also a pupil, began his study of the history of philosophy where Mercier ended it, and has consequently acquired a far wider view of that field than his master. But we must remember that Mercier had many other duties to attend to while he had the Archbishopric, but that even if these forced him to abandon the formal study of philosophy, he always remained a philosopher in spirit, for the orderly processes of reasoning in the analysis and synthesis required for the solution of any problem always betrayed his philosophical mind which could not hide its light under a bushel.

His actual accomplishment in philosophy, however, was very great. His general plan, running through all he did, was to unite Thomistic philosophy with modern science and the modern need of new ideals. He wished to avoid both the extreme of callow and unthinking modernism which carelessly brushes aside the past, and the extreme of orthodoxy which objects to everything modern merely because of its modernity without investigating its soundness or unsoundness in principle. Mercier was confident of his position because he knew both ancient and modern and the relation between them. He did not reject one or the other, for he knew they were harmonious. Faith and reason for him were united by a fundamental concord. "The Catholic scholar is certain of the truth of his faith. . . . Hence, if he worries about the eventual future of science, he is lacking either in faith or scientific spirit." Over his whole neo-Thomistic system there ruled one main idea, that philosophy is essentially a work of synthesis. It must unite all the powers of the mind, all the data of science, all the points of view which partial analysis of reality reveals about things, all the isolated reflections that form the history of thought. Unity was the fundamental characteristic of scholastic philosophy, and the ultimate reason for its remarkable fecundity.

Mercier's own contribution to this was rather that of a formulator of problems than that of one who builds up brilliant conclusions. When problems have been discussed for some time there usually follows a synthesizing of all the discussions into one coherent conclusive solution. These are important, but equally important are the works of men who first began the original discussion, who opened up the problem by making people aware of it. Of these was Mercier. He gave thought a new direction, discovered and opened up new and fertile paths. This is the work of genius.

Mercier always felt that the most important aspect of his work was his living work, the founding of the school and the sowing of fertile ideas in the minds of his students, a work accomplished by coming in direct contact with them instead of reaching them through the indirect medium of writings. He started a movement of study, research, and philosophical reflection which soon spread and made itself felt in the world outside Louvain. The masterly way in which he planned and organized his Institute forestalled its early death, and prevented it from becoming just another fossil among the many such academic and philosophical endeavors. This unceasing effort to make his work living is well seen in a passage from *La Conscience Moderne*:

> More than once we have been asked to expound in a few succinct pages the essence of neo-scholastic philosophy; how it is differentiated from mediæval scholasticism on the one hand and from modern philosophy on the other. Such an exposition is impossible, and we should be faithless to the spirit of our work if we were tempted into offering one. . . . The essential works of a school must be *living*: it is method, spirit, rather than doctrine.

Such an explanation of aims may have seemed quixotic at the time; nevertheless, he set out to show that it could become fruitful as a practised ideal. To launch the undertaking of his living work of the school he wrote prodigiously and with astonishing rapidity, always in the face of great odds, such as the duties of administration, the interruptions of visits, and an ever-increasing correspondence. To produce important works of writing was to Mercier an essential activity of a living, progressive school such as he wanted his Institute to be. It was the duty of every serious student by profession, it was the necessary condition of a living science which wishes to advance into the future and not merely live on the past. To fulfil this condition he pushed his disciples with feverish haste, and he gave them a perfect example in himself. To give voice to the school, to the method and ideas for which it stood, as well as to express his own ideas, he founded, besides the *Revue Néo-Scolastique*, the press of the Higher Institute of Philosophy, known as the *Bibliothèque de l'Institut Supérieur de Philosophie.* Its first publications were written by the founder, Mercier. These were his successive volumes, *Cours de Philosophie, Psychologie, Logique, Criteriologie, Ontologie.*

In his *Criteriologie* he dealt with epistemology, setting himself in opposition to the neo-Kantian positivism which dominated philosophy at that time. Mgr. Léon Noël, in *La Philosophie en Belgique,* in speaking of Mercier's contribution to the problem of knowledge, says,

Before the time [of Mercier] this problem had scarcely been faced in a frank way by philosophers of Thomistic inspiration. The apparent silence of scholastics on a question unknown to their age, had been taken as a solution by too timid disciples. One must, they thought, deny that there was any question, refuse to discuss it, to examine before all else the aptitude of the mind to know truth. But this prejudice instead of inspiring confidence could only shake it. In its place, Mgr. Mercier courageously substituted the tactics of radical sincerity. . . . He showed how St. Thomas and Aristotle had already recommended this method; following the example of St. Thomas, he turned the mind back on itself, and instead of affirming gratuitously its aptitude for truth, he had the mind attain it in its immediate judgments.

And it was entirely owing to the work of Mercier that at the International Thomistic Congress held in Rome in 1925, one-third of the discussions were devoted to the problem of knowledge. The *Criteriologie* also dealt with metaphysics. It contained a justification of metaphysics against the positivistic scepticism. Here Mercier tried to discover a solid foundation for Realism which would insure the doctrine of substance and the existence of God. In all his treatment

he never lost sight of his starting point, experience. In
logic he showed the importance of the syllogism as opposed
to the logical confusions of positivism. He also examined
the problem of induction on the metaphysical plane. In
ethics he showed that the foundation of obligation was not
in the will of the Creator, as it has often been arbitrarily
asserted to be, but is in the rational nature of man. In
psychology he confronted Aristotelian vitalism with modern
discoveries in the biological sciences. With far-reaching
vision, Mercier placed his confidence in the newly born science of experimental psychology and equipped his Institute
with a laboratory which was one of the finest. We may view
as a tribute to the work of Mercier the recent ruling of the
present Pope which required that experimental psychology
be taught in all Catholic seminaries. This was only carrying out what Mercier had said forty years previously, in
1891:

Psychology is undergoing today a transformation from
which we would be blameworthy to remain aloof. . . . Here
is a young, contemporary science, which is in itself neither
spiritualistic nor materialistic. If we do not take part in
it, the psychology of the future will develop without us, and
there is every reason to believe, against us. Do we want to
conquer the right to have a directing influence? Then we
must prepare workers who will produce their own works,
original experiments, which no one can overlook without
ceasing to be familiar with the science.

All this activity produced favorable results both for him
and for the school. In 1907 the Royal Academy of Belgium
conferred on him the decennial prize for philosophy, in spite
of its traditional conservative tendencies. The quality of his

work was recognized from the very beginning in Germany by authorities such as Rudolf Eucken and Fritz Medicus, and in France at the Sorbonne. His works ran into numerous editions and were soon translated into many languages. The Institute too was soon bearing rich fruit as a result of its activity. It produced many books. Three other reviews were established besides the *Revue Neo-Scolastique.* In other countries many reviews were founded which owe their origin to the one at Louvain, as is shown by their names. *The New Scholasticism, Rivista di Filosofia neoscolastica, Scholastik, Ciencia tomista.* The attendance at the Institute soon increased tremendously with its increased reputation. Students came from all parts of the world, and returning home sent new pupils back. The influence of the Institute can be seen in the establishment of other similar enterprises, such as the Catholic Institute of Paris, the new University of Milan, and others at Innsbruck, Cologne, and even at Rome itself. And the present Pope, in his recent reforms for Catholic education, seems to have been influenced by the work of Mercier at Louvain.

That Mercier's influence extends far beyond his own time and place is shown by the many recent references to Thomistic philosophy. Mercier's ideal has been realized; Thomism is respected wherever philosophy itself is.[1] St. Thomas is now recognized everywhere as an important philosopher. That this is due to Mercier's untiring activities there can be

[1] In 1924, at the International Congress of Philosophy in Naples, Doctor Liebert, President of the *Kantgesellschaft* and one of the most influential of German thinkers, thought it fitting in commemorating a centenary of Kant, to draw a parallel between the master of Königsberg and St. Thomas. And the same congress asked Doctor Gemelli, Rector of the University of Milan, to commemorate at another solemn gathering the sixth centenary of the canonization of St. Thomas. In 1926 the organizers of the International

no question. He wanted Thomism to be heard and understood by modern thinkers. And his dream has come true.

Mercier's work with the Institute lasted in all about twenty years. It was brought to an end in 1907 by the death of Cardinal Goossens, Archbishop of Malines. By then, Pius X had succeeded Leo XIII on the Papal throne. There may have been no doubt in his mind who should succeed Goossens; it did not take him very long to decide, but the interval was one of suspense to Belgium, of tense anxiety for the officers of the Belgian church who cherished secret ambitions, and of lively interest and importance in political and social as well as in ecclesiastical and academic circles. There were bishops who stood high, conspicuous in the urban dioceses of Liège, Ghent, Bruges, Tournai, and Namur. Any one of them would have been justified in feeling that his rank and station entitled him to consideration. But it was too important a post to be filled on a basis of mere seniority. Malines is the largest diocese in Belgium. It comprises two and a half million souls, eight hundred and fifty parishes, numerous important seminaries and colleges, and for the service of all these, two thousand four hundred priests, monks, and religious servants. In one year the Government had voted an appropriation for the religious establishments and institutions of the Roman Church of seven million francs. Clearly the appointment was one of national political importance.

Congress of Philosophy at Harvard included among the topics on their program: *"Neo-scholasticism:* A discussion of the value of scholastic philosophy in terms of the present." Several representatives of neo-Thomism were asked to expound their doctrines. And at the Sorbonne, a distinguished professor of mediæval studies has held the thesis that modern philosophy must be dated not from Descartes but from St. Thomas.

That is not to say that the Catholics are always the dominant political party in Belgium; they form only one of five or six parties. In Mercier's time, the Conservative party was the Catholic party in name as well as in object. Traditionally it consisted of the higher clergy, the aristocracy, a small part of the urban bourgeoisie, and most of the agricultural laborers. It was in fact conservative in its program; it left to the Church the organization and care of education, it was hostile to military expenditures and all obligations not originating in the Church, it opposed all innovations, and had marked protectionist tendencies. The Christian Democratic party adhered less closely to the Church. It contained most of the secular clergy, some of the regular clergy, many farmers and industrial workmen, and a few of the city and country bourgeoisie. Its platform was syndicalistic with strong socialistic tendencies. It demanded supervision of all instruction, but would not have removed it far from the Church, for all the societies and associations which it formed were connected with the Church, each under the direction of a cleric. The Socialist party did not oppose the Church, but rather disregarded it, particularly in its demand for compulsory lay education. Its platform was colored with international socialism of various shades, calling for universal suffrage, free thought, suppression of capitalistic enterprise, and the like. The Liberal party faced in two directions. The right wing was the traditional Liberal party. It called for free thought, free trade, and individual liberty, compulsory national education, and opposition to clerical mortmain as a social danger. The left wing was the progressive or Radical liberal, composed of ardent

84

young men of the educated classes, the middle and lower bourgeoisie, and the best of the workmen. Its platform, so far as it had any, differed from that of the right wing of the party in demanding state intervention where employer and employee could not agree, but its political weakness was its inability to agree or to establish party discipline. On most occasions each party worked to its own ends; occasionally on non-partisan matters they all pulled together for a national purpose.

In spite of the many political factions and divisions, Belgium is strongly unified by Catholicism. As the head and front of a religion that is as nearly national as a religion can be, the Archbishop is a very influential figure in all departments of Belgium's national existence. The King must have an Archbishop who co-operates with him. The clergy must have one who unites them in leadership and purpose. The people must have one who inspires them by gesture and personal example. The Pope must have one who is in every sense his deputy. The appointment rests wholly in the hands of the Pope, but it would be neither courtesy nor policy for him to appoint one who was *persona non grata* with any of the important persons or parties in the archdiocese. The Pope does well to give good heed to the voices of the King and the Papal Nuncio, and their responsibility in turn is not alone to themselves, but to all others, the Church, and the Nation. The King was Leopold II, and the Nuncio was Cardinal Vico.

There was considerable speculation and excitement at the Institute. To its little world there was only one hero and only one possible candidate, and unless the authorities were blind, their beloved president would move to Malines. But what did they know about it? Among the important persons still belonging to the old Abbeloos faction at Louvain were de Becker and Dordolot, who were doing their utmost to hinder Mercier's candidacy, while the vicars-general of Malines, to whose chapter Mercier had now belonged for some twenty-four years, were all in favor of *him*. Some of them insisted on urging his candidacy with the Nuncio, despite their fear that Mercier would not for a moment accept the Archbishop's throne. The sacrifice of giving up his philosophical studies would, they feared, prove too great. As for King Leopold, he wanted none of the Bishop of Namur, who had been so unsympathetic to his Congo schemes. Among the Ministry, van Trooz was a solid friend of Mercier.

Such churchmen as could see clearly in the midst of all the excitement, realized that in reality it boiled down to three likely candidates: Mgr. van Heylen, the Bishop of Namur; Mgr. Waffelaert, the Bishop of Bruges, and Mgr. Mercier, the president of the Institute.

The Nuncio hustled about here and there with his ear to the ground, sounding opinion among the upper hierarchy as well as in high governmental circles. What was Mgr. Evrard, the Dean of Ste. Gudule's opinion in the all-important matter? Evrard was a diplomat, and hoped desperately Mercier might be selected. He replied cautiously to His Holiness' representative that he believed no order priest should be selected, as also no priest from outside the diocese, and certainly no one whose knowledge did not extend beyond that of the Church fathers and doctrine. The Nuncio noticed that that debarred both van Heylen and Waffelaert.

Mercier's first intimation of what was in store for him came one day when he stood in the hallway of the Seminary Leo XIII chatting with its spirited young director, Simons, to whom he said in response to some jest about the Archbishopric that it was no more for him than he for it. Just then the porter handed him a letter bearing the seal of the Chapter of Malines. It notified him that they had selected him to deliver Goossen's funeral oration. Here was a clear enough indication of the trend of opinion. As soon as he could get away after the ceremony, he turned his back on the question of high place. He and his brother Léon, the Brussels physician, had bought with the savings of years of economy a cottage near their native village of Braine l'Alleud, in the hamlet of L'Hermite. There they went for rest and family reunion, and there they found happy retirement amid the familiar scenes and faces they loved. There he was tranquilly working when late on February 7, 1907, the Papal Nuncio called at the big new Royal Palace in Brussels to inform His Majesty of the nomination made that day in Rome. There again he was, absorbed in his work, the next morning when a messenger from the Post-Office came through the cold and the fog on his bicycle with the telegram that told him of his appointment to the Primacy of Belgium. He read it, turned back to his writing table, and finished the preface for one of his books on which he was at the moment engaged. Then quietly he took down his hat and cape and went to the village church for a few moments of prayer, and then took the by-path across the fields to the railroad station. His friends, it would seem, had heard of the appointment before he did, for the post-man's wife was writing out the telegrams of congratulation as fast as her baby would let her, and the church bells were already ringing out the news to the country-side. The news was ahead of him in Brussels. He might have heard, if he were not too preoccupied, the newsboys crying it in the streets as he hurried to the Nuncio's palace where he had been ordained twenty-two years before. He paid his official visit of filial submission and then hastened to the *Gare du Nord* to catch the first train to Louvain. There he had to face a celebration that crowded the largest hall in the College of the Pope. For the moment it was rejoicing over his advancement, but doubtless many a heart was sad at the prospect of parting with the president who had made the Institute what it was.

Doubtless Mercier's own heart felt sadness under the outward guise of rejoicing. Later, when the time came for him to say good-bye, his expressive face, every line of which bore witness to the noble and thoughtful life he had lived, was twitching with emotion as he gave his farewell message:

I have not desired the honor to which I have been called. Although my name is mentioned, it is difficult for me to accustom myself to the idea that I am the person. It seems to me it must be some one else. I had lived in the hope of passing the rest of my days in this home where everything is dear to me and each object is part of me. I considered it as my nest. . . . This feeling still permeates me at this moment when Providence has changed the destiny I desired. But if the work to which I have been called separates me from you who are my family, my heart remains with you.

Chance words here and there in his later utterances show

that he looked back at his years at the Institute as the happiest of his life. Later in explaining the unexpected granting of a petition he said, "Oh, well—he hit me in my weak spot; he appealed to the professor of philosophy and not the Archbishop of Malines."

Out of devotion to Mary, his Heavenly Mother, Mercier chose the Feast of the Annunciation, the 25th of March, 1906, as the day of his consecration to the Archbishopric, and Malines made much of the celebration. Jef Denyn, the master *carillonneur*, high in the massive tower of St. Rombaut, rang the bells which for centuries had expressed the joys and sorrows of the people of the Flemish plains. The balconies of Margaret of Austria's Palace, where the great Emperor Charles had spent so much of his life, were gaily decorated. Every sculptured saint was decked with flowers and banners. Elizabeth, Queen of the Belgians, sent the flowers which decked the shrine of the Blessed Mother in the Palace. All the portals of the Cathedral were draped. Crowds packed the streets; Chapter and Canons in newly starched linen and lace were swarming like ants. The new Archbishop was on his knees in the little chapel of his strange cold palace, alone with his God.

At length he came out to walk the few steps from his palace to the Cathedral. The Second Artillery was drawn up, cannons boomed, the crowd bowed before him as he came, here and there a mother held up a child for his blessing. He came slowly in mitre and cope, his train borne by an acolyte, before him a cross, on each side a priest, behind him in processional order the priesthood of Belgium. In the shadow of the portal stood Cardinal Vico, the Papal Nuncio.

"Your Excellency," said Mercier, "tell the Holy Father that I will be a true bishop. I will serve Christ in all things. It shall be my object as long as I draw breath to protect the interests of the Church in my country."

Before consecrating him, the Nuncio questioned him as to his faith. The subject of the examination was the dogma of the Trinity, of the Incarnation, of the Church and the divine origin of the Testaments. Mercier answered the examination by an act of faith. "I knew," he said with unfailing modesty, "that I had permitted myself to become too engrossed in the study of profane problems by external works, but I felt that I hungered and thirsted for union with God."

Such was his induction into the work which he well knew to be great, but which turned out to be so much greater than he knew. In the very beginning of it, on April 15, 1907, he was appointed Cardinal, and took his title from the little church near the Colosseum, which, because it still contains the chains which bound the Fisherman of Men is called St. Peter's in Vincoli, St. Peter's of the Chains. Thus prophetically he was bound to "prove himself brave unto death and unto the shedding of his blood for the exaltation of the holy faith, for the peace and tranquillity of the Christian people, and for the maintenance and propagation of the Holy Roman Church."

"And I will give you pastors according to mine heart, which shall feed you knowledge and understanding."
—JER. iii, 15.

CHAPTER V

HUMILITY IN SERVICE

MERCIER had laid down the work of the teacher and had taken up the work of the apostle. It had been very difficult for him to give up his teaching. In his last words to his Louvain students, he had given them his doctrine and plan of action:

Toward what, then, is aimed this play of Secondary Causes, the threads of which Providence held in our past?—Toward one thing alone, to prepare the present moment. It is the moment, then, this providential preparation of today, which we want to consecrate, to bless, and be it with anguished heart or even with horror, to face dauntlessly.[1]

No man better exemplified this teaching than Mercier himself. All his past preparations as pupil and professor were converging in the present entering of his new life of spiritual leadership, making it one of supreme and enduring value and achievement.

The great principle of his life was order, and this took

[1] Whittier expressed a similar idea in "My Soul and I":

The present, the present is all that thou hast
For thy sure possessing.
Like the Patriarch's angel, hold it fast
Till it gives its blessing.

91

the form of unity in multiplicity. It was this principle in his spiritual life that made for his simplicity of character, a quality which marks great men of all ages. He could be at once absorbed in the pursuit of his spiritual ideal and intensely engaged in realistically practical activities. He was so great that he seemed hardly to understand petty characters, yet he could unobtrusively descend to the level of his meaner companions without losing touch with great things. He never lost his sensitiveness to the least vibration of the good and the beautiful. He had that superior understanding of humanity in all its aspects which the Danish philosopher, Höffding, calls "the great humor." A friend of Mercier says that "when he was about to utter some noble ideal, of a sudden he would draw himself up, rays of youthful impetuosity would shoot from his eyes, his broad forehead seemed to be aglow, and his whole being gave forth an irresistible suggestion of confidence and fire."

Mercier was more than a Roman Catholic whose faith came by birth or environment. His religion was the result of the inevitable and spontaneous development of his whole spiritual nature. Hence he was greater than any sect or religious denomination. To him, Catholicism meant the widest possible spiritual life. He said, "Christ does not invite humanity to intellectual bondage, but to share the highest liberty of the children of light." The liberalism of his outlook and the meaning of the religion to which he consecrated his life, are seen again and again in his writings and speeches.

Professing the Christian faith should cause no obstacles to the scholar's initiative, or even to the daring of genius.

There are hours—those of scientific research—when we are commanded to be neutral. We must not take up scientific problems with the preconceived idea of finding a confirmation in them of our religious beliefs.

The more our Christian faith is sincere, the more it is protected from the preoccupation which trouble the spirit or paralyze the will.

Error is the predecessor and the constant companion of truth. A true conclusion is often merely the result of a long series of errors. A discovery is very rarely made suddenly, by a flash of genius. It is the common law of all progress that following generations approach one another by fragmentary inductions, and often at the price of more than one mistake, before arriving at what finally constitutes progress in thought. You who aspire to scientific conquests must be able to bear that he who has an idea should follow it through to its consequences.—Do not be in a hurry to recriminate if it does not make straight for its goal. The by-ways where it may be straying are its most practicable route, and after all, perhaps the most direct, towards the truth.

Mercier was a true member of his church. The day was passing when men entered the church for non-religious reasons. The eighteenth-century Abbé who, neither learned nor religious, was a mere drawing-room ornament, has largely disappeared. The Monsignore and Bishops of the Church in Belgium are men of high education and devout Christianity who have entered the church for the service of their fellowmen and of God. Of such was Mercier, the greatest of them all.

There were many reasons why Mercier became a beloved apostle and a great pastor of his people, a *pastor vigilantissimus*. The chief of these, however, were his faith and his charity.

His faith in Christianity was supreme. For him, as for Bossuet, the establishment of Christianity was the only really important event in the whole history of the world. With this always before his mind, he tried to fulfill the ideals of Christianity every minute of his life. And this enabled him to retain his serenity through the most trying times. In spite of the urgency of parochial calls, he never allowed the slightest suggestion of "high-pressure" of "mass-production" methods to enter the calm of his library in the Archbishop's palace. He saw to everything with smoothness and simplicity, without haste, and yet always accomplished his duties in the necessary time. He heeded the words of Isaiah, that "he who has faith need not hasten." All his effortless accomplishment was owing to his supreme faith. He had the faith that moves mountains. It enabled him to walk both earthly and heavenly paths, to breathe equally well the air of the heights and of the valleys. His faith made him an unflinching optimist. His whole manner expressed his confidence in the supremacy of faith, but he did not cease to exert himself to establish its reign.

His charity he learned from his Master. Mercier felt that the world needed tolerance of human frailty. Many years before, the Master once had a conversation with a woman who had been caught in sin. He did not scold her, but while those around Him were preparing to stone her to death, according to the kindly Hebrew custom, He quietly wrote with his finger in the sand until all except the guilty woman had sneaked away. Then He told her to go and sin no more.

St. Francis de Sales' likeness had not hung fruitlessly in Mercier's study, either, for from him too had he gained the wider vision which brings charity and forgiveness. He knew that love, because of its life-giving power, is the only really creative passion. *"La grande maladie de l'âme, c'est le froid,"* said Tocqueville. And Mercier knew that the great blessing of the soul was love. He gave of this fully and freely, and because of this he had more religious, social, and racial tolerance than is common among prelates.

Mercier's political and educational work at this time was very great. In order to understand it we shall have to look into the political history of Belgium a little. Having no natural frontiers, and consequently open on every side to attack, it has been invaded in turn by Gaul, Roman, Frank, Burgundian, Spaniard, Austrian and Dutchman. It has thus been the scene of struggles since time immemorial, always the bone of contention between the larger powers of Europe, and always the arena in which they did their fighting. It has been so subjected to change and partitioning that it is a wonder that it attained any national independence at all. The long and devastating Spanish-French wars so ravaged the land that there was left hardly a pig or a cow in the countryside. Then after Marlborough's victories, the French armies were finally driven out of the Belgian provinces, and by the peace of Utrecht, the long connection between Belgium and Spain was severed. For a century the provinces were known as the Austrian Netherlands, and Holland furnished the garrisons for the important fortresses and cities, while Austria provided its archdukes and duchesses for governors-general. After that the French revolutionary armies swept over and conquered the country, keeping it as part of France throughout the Republic and the Empire. After Napoleon's fall, the Congress of Vienna gave Belgium to Holland, and so it became once more a Dutch province. That rule was overthrown, however, in 1830, when the Belgian Catholics and Liberals united and drove out the Dutch. They framed a constitution and set up Leopold I as their King. To insure the national integrity of this small country, England, France, and Prussia signed a treaty guaranteeing their regard for its neutrality. The person originally responsible for this guarantee was the German doctor Stockmar.[2]

Not only has the country suffered from external attempts to tear it apart, but it has had internal dissension as well. If you draw a straight line from east to west through the heart of Belgium, you will divide the country into two parts which are nearly equal in area and population. This division corresponds to the actual division between the Flemings and the Walloons. The northern part is Flemish; the native speech is a Teutonic dialect, close to Dutch. These people are hardworking and stolid, with narrow and not easily changeable ideas. And to their ideas they are devoted with an unshakable conviction. The southern part is occupied by Walloons, who are more French in language, manners, customs, and character. They are less credulous, less inclined to unquestioning devotion, more sceptical than their Flemish neighbors. They live with a lighter touch, with less regard for consequences, with more of an enjoyment of the moment. This natural division of the country into two sections of such differing temperament has aggravated the three principal

[2] The Chancellor of the German Empire in 1914 pronounced this treaty as insignificant as a mere scrap of paper.

disputes which have for long agitated Belgium: that of schools, that of language, and that of suffrage. In each of these, Mercier played an important part. It is interesting to note that he was able to sympathize with both types of temperament because he was born near the division of the two sections and was therefore used to both strains of mentality.

The problem of schools was an ecclesiastical one, cutting deep into the very heart of the Church's activities. The Liberals, abetted by the Socialists, were urging the introduction of a state-controlled compulsory system of education. The Catholics, who were the Conservatives, said this would be hostile to the spirit of liberty. What they meant was that state control would loosen Catholic control. The Church has always recognized the importance of gaining an influence over children at an early age, so that it has insisted upon religious instruction in the schools. If the state made education compulsory, this hold upon the schools which the Church had would be materially weakened. When Mercier became Archbishop, Belgium was the only West-European country which did not prescribe primary education. The organic law of May 9, 1914, introduced for the first time primary education in Belgium. The royal decree, co-ordinating all Belgian legislation relating to primary education, was published and signed during the next two months. Both as teacher and churchman, Mercier was interested intensely in this seething controversy.

The language question was more of a political one, and one that grew more directly out of the Flemish-Walloon division of the country. When the Dutch had the upper hand in the country following the Congress of Vienna, they attempted to make Dutch the official language. But then the tables were turned when, after winning their independence, the Walloons showed an equal intolerance for the language of their Flemish countrymen. The controversy was raging throughout Mercier's career, and has reached an even more acute stage now. There was no question in Mercier's mind but that the Flemings had long been unjustly neglected and despised. The Belgian bishops published a collective letter in 1906 emphasizing the necessity of a just appreciation of the Flemish language in Belgium. Some time later Mercier said that not only the language but the Flemish people, the Flemish spirit, in fact, must be more highly regarded:

Belgian unity is not only brought about by legislation, by discipline, by foreign trade, and working shoulder to shoulder. It is brought about, or rather should be brought about, by mutual sympathetic understanding or a desire on both sides to share equally in a common life and in rising, in common, towards a higher ideal.

Walloons and Flemings learn to know each other better and more fraternally and to respect and favor each other's legitimate hopes. You are brethren; do not treat each other as strangers. The peace of Belgium is at stake. True national prosperity depends on it.

Though he continued throughout his career to appreciate the Flemish cause, he could always see both sides. Since three-quarters of his parish was Flemish he constantly spoke this language in addressing the masses. But he was not as violent an advocate of the Flemish cause as many of his associates expected him to be. Indeed, some of his young priests were so violent in their zeal that they were expelled from the St. Rombaut school. Their behavior wounded Mercier deeply, for he felt that nothing should be done to aggravate the trouble.

During a bitter period in the Flemish controversy, a number of the Flemings felt that the Cardinal was lacking in sympathy for their cause. As a result, they refrained from going to Malines for their seminarial training and the number of seminarists decreased materially, to the Cardinal's chagrin. Thus as the bitterness increased, he became more and more anxious, begging for tolerance, insisting that every Belgian should understand his country's two languages while each language should be officially used in the parts of the country where it was native. As is so often the case in disputes that involve deep feeling and excitement, the man who holds apart and views it impartially, refusing to give way to the extreme passions of either side, is grossly misunderstood by both parties. The leaders of the Flemings accused him of not understanding the Flemish mentality. To his accusers he replied that he was sure they did not realize the danger of the movement. "I tell you," he wrote to a deputy, "that the Flemish race has few more fervent admirers than the Archbishop of Malines, and if you think I am sincere, I beg you to do all in your power to further their cause in the Chamber, in the Provinces, and in the villages." While thus emphasizing his loyalty to the legitimate aspirations of the Flemish people, he nevertheless refused to be swept into an unreasonable and extreme position. He was a university student and a philosopher to whom world culture was essential. How could the prestige of his great Catholic seat of learning become world-wide with only the Flemish language to work with? Education must transcend national barriers; for the progress of science, art, and philosophy, only an international language should be used. English, German, French are all equally international. And Belgium was fortunate enough to possess French as a native language of many of its people. It would thus be unreasonable not to take advantage of that and promote the spread of French, the international language, instead of Flemish, the local language. He also felt that a separate Flemish university was unnecessary, for training in the Flemish language was useless for any kind of research or international publication.

After ten years as Archbishop, Mercier saw certain aspects of the controversy in a somewhat changed light. He advocated the increase of Flemish courses given at Louvain, though not to the extent desired by the Flemish. It was a very delicate situation for Mercier. He was in a Flemish-speaking district, surrounded by many violent "Flamingants," many of whom were churchmen or former pupils of his own. They never quite forgave him for not fighting more violently than he did for the Flemish tongue. But he was sure of the wisdom and justice of his position. He believed in evolution and not revolution as the best means of furthering the Flemish cause. He said once, "If the Flemings ever obtain what their most rabid adherents demand, then—*finis Belgiæ*."[3] He did not believe the good of the whole should

[3] It is interesting to note that during the war this split in national sentiment was a powerful instrument in the hands of the German authorities, who did their best to use it to foment separatist movements in the Flemish sections of the occupied territory. The evil effects of their work have not yet entirely disappeared. So efficient was it that even some of the clergy were involved, backing up the efforts of the Germans at the expense of their

be sacrificed for the good of the part. He saw farther and wider than those about him. In this cause more than in any other it was necessary to insist on the truth of the Belgian national motto: "*L'Union Fait la Force.*"

To the world, Mercier must have appeared a political and social worker. But this was the mere surface pattern of his deep spiritual life. His inner life was one of extreme simplicity, asceticism, and devotion. To all appearances he was a Prince of the Church, living in a palace. But actually he was an ascetic and his palace was a monastic cell. He exemplified the famous saying of Marcus Aurelius, "Even in a palace life may be lived well." For in spite of all the opportunities he had for self-indulgence, he hardly even allowed himself the barest comforts. Eating, sleeping, writing, at prayer, and at conferences, he maintained that severity of self-discipline that marked him and set him apart from other men. This can be seen in the contrast between his high position and his way of life.

The Archbishop's palace is a dull and rather shapeless Italian Renaissance building of the eighteenth century. Germany has many *Kurfürstliche Residenze* in the same style. It is neither good nor bad, architectually, but inoffensively mediocre. The builders, Cardinals D'Alsace and Franckenburg, might have done better, but they might also

patriotism. A number of traitorous Belgians formed a group called the *"Conseil des Flandres"* and among other things attempted to damage Mercier's reputation at Rome. This cut Mercier deeply. He said of it later:

"At an exceptionally delicate moment, a few Belgians joined with the Germans in an attempt to make the Holy Father believe that I was betraying the true interests of my flock, the Belgian people. In a calumnious pamphlet which they hoped to pass to the Vatican by the instrumentality of the Apostolic Nuncio, the members of this so-called *'Conseil des Flandres'* petitioned the Pope for my dismissal. . . . The Nuncio refused to forward this, and they had to send their message to Rome by other means."

have done worse. The French Revolutionary armies are to be excused for burning a portion of it, for they vented their wrath on an architecturally unimportant building instead of desecrating the adjoining church of St. Rombaut. The inside of the palace is cold and repelling and devoid of all luxury. Its adornments seem to consist chiefly in a scattering of saints and virgins, a bust of Leopold I, portraits of former archbishops, huge, bad canvases by Wooters, linoleum, and colored stucco. There is a great staircase of the hard, Belgian bluestone. The large Victorian reception-room is marred by a false fireplace, which besides being annoying for its sheer falsity, disappoints in such a chilly interior by shattering the hopes it raises of a blaze. The only object in good taste is a fine *Pietà*, a gift to Mercier from his friend, Meunier, the sculptor.

The large throne-room is suggestive of tiresome formalities. It is used only on ceremonial occasions. The Pope's throne stands on the daïs facing the wall, symbolizing (until the recent settlement) his imprisonment in Rome. On the wall now hang portraits of Archbishop Franckenburg and Janssen's splendid likeness of Mercier. It was in this throne-room that Mercier taught the shy Crown Prince the true values of life.

At the head of the staircase is the chapel. It is garish and ugly to a Protestant's eyes. Above the altar is a circular window depicting the Christ with the Lamb on his shoulders. This is surrounded by colored stucco figures, imitation marble pilasters, brass candelabra, modern oak panelling, all in the worst possible Victorian style.

Mercier's bedroom was severe as a monk's cell. It had

no carpet on the floor, the mirror was microscopic, the iron cot was too short for Mercier's long legs, and it had only a straw mattress. The wash-basin was a plain enamel one, and the only ornaments were a crucifix, a Botticelli "Annunciation," a crude chromo of the Heart of Jesus, and on the mantel a statue of Mary the Mediatrix. In the corner was a hanger holding well-worn capes and soutanes, with a row of huge buckled shoes underneath. By the bed stood the *Prie Dieu.*

The palace had two wings with the garden between. In one wing was Mercier's library, bedroom, and the refectory. In the other was the vicariat where every evening promptly at seven the vicars-general, Van Roey, Van Cauvenbergh, de Wachter, and Legraive, went over their work with Mercier.

Mercier's library thus overlooked the garden. It had a large bay window which gave it a commanding view of the luxuriant spread of flowers and admitted floods of light. On the wall hung a portrait of the saintly Madame Barbe, with much of her son's look in her serious face. She wore her very best Sunday ruffed cap with two crimson bows, one on the crown and one under her chin. On the wall also hung the architect's drawings for the *École Supérieure de Philosophie* at Louvain. (Under the worn-out brief case on the chair were the jubilee numbers of "*Le Patriote Illustré.*") On the writing desk was a fine crucifix, a Virgin with the Christ child in her arms, a portrait of King Albert and one of Benedict the Fifteenth, and a picture of St. Francis de Sales, who never wrote except to make God beloved. There were books and papers scattered everywhere, for this was the workroom of one who read and wrote and thought a great deal. There were many sheets on the desk covered with philosophic writings. Many of these were written on the backs of circulars and the spare sheets of wedding invitations or obituary notices, so as to save stationery. Next to the writing table stood a swivel bookcase, with the books of reference which he needed near at hand. Here were such books as dictionaries—Bossuet's "Meditations on the Gospels"—"*La Sainte Bible Polyglote*"—"*La Charité Sacerdotale*,"—Swete's "The Holy Spirit in the Ancient Church"—"The Holy Spirit in the New Testament"—De Regnon's "*La Sainte Trinité*"—Belet's "*Bibliothèque Théologique*"—Fortescue's "The Mass and the Study of Liturgy"—the Bishop of Newport's "*Lex Levitarum*"—Tyrrell's "*Nova et Vetera*"—Maller's "*Histoire Contemporaine*"—"*Histoire de L'Église*"—Alfred Plummer's "Exegetical Commentary on the Gospel According to St. Matthew"—Doctor Maumigny's "*Pratique de L'Oraison Mentale.*" We can see the variety and amount of his duties by the contents of the "live" files: *Lettres Pastorales, Enseignement Primaire, Vie Diocésaine, Finances, Congrès, Seminaires, Liturgie, Réunion D'Éveques, Question Flamande, Académie, Congo, Communautés Religieuses, Écoles, Conciles, Presse, Associations Scient. Internationales, Conférences Ecclésiast. Nouvelles Paroisses, Syndicats, Alcoolisme, Institut St. Thomas, Nominations Curé, Grand Séminaire, Confirmation, Clergé, Allocutions de Circonstance, Associations des Anciens, Question Sociale.*

The palace embraced three sides of the garden, whose horse-chestnut trees softened and obscured the steep-tiled roofs and sixteenth-century gables, mellow, crumbling in

Photographs by L. Bossut, Malines

Mercier a short time before his death

Mercier in his garden

orange and ochre. The garden was a favorite haunt of Mercier. Paths wandered among the roses, lobelia, lilies, dahlias, red and white geraniums. The verdant bursts of laurel, rhododendron, and holly were a joy to wander among; in spring the lilacs flooded the air with their scent; in summer the taller birches, poplars, maple, and beech made a cool shade for Mercier's promenade. He said the flowers reminded him of his mother, who spent all her spare time in her garden. It was among the flowers that he used most often to read his breviary, "that greatest of books of prayers," filled with his own Greek annotations. Often he would sit with his pad and pencil under the row of lindens or in the little summer house where there was a statue of the Virgin, writing for hours undisturbed by secretaries and vicars. St. Rombaut's steeple was just above him, and sometimes its bells would clang thunderously overhead.[4] But he was so used to them that he went on writing undisturbed. The only time he would stop his writing to listen to the music that poured forth from them was when Jef Denyn was their ringer. He was the greatest of *carillonneurs*, and when he was handling the bells the music was worth listening to.

[4] St. Rombaut, for whom the Cathedral was named, was one of the earliest missionaries in the Low Countries. He had no easy time of it with the savage inhabitants of the eighth century until the God he worshipped gave proof of His real strength. Through His help, Rombaut was not only able to make the blind see, and throw out many an evil spirit, but actually to bring back to life a young nobleman. The simple folk of that day recognized that there was no disputing Rombaut then; it were wiser to kneel before his cross. One day Rombaut was, however, so rash as to flay with his tongue, and in no measured words, a young fellow who was, even for the license of those days, leading a most vicious existence. The culprit lost his temper, grabbed a handy hoe, and brained the lecturer. Though the incident cost Rombaut his life, it gained him canonization. The Lord permitted him often to return to earth so as to help his good Malines converts, and always to bring the hoe with him whenever he appeared.

Mercier's day was strenuous. He rose at five o'clock, even in the chill dusk of winter. He went immediately to the chapel where he knelt for half an hour in meditation, his tapering Gothic fingers pressed together, the thumbs crossed, his body erect, and his head slightly bowed. Then he celebrated Mass in the presence of the household. It was only after this that he ate breakfast in the plainly furnished room, which was as cold and as bare of ornament as were all his quarters designed to serve his physical needs. It did not dampen his spirits or make his day gloomy, however. Upon entering this breakfast room one day in later years, Mercier, in talking to his guest, an American friend, pointed to the ceiling, which had been riddled by a German shell, and said with a good-humored smile, "You must excuse appearances; those are *'freschi tedesci!'* " During breakfast he read his letters and papers, sorting them out for the attention of his secretary and assistants. His next relaxation was the scant hour for lunch, to which he often invited guests, usually his seminarians. He would quickly put them at their ease, for he had the sympathy of St. Paul, the gift of understanding others and entering into their feelings as if they were his own. After lunch, if he could afford the time, he suggested a walk to the Seminary's recreation ground. Generally, however, he made another visit to the Tabernacle before he resumed his work, and then went to the Vicar-General's office for the long conferences with his collaborators in the administration of the diocese. And then twice a week there would be audiences that lasted interminably. When the work was finally cleared up, or the visitors gone, Mercier returned to the Blessed Sacrament for the

106

third time for a half hour of prayer. Then came the modest evening meal, followed by the gathering of the entire household in the chapel to say the Rosary, usually repeated by Brother Hubert. Mercier would give them his blessing, and they would withdraw, leaving him alone before the Blessed Sacrament to meditate with his God. And even then he would not always go to bed, for sometimes he would steal out to visit some sick or dying neighbor. He never knew how to refuse a kindly act. His faithful valet, Franz, who always used to see that he had on his old padded great-coat before he started, often would shrink from telling him that there was another message to come to a dying parishioner, for he knew that, however tired his master might be, he would never refuse, but would go miles in the cold and dark.

He was equally charitable with his audiences. Though those around him did their best to protect the Cardinal against callers and their importunities, this was no easy task, for, without haste and effort, he would see all who came lest he miss an opportunity to help. Better to see them all than let the hundredth sheep go astray. As a result, he saw all kinds of people: hesitant seminarists raked with doubt, silly society women trying to reconcile self-seeking with the seeking of Christ, spent working women, laborers mistaking license for liberty, and cabinet ministers hoping to combine selfishness with a calm conscience. His secretary, Dessain, tells the story of how one day Maurras had an audience with Mercier. When he was leaving, he said to Dessain,

"Your cardinal is dictatorial."

"Why, sir," replied Dessain, "he *is* authority, he rules."

Dessain went in to Mercier and told him what Maurras had said.

"Oh, I know why," answered the Cardinal, "I said to him, 'Monsieur Maurras, you are mistaken, you put the Church at the service of law and order, while they should be at the service of the Church.'"

After listening patiently to Maurras' arguments, Mercier had summed them up and expressed his disapproval. No one had ever spoken to Maurras in such a way before. Another time a distinguished French diplomat had an audience. When he left, he confided to the secretary, "That Cardinal is a dangerous man; that is evident in the fact that at his age he has still preserved the genuine laughter of a child."

Mercier was a tertiary of St. Francis. He followed him in his practice of poverty and self-abnegation. The way in which he deprived himself of food and the smallest necessities of life almost drove his cook Virginie and his valet Franz distracted. The master was a hero to his servants, and the circumvention of the desired mortifications of his flesh called for their utmost ingenuity. He had a bird's appetite, despite his giant frame and indefatigable physical and mental activities. If any little delicacy found its way surreptitiously to his table, it was passed in vain to him. The wine poured in his glass he merely touched to his lips out of courtesy to his guest. Though he never smoked himself, he would occasionally surprise his host by slipping the cigar that was passed to him into his pocket, but only so that he could surprise Franz with the gift. Once the bedroom mirror broke, and Franz purchased a better one. But it was too good, *"trop de luxe,"* so that it had to be exchanged for a smaller one. When the shaving brush cracked and Franz provided a new one, he found Mercier in the gray hours of the morning standing in his underclothes examining the new shaving brush through his pince-nez. He gravely handed the offending novelty to the servant.

"Franz," he said in an injured tone, "take this back to the shop and tie a string carefully around the anatomy of the brush I am using so successfully."

The old brush was repaired and served long thereafter. One day Franz noticed how unusually old and used was the straw on the bed. He secretly changed it, hoping that even though his master did discover it, he would let the matter pass. But the next morning Franz was good-naturedly taken to task.

"Franz," said the Cardinal, trying to be severe, "you do not seem to understand that it is for my good that I deprive myself of comforts."

"No," ventured Franz, stubbornly, "I believe there is a limit to earthly discomforts, and when Your Eminence works as hard as you do, you need a little sleep too."

The soft, kindly look returned to the luminous eyes.

"Ah, Franz, we must constantly mortify the flesh, and never become dependent upon the luxuries and comforts of this world."

The shoes were Franz' especial despair. Mercier would never get new ones. One pair that had been soled many times before, Franz refused to take to have re-soled, for the shoemaker had said the last time that they would fall apart even with new soles.

"Very well, Franz," said Mercier. "The point of disagreement is not a critical one. I will take them myself to my friend in Braine l'Alleud; possibly he will do me the favor of mending them once more."

New clothes were almost out of the question, and yet, strange to say, Mercier took an innocent child's pleasure in his dress if the occasion demanded his tasselled and gold-laced crimson hat or his *"Cappa Magna,"* or the bavette. "It is all for the glory of God," he said to the delighted Franz who proudly handed him the staff that was given to Mercier after the war. On this staff the goldsmith, instead of the usual Paschal lamb, had depicted the dragon (with a German physiognomy) being speared by St. Michael.

From time to time Mercier was given fairly large sums of money, but he never kept any part of the gift for himself. When he won the government prize of 10,000 francs, instead of replenishing his wardrobe, he gave it right and left to the poor. It left him as poor as before, with Franz shaking his head over the meagre contents of the bureau drawers.

"I am the good shepherd: the good shepherd giveth his life for the sheep."—ST. JOHN x, 11.

CHAPTER VI

LEADER OF THE FAITHFUL

MERCIER took over the leadership of the Belgian clergy as a spiritual fatherhood, with high ideals, a strong sense of responsibility, and an eager feeling of opportunity. He had the vision to see what not all of his colleagues saw, that the country is what its people make it, the people are what their clergy makes them, and that the clergy might be shaped to his ideal. He could read the example of English history, and did not need Emerson to tell him that for a thousand years the English clergy have been the scholars of the nation, and that no church has had more learned and industrious men. Perhaps he thought of their names in shining procession, Cardinal Wolsey, Sir Thomas More, John Colet, Robert Burton, Archbishop Usher, Bishop Lightfoot, Palgrave, Newman, Channing, and all the rest. What these did for England, an enlightened and devoted clergy could do for Belgium. Perhaps the Belgian clergy might have done as much had their history been different, if they had worked in a "tight little island" instead of in the "cockpit of Europe."

In the sixteenth century the political-religious revolution directed against Philip II was followed by the dismemberment of the Netherlands, bringing with it important conse-

111

quences in the formation of the mentality of the Belgian clergy. Placed in the vanguard of Catholicism, in the midst of the northern Protestant powers, this clergy was not only imbued with a fighting spirit, but was also alert to keep its faithful in strict obedience.

Its mental alertness became even more pronounced in the eighteenth century, when it was forced to fight against the philosophical spirit which came from France across the south Belgian frontiers, as also against the "enlightened despotism" of Joseph II. Several of this Emperor's reforms were excellent, but they were instituted in so clumsy a manner that they brought about the "Brabançonne Revolution" in 1789, very largely engineered by the clergy. Certain political parties appeared. The so-called *"Statistes,"* who adhered to the sovereignty of the old states or provincial assemblies, with the clergy as their leaders, may be considered as the forerunners of the Catholic Conservatives; while the *"Progressifs,"* consisting mainly of lay members eager for reform, may be considered the predecessors of the Liberals. The clergy desired, with the support of the *"Statistes,"* to reap all the benefits of the revolution, and the so-called *"Progressifs"* were crushed. This internal strife had the deplorable result of facilitating the Austrian restoration in 1790.

The fighting spirit of the Belgian clergy was further developed by the resistance to the French rule from 1795 to 1814. It waged war not only against the foreign domination, but also against the modern ideas which had given birth to the French Revolution. The same spirit of resistance dominated the Belgian clergy from 1814 to 1830. They resented having their country handed over by the powers to the Protestant Prince, William of Orange. The conflict became acute as soon as the clergy had in its "doctrinal judgment" of 1815 condemned the fundamental law of the Netherlands, and forbidden Catholics to swear allegiance to it. The active opposition did not cease and even increased in bitterness after William had tried, in 1825, to oblige all candidates for the priesthood to follow courses of instruction at the philosophical college, which had been established at Louvain in a *"cesaro-papiste"* spirit. The hostility of the clergy towards the educational and religious policy of the King of the Netherlands resulted in the Belgian Catholics temporarily forgetting their quarrels with the Liberals. As these also had grievances of their own against the government, which was persecuting their press, a national union of all Belgians was formed against the government, which consisted almost exclusively of Dutch members. The union resulted in the successful revolution of 1830 and in the independence of Belgium.

Catholics[1] and Liberals remained on good terms for ten years. In all discussions of the constituent assembly, the two parties made mutual concessions, and the Catholics were very broad-minded. The highest ecclesiastical authority, the old Prince of Méan, who was Archbishop of Malines, wrote as early as November 17, 1830, to the National Assembly:

"It is my wish that the Catholics ask for no privileges. Entire liberty, with all its consequences—that is the only object of all their hopes, that is the advantage they wish to share with all other citizens."

[1] The conservative party unfortunately carried the name "Catholic," which should be reserved for the church.

Unfortunately, this good understanding between the two major parties disappeared as soon as Belgian independence was definitely established by the treaty of 1839. The Liberals were the first to repudiate unionism. The Liberal Congress of 1846 marked the beginning of the electoral struggles. The principal point of discord was the so-called "*question scolaire*." The Liberals' demand of entirely official governmental, non-sectarian instruction seemed unreasonable to the point of anathema to the clergy, who feared, and not without reason, that non-sectarian instruction meant either no religious instruction whatever, or what was worse, anti-religious education.

The feeling between the two parties became particularly bitter when the Liberal ministry of 1879 passed a law excluding all religious instruction from the public, primary schools.

The Belgian bishops took the strictest measures against all teachers of lay schools and all parents who sent their children to them. The result was the so-called school war, and the consequent spirit of intolerance. The elections of 1884 ended in a crushing Catholic majority, and the Catholic party remained in unquestioned power up to the time of the World War. As a result, at the time that Mercier was preparing for his great work and was already beginning to exert an influence on students, the clergy found itself in a most favorable position and was able to direct and mold through education the attitude toward the social question, which, after 1886, became very acute in Belgium.

A socialist party had, in the meantime, arisen, and had lost no time in gaining many adherents among the laboring classes in all industrial centres. The clergy, on the other hand, expended its organizing efforts mainly in the country districts which had remained essentially Catholic. Through the religious, economic, and social organization of the *Boerenbond* (peasants' league) the clergy was able to retain its authority among the rural population, the urban population and labor unions being composed largely of unbelievers.

Higher education was rather rare in the ranks of the Belgian clergy. Before the war, its members came largely from the country districts. Such young men from the aristocracy or bourgeoisie as wished to enter the Church, generally preferred to go into one of the great religious orders, and particularly that of the Jesuits, with its high intellectual standards. Only a small number of the candidates for the priesthood went to the University of Louvain; the majority were not concerned by the fact that its scientific courses compared favorably with those of the world's first universities. After passing through the lower seminary, which corresponds to a "college education" in the United States, they finished their studies in the upper seminary, where they perforce specialized almost exclusively in theology. This naturally resulted in many churchmen forgetting their broader culture. There are, of course, many shining exceptions. The proportion of well-to-do and cultivated young men who have become highly educated members of the Belgian church has increased considerably since the war. The city clergy count many first-class men who command universal esteem, not only owing to their faith and teaching, but to the example which they set. Though many of the country clergy are today not men of intellectual attainments, they are otherwise fully equal to the mission en-

115

trusted to them. They are constantly looking after their flocks, comforting them in their misery and assisting their needs, exhibiting inexhaustible goodness. They exemplify what levels may be attained by living a good and simple life. Though they may lack elegance and refinement, it must be remembered that they have to do with peasants, and to know how to act in order to inculcate good principles and exercise an influence over them is no mean accomplishment. They understand the peasants, because they, themselves, often have been peasants.

It was difficult for the parochial clergy to participate actively in the intellectual life of the nation or to have much influence among the cultivated classes. As they were usually in touch with only the lower classes, they far too often took refuge in their own authority and proved sadly lacking when obliged to take up the cudgels against well-informed persons.

Thus, although the Belgian clergy's life and habits were generally irreproachable, it did not enjoy universal consideration.

The Catholic Church in Belgium derives its income partly from gifts of the faithful and partly from the Constitutional obligation entered into by the Government, by which it contributes an insignificant amount towards the livings of ministers of all faiths. For long the Catholic Church, along with all others, had to submit to the nationalization of all church property (subsequent to the French conquest of 1795). Only the church buildings proper, which constituted a civil person, enjoyed civil rights and did not belong to the state. For practical purposes, the trustees were sometimes obliged to carry assumed names, and the church property legally belonged to intermediaries, a situation which resulted of course in all kinds of difficulties and hindered control or use of the property. The law of June 27, 1921, governing "Associations without lucrative object," put an end to that system. In return for publication of their laws and balance sheets in the official journal, the *"Moniteur,"* and upon the annual capital payment to the Government of a tax of one per mil, all associations whose main object is not lucrative receive a legal status distinct from their members, and have thus the legal right to possess property.

There was a time when the Belgian clergy, particularly in the country districts, was obliged to depend upon the generosity of the parishioners for part of its school funds. This resulted in the clergy's lacking independence of the *chatelain* or the rich landowner, and the difference in their social status caused a sometimes excessive deference on the part of the *curé.* This situation changed greatly after the revision of the Constitution in 1893, and the power and influence of the clergy grew with the spread of democratic ideas; henceforth, in the political campaigns the priests often became the village leaders, fighting against the great landowners as well as against the government school teacher. Men who were of the *curé's* mode of thinking were elected to the village administrations. A class among the clergy was thus formed, called the *"petits vicaires,"* mischief-making, ambitious, tactless, and lacking in dignity, who often came into conflict even with the ecclesiastical authorities. Often social work was to these bellicose priests merely a means to insure their own influence. This became particularly evident after the Flemish question had arisen. While French had been the language of most of the cultivated, as well as of the bourgeoisie, certain churchmen for demagogic reasons took up the fight in favor of "flamingantisme," and often poisoned the linguistic conflict by mixing it with religion, as they had previously mixed religion with the political struggles.

As a result of these various circumstances, many of the Belgian clergy often exhibited in a clumsy way what its adversaries called "priestly arrogance," provoking reactions inspired by narrow sectarianism. Thus religion had unfortunately often descended from its high level into electoral conflicts.

Such was the material and organization that came under Mercier's leadership. It was stubborn material, with much cross-grain and many knots to thwart his shaping it to the image of his ideal.

Against the worldly influences on his priests, Mercier set up his ideals and his example of asceticism and withdrawal or detachment. He did not consider it necessary or desirable that either a village priest or a cardinal should desire any more of worldly goods than would suffice to keep him alive; beyond their daily bread, he sought nothing for them. Indeed, when during the war many of them lost practically all they had, he felt it rather a benefit than a loss because poverty would help them toward salvation. His success lay not in advancing them in rank and salary and social and political importance, but in raising their intellectual and spiritual level as the only means of increasing their influence and at the same time insuring that it should be for good.

They must, to be sure, be men of action, but if action is to be for the good of the world, it must be directed by contemplation in withdrawal, and detachment of desire from worldly things and worldly goods. This he constantly set before his clergy, in the written word, in the spoken word, but most potently in example.

When Mercier was making his retreat at Esschen in 1911, his confessor, Dom Columbia Marmion, came to visit him, and finding him miserably lodged in one of the common cells, insisted that the Prior give him a better room and a comfortable mattress. The Prior made the change while the Cardinal was at prayers in the chapel, but he had to move everything back to the original cell as soon as Mercier found it out. And as he himself lived the sacrifice of the Mass with the utmost intensity, so he told his priests, "You must be holy, for you cannot give what you do not possess. You and I must devote a definite period every day to prayer, preferably at dawn; otherwise we are caught by the agitations of the day and the complications of our activities. In the early morning, we have not as yet been seized by the day's whirlwind. And remember, the greater the fear of God, the less the fear of man." He told them that the knowledge of God they could gain only through silence and solitude. He advised them to be men of contemplation and men of action; of contemplation in order to approach Christ; of action in order to fulfill their apostolic duties. Contemplation, he told them, was the source from which they should drink, action the canal by which they should relieve the thirst of the flock of Christ. He found support in the words of the ancients and the moderns; in Plato, who said that if anything gave peace to human life it was the contemplation of perfect beauty; in modern psychology, which recognizes that meditation gives clearness and force to will and intelligence. Most directly did he point this counsel against the dangers of political activities. *"Pas de politique! Tenez-vous en dehors et au dessus des parties."*

All this came to them often from his lips, oftener from his pen, always from his example. He preached the retreat to his priests and to his seminarians; his words might be always with them in his book, the *Retraite Pastorale*, and his example before them when year by year he made his retreat in late summer or early autumn. Beyond example and moral exhortation, he gave them explicit theological instruction which they could follow without doubt or perplexity. In hope of bringing his influence to all as directly and as regularly as possible, he instituted his periodical, *La Vie Diocésaine*. It was on his priests that he set his hope for all the high things he hoped to do for his people, and to them he gave his noblest efforts of inspiration.

In a sense it was a continuation of the work of education in which he had been so long engaged, only now instead of speaking by word of mouth to small groups of neophytes, he sent his voice out to all, speaking as one having authority. The eagerness for the advancement of his work in the Institute was for the spreading of the truth that should make men free. The same eagerness and directness of appeal are in the conversational tone of his pastoral letters. There is more intensity in what might be called his ascetic works, *À Mes Seminaristes, Paix Dans la Fraternité, Action Sociale de nos Évêques, Retraite Pastorale*, and *La Vie Intérieure*, the expressions of his inmost thoughts. And even his doctrinal works, not excepting those in pure theology, are very human. Indeed, some of those who stood nearest to him felt that this quality of ease came more readily from his pen than from his lips.

The influence of his works had behind it the pressure of his tireless energy in producing them. In range of subject they cover widely diverse fields, including economic, social, religious, artistic, and political questions beyond his own fields of philosophy and science; touching subjects concrete and abstract, education, married life, peace, war, charity, mystic contemplation, the liturgy—nothing human was foreign to him, nothing divine was beyond him, nothing urgent escaped him. Between 1906 and 1919 he published three volumes of his pastoral letters, and in the following years four more. All this work varied of course in literary quality. In general the quality is high considering the amount of the work, and certainly the best of it is that addressed to the more intellectual readers. But the clearness of his thinking gave the best of values to his style in all that he wrote. He used French more than the other languages of which he was master, not only because it was his mother tongue, but because he thought it most flexible, and useful for the expression of finer shades of idea and feeling. The beauty of his literary work is not the beauty of conscious artistry, but the beauty of his character, the beauty of sincerity, simplicity, directness, austerity.

Such in general was the effect of asceticism on his art; its mistrust of the sensuous excluded a wide range of values, but developed the best that was in those which remained.

The bareness of Mercier's physical life, in childhood enforced from without and in manhood enforced from within, left his tastes undeveloped beyond narrow fields, but excellent within their range. Mercier loved the beauty of art that comes from sincerity, but sham and make-believe offended his æsthetic sense. To the average Protestant, many a Catholic church is disfigured by gruesome crucifixes and ghastly statues, sometimes grotesquely dressed like dolls in tinsel and trappings. But asceticism need not necessarily lead to insincerity or shabbiness in art, for we find it in the works of masters expressing their loftiest aspirations. Mercier expressed his distaste for what in the churches offended his æsthetic feeling.

Strip off from your altars those tattered and dusty paper ornaments and those vulgar tin objects which, with equal contempt for nature and art, are called artificial flowers. Each season which brings to us its varieties of color and perfume invites in its turn the chrysanthemum, the wild holly with its scarlet berries, the hyacinth, the azalea, the lilac, the lily, to give praise in our churches to God's greatness. *Benedicite iste sanctus est et ego nesciebam. Vere Dominus est in loco isto et ego nesciebam.* Do not empty into the house of the Lord the contents of the pawnshops, nor block up the temple walls with caricatures of the noble figure of Christ on his way to Calvary, and lifeless imitations in cardboard of apostles, martyrs, and virgins. For the honor of God, respect the dignity of His temple. Encourage Christian artists and employ real works of art for the edification of the faithful, and do not assist in smothering their effects under the weight of commercial competition and machine-made articles.

Bare indeed was his altar in later years, a rude board structure against the boarding which supported the shell-riddled walls of St. Rombaut! Then the very bareness was a beauty, the beauty of the naked flame in the indignation of his protest. Beauty Mercier knew well, both with the mind of the philosopher and the feeling of the man. M. le Grand says of him,

As a philosopher, his sensibilities were too keen and too rich not to appreciate to the fullest extent the rôle which art is called upon to play in the expression of all thoughts and feelings, and in bringing out the best of our faculties.

Mercier felt that something was lacking in a character if beauty did not occupy a place in it. He said of beauty and art,

Beauty is founded on truth. The artist takes the elements of his ideal from the reality which surrounds him and appeals to his senses.

The intrinsic aim of art is to move and make an impression. A work which does not contain within itself a genuine source of emotion is not a work of art.

For music, Mercier had little endowment of ear or voice, little, indeed, of interest because of his incessant occupation with ideas. In the beginning of his clerical experience, he gave little thought to the religious and emotional possibilities of it for the purposes of the liturgy. A visit to London in 1909 awakened him to the advantages of music to the Church, a visit to Rome stirred him to action. Pius X, who was truly a musician, was moving toward reform of the liturgy and improvement of ecclesiastical singing. He sent Mercier with his choir-master, Perosi, to hear one of Perosi's oratorios. Its effect on him amounted almost to a revelation when, opening his Bible after the performance, his eye fell first on St. Paul's advice to the Colossians on the value of singing sacred hymns. In his characteristic immediate fashion of translating enthusiasm into action, he set out at once on his return to Malines to learn music and to work with masters of it to give to the liturgy all of the best that music could impart. There were limitations, notably the encyclical of 1903 (not then universally or strictly observed) forbidding the music of Haydn, Mozart, Cherubino, Beethoven, and Gounod. But even so he saw much that he could do. He sent for the music master of the seminary, inspired him with energy and importance, and set him to work on his own choir and encouraged a burst of fresh activity in the training of the seminarians. The plan was to revive the Gregorian chant to give the congregation an active part in the Church offices. Mercier had little knowledge to depend on, but his enthusiasm carried him on. He envisioned church music as a power to spread liturgical studies; he would use its splendor to bring the congregation to worship in the spirit of true beauty. It must be vocal, with no instrumental accompaniment but the organ; it must be collective, and respectful of the liturgy; it must be spiritual and at one with the service, not sensuously alluring; it must employ no device of rhythm, melody, or harmony save such as are fitting for a state of prayer. His energy brought prompt results. Before long he had at St. Rombaut a choir of which he was justly proud, and in later years his contemporaries praised as one of his achievements the work he did to beautify and solemnize the liturgy in the churches of Belgium.

Mercier's enthusiasms were intense, but he was no fanatic.

One day in the fields of l'Hermite he stopped a little girl and asked her if she went to school.

"*Mais non, Monsieur.*"

Had she received her first communion?

"*Mais non, Monsieur.*"

"But aren't you a good little Catholic?"

"*Mais non, Monsieur, je suis Protestant, moi—je m'appelle Françoise.*"

"Ah, how sorry I am," said the friendly old man.

"What a disaster, that there should be Protestants in the neighborhood," he remarked to Julie, the cook, when he reached home.

His feeling was not to damn Protestants with hell-fire, but to bless them with the wish that they might be converted. So he felt toward Americans who were stanch help to him in time of need. To one of their beneficiaries he wrote, "I send you some quarts of condensed milk. Pray for the conversion to Catholicism of our benefactors." When he was in the United States, he was delighted by the affection shown him by Protestants as well as Catholics. He told his friend Thiery, "Just as many Protestants as Catholics greeted me warmly. That would have been impossible with those of different faiths here at home." His essential kindliness, however, never clouded the issue. He makes the distinction between Catholic faith and Protestant with unimpassioned precision:

Luther contests the Church's right to teach authoritatively to Christian society the revelation of Jesus Christ. He pretends that to be a Christian it is sufficient to know one's faith. He does not want hierarchical authority constituted within the Church for the purpose of faithfully transmitting to the world the revealed teachings, nor does he consider the interpretation of them by such authority with right and assurance necessary to protect their integrity. Therein lies the essential point of difference between Catholicism and Protestantism.

And again,

Catholicism says that Christian faith is communicated to the faithful through an official organ of transmission, namely, the Catholic episcopacy, and that faith is based on acceptance of the authority of this organ. Protestantism says, on the contrary, that faith is exclusively a matter of individual judgment, based upon the interpretation of the Scriptures. Authority on one side; individuality on the other.

And in another letter,

Protestantism, the negation of the divine authority of the Church, still pretends to maintain the integrity of the dogma and the unity of the creeds, under the invisible inspiration of the Holy Ghost. But lacking authorized guidance and legal supremacy, doctrinal differences degenerate fatally into irreducible conflicts of incredulity and indifference. At the present moment there is not a single dogma on which the various kinds of Protestants agree.

This unyielding acceptance of doctrine and dogma did not prevent him from winning the hearts of Protestants, for he met them as he met his little neighbor Françoise in sorrow rather than in anger. The zeal of righteous indignation stood him often in good stead, but vindictive anger was not in him nor in his God. His was not the angry Jehovah of the Old Testament, and hell was to him no place of brimstone and flame.

126

Hell, against which numerous spirits rebel with a scarcely justified incredulity, is, essentially, nothing but the obstinate refusal of a soul to love. Eternal misfortune results from refusing to love, just as happiness is the result of it.

And it might surprise Protestants who think that the Catholic Church does not encourage the reading of translations of the Bible by its children to learn that Mercier declared that every educated man should have among his books either the whole text of the Bible, or at least the New Testament, and in addition the catechism of the Council of Trent, a manual of the dogmatic teachings of the Church, a Roman missal, Thomas à Kempis's *Imitation of Christ*, Bossuet's *Meditations on the Gospels*, and St. Francis de Sale's *Introduction to a Devout Life*. His preference for the New Testament he declared freely:

The Gospel of St. John is the most moving and instructive reading imaginable. There are four chapters towards the end of it which are, in my humble opinion, the marvel of marvels. I have read them twenty times—a hundred times —and each time I find a new meaning and a seductive charm. At least get a New Testament so that you may read it every day. And read the Psalms, and then the Prophets, and I promise you pleasures of the intellect and the heart such as you never suspected. And remember that the breviary is the greatest of all books of prayers.

"Le sacrifice est la loi des hautes affections."
                                    —CARDINAL MERCIER.

CHAPTER VII

"PATRIOTISM AND ENDURANCE"

I<small>N</small> the summer of 1914, history repeated itself. A small insignificant country, before that time but little noticed, attracted tragically the notice of the world. It was the country of the people whom Cæsar proclaimed the bravest of all the Gauls—*Horum omnium fortissimi sunt Belgae*—and his word remains as true today as when he spoke it twenty centuries ago. Like the name of Thermopylæ were to become the names of Liège and Namur, where Belgian soldiers were to lay down their lives that their country's honor might live. And from the long-drawn conflict to follow a figure was to emerge greater than all the others. Of all the captains and statesmen of the great war, none was to stand forth in this conflict as the churchman, the man of peace, Cardinal Désiré Mercier. It became his lot to personify the soul of his fatherland and embody western civilization's ideals of right and justice. The position in which the German occupation of Belgium placed him gave to his strength of spirit, his intelligence, his wisdom and responsibility, an opportunity to make themselves felt such as seldom falls to the lot of any one. Mercier measured up not only to all demands of the situation, but even to its possibilities. His history during the war was very nearly the history of Bel-

128

gium. To say so is in no way to belittle Belgium's Soldier King, who was on the field of battle; he and his Queen lived on the blood- and mud-soaked fields of France, and on the last narrow strip of Belgian mire washed by the Channel waves. What they did they did as their duty, and it brought them their glory. To Belgium it brought the history she had never before had, and the new and burning patriotism of her people. To Mercier it brought, as war brought to Lincoln, his full stature.

The invaders entered and locked the doors, and straightway Belgium became Europe's infectious ward, cut off from the rest of the world, and disinfected by *Vermittlungstelle* and *Meldeamte;* destroyers to the west scurrying after submarines; trenches and armies south and east; high-tension currents meaning death to those who braved the wires on the northern frontier. It was a national isolation unparalleled in history. Nothing came through but American food and Prussian propaganda; there was no post, no telegram, no telephone. Within the barriers there was nothing but the steady day-by-day depression comparable only to a family funeral. Motors and bicycles were only for the conquerors; for the conquered, special permits to circulate outside their own bailiwicks; for the rich, narrowly restricted diet; for the poor, breadlines; for women and children, loneliness and anxiety on behalf of the men who were on the other side of the ceaseless distant boom of the guns. The Belgian Government, on alien soil, had only itself to govern, and was not always successful even at that. But the Belgian provinces, for centuries accustomed to decentralized government, managed their own affairs astoundingly well, and the National

Committee set up in Brussels kept pretty well clear of its imminent difficulties. The spirit of self-sacrifice and self-forgetfulness so pervaded all classes that their differences of faith and politics for the time disappeared, burned away by the common calamity. Rancors melted; quarrels and rivalries went; pettiness vanished; political parties disappeared and class distinctions were forgotten. Except for the enemy, those who were left inside the barriers were Belgians and nothing else. The duchess poured the milk of the children of the poor; the princess nursed the unknown sick; every heart was open to one and all—except the enemy. Every one had the same wish, news from the front; every one had the same fear, the Germans; every one had the same love, *La Patrie*. Every man was his brother's keeper. That it should have been so need surprise none; the miracle was that it lasted for four years without a human let-down. The situation that brought about this spirit seemed even to those who caused it to have no parallel. Prince von Bülow, who preceded von Bethmann-Hollweg as the War Chancellor of the German Empire, referred later in his *Memoirs* to his own country's treatment of Belgium as that of "a nation which, by infringing Belgian neutrality, did unheard-of violence to international law and to treaties which it had sworn to maintain."

Such was the crisis which called upon Mercier, student, thinker, intellectual, at the age of sixty-three to become the man of action. By character he was fitted for the part; he had the indomitable will that was necessary, the self-control, the sanctity, wisdom, authority. And is it too fanciful to suggest that the war gave him opportunity to test in practice the philosophy he had so long pronounced in theory? St. Thomas postulates three elementary requirements for the waging of a righteous war. First, the consent of public authority (those ruling by consent of the people) typified in the person of the Prince, *Auctoritas Principis*. Second, a just cause, *Justa Causa*. Third, a right intention, *Recta Intentio*. To St. Thomas, the end and object of war was the re-establishment of peace. His concept, which excludes, of course, all aggressive wars, was very familiar to Mercier, to whom an aggressive war was a heinous violation of justice. As a devout Catholic, he saw war as a sin against charity. His opinion of it may best be summed up in his own words:

No might is right! The use of force may be legitimate or illegitimate, that is to say, it may conform to or be contrary to right; but the only legitimate use that any human government whatsoever can make of force is to place it at the service of Law, to the end that Law may be enforced and respected.

And again:

Right is a moral force, the exercise of which is guaranteed and sanctioned by force. The easier it is to use force, the more dignity commands the restraint of its use.

Mercier approved heart and soul of the decision of King Albert and his advisers to resist as long as possible the German advance across the neutral soil of Belgium. Like one of the great bishops of the fifth century, he stood erect with his country's banner in his hand, waiting undaunted the enemy's approach.

On August 20, 1914, Pius X breathed his last. His death placed upon Mercier the immediate duty to go to Rome to attend the conclave for the election of a new Pope, and to make the most of the opportunity to discuss Belgian affairs with him for guidance in his episcopal duties. But he could not leave his flock without complete assurance that the Germans would let him return, and well he knew how glad they would be to get rid of him, how reluctant to see him return. It took the whole influence of the Roman Church to get him such assurance, but get it he did; *laissez-passers* came through for him and his secretary, Canon Vrancken, probably because the attitude of Rome was a matter of much importance at that time to Germany and Austria, and they were seeking to cultivate the good-will of the Holy See by careful propaganda among their Catholic people. It goes without saying that if Mercier had not had assurance of his return he would not have gone. He left just in time, only an hour before the Germans cut the Malines-Termonde railroad, and travelled through Lille and Paris amid sights strange and foreboding, endless columns of poilus, artillery, supply trains, trucks, and cars of ammunition.

In Rome he found on the whole more of sympathy than comprehension. Among his good friends he found some who felt that Belgium had done all that could be expected for her honor, and that further resistance to the German invaders was suicidal. An important officer of the Church who called on Mercier asked him, perhaps with too much of condescension or complaisance, what on earth the Belgians expected to accomplish by continuing the useless sacrifice. The blundering instrument of stupidity touched in Mercier a quivering nerve. He sprang from his chair and put his hands on his caller's shoulders; his voice trembled with emotion.

"But, Prince," he cried, "you don't think—you can't think —what you are saying! No one thinks that way at home."[1]

Mercier took part in the mourning of Rome, the beautiful and impressive services which Periosi conducted in the Sistine chapel. He went down into the crypt where Pius lay for the time, to weep and pray beside him in private. Then he and his colleagues turned to the duty of the hour. The election was painful, for the situation was inevitably strained, and conversation between the cardinals of the warring nations was embarrassed and forced in intervals which should have been times of relaxation. The correspondent of *The London Times* may have been well informed when he reported dissension and excitement in the conclave before it could reach agreement. Despite Mercier's nationality, his chances of election were not entirely negligible. The College was at the time about equally divided in number between Italian and foreign cardinals, and many of the foreigners, French and British in particular, are said to have voted for Mercier as a protest against German action in Belgium. Indeed, Mercier's indignation is said to have led him so far as to call the conclave's attention to the outrages daily taking place in his country, a protest which is said to have called forth a lively remonstrance from the German and Austrian cardinals against the introduction of political subjects into such an assembly. But at last the smoke of agreement arose to heaven. The choice was Cardinal della Chiesa. The college dispersed, but not before Mercier had received bad news.

[1] Henri Davignon, *Le Cardinal Mercier et la Guerre* in *La Revue Hebdomadaire,* Jan. 30, 1915.

On August 27, when the noon-day meal was over, Mercier's old friend Cardinal Vico, late Nuncio at Brussels, took Mercier's arm and suggested a few steps together in the Raphael gallery. When they were alone together, Vico held up a newspaper.

"The news is bad," he said.

Mercier braced himself for a shock.

"The University of Louvain is burning. Your palace and your cathedral have been under bombardment."

Mercier, stunned, opened and stared at the newspaper. His palace was torn by shells, and the nave of his cathedral was a heap of debris. Tracery, glass, and masonry were shot to pieces. About one-sixth of Louvain was gone; the precious library was entirely burned with all its rarest books, and burned was many a former colleague's home. The *Vieux Marché*, the *Palais de Justice* and the *Théâtre* were all in ashes. The dead bodies of his peaceful students were being burned. In the goodness of his heart, Mercier, though he realized what war meant, had believed no civilized nation capable of such acts of vandalism. In his first misery he murmured, "Why all this sorrow, Lord? My God, my God, hast thou forsaken us?" Then, as he looked at his crucifix, the complaint died on his lips, and he added, "A disciple is not above his master, nor a servant above his Lord," and throwing back his head, sustained by an inner force that made Vico marvel, he said, *"Nous rebâtirons!"*

Mercier expressed his feelings to a Roman friend, Dom Ernest Vercesi, who repeated them to a reporter of the *Corriere d'Italia*, for whose mill it was obviously the best of grist. At its appearance in the paper, the German Ambassador to the Holy See was infuriated. He informed the newly elected Pope, Benedict XV, that unless the Belgian Cardinal made a public retraction he would not be allowed to return to Belgium. Mercier's only reply was, "One does not disavow the truth." Testimony since the war is in Mercier's favor. Hugh Gibson, Secretary of the American Legation, was in Louvain at the time of the burning and killing. In his *A Journal from Our Legation in Belgium*, he tells of hearing from German officers he talked with in the streets that they had every intention of wiping out the city. He recorded in his diary that it was a cold-blooded and calculated plan to terrorize the civilian population, and "it was not until the German Government realized the horror and loathing with which the civilized world learned of the fate of Louvain, that the orders were cancelled and the story sent out that the German powers had tried to prevent the destruction." Perhaps that was why the Ambassador did not insist. Mercier's safe-conduct was not recalled. In company with the three French Cardinals he went to Marseilles. There, while the tramp of the poilus sounded on the pavement outside, the four Princes of the Church knelt at the altar and prayed that the Virgin would bring to the arms of France and Belgium the benediction of her Son. Then he took up his journey over fighting France, where the Battle of the Marne had just been won.

As he neared home he had to go deviously about. Only a narrow strip of western Belgium remained free. On a portion of it Belgian soldiers, reinforced by British marines, still cherished illusions as to the strength of the Antwerp fortifications, while disillusioned civilian refugees crowded westward in tens of thousands to throw themselves on British hospitality. After reaching England, Mercier recrossed the Channel against the current of the exodus to take charge of his distracted flock in the face of the storm, in the spirit expressed in the words, "I am the good shepherd and I know my own, and my own know me." There he took the position described by the French writer, Victor Giraud:

The Archbishop of Malines faced Germany coolly, resolutely, audaciously, demanding from her his full right, especially the right to do his full duty; he spoke, he wrote, protecting, organizing, consoling. Over four years' time, this tall lean prelate, with the pale, ascetic countenance, the deep burning eyes, the grandest figure in the Catholic world of our day, may be said, along with King Albert, to have personified the very soul of sturdy little Belgium.

He spent a night in Antwerp with his friend Count Moretus, and then, as early as possible the next morning, set out for Malines with a *gendarme*, and a *garde civique*, in a military motor. At the palace Mercier's heart sank at the clang of the bell in the deserted building, but there was Franz with a smile of welcome on his worried face. Mercier embraced, blessed, and comforted him with a word of praise in Flemish, "You have done well, Franz, you never left!" Then Père Rutten,[2] the Dominican of the Christian Syndicates, came running to join the welcome and tell of all that had happened. The wounded had only just been evacuated from the throne room, which had been turned into a hospital. The walls of His Eminence's own bedroom had been rent by two shells, the dining-room ceiling was half down, but the Blessed Virgin had diverted the shells from

[2] Now (1932) a Christian-Socialist Senator in the Chamber of Deputies.

the little chapel where everything, God be praised, was still unscathed. Mercier went there first of all. As he rose from his knees he murmured, "God alone can pardon them." His next thought was, of course, for the cathedral. The streets of the city he found swarming with confusion like a disturbed ant-hill, hurried, dismayed citizens, householders pushing through the crowds with carts, trucks, and wheelbarrows crammed with household goods, children perched on the tottering loads, and a long queue of hungry people waiting for bread which the good burgomaster, Dessain, was distributing from the *Maison Communale*. When they came in sight of the cathedral, Père Rutten saw a look of indignation mingled with disconsolate tenderness come over the Cardinal's face. But, thank God, St. Rombaut had been built to withstand centuries of assault, and was as yet comparatively unharmed. *"Comme elle a bien résisté, la brave église,"* said Mercier. Then, to fulfil his agreement with the military authorities, he turned away to go back to Antwerp. But his affection for his people, and the impetuosity of his eagerness for his duty to his charge, brought him back to Malines the next morning, and there he remained until the Germans for the third time bombarded his open and unarmed city.

September 27 was a Sunday on which the Cardinal had to celebrate mass in St. Rombaut, but two bombardments made it impossible. As the shells fell, Mercier, slowly telling his rosary, walked down the garden path that led to the cellar, where he remained with his household until his secretary, Canon Vrancken, told him that the authorities could no longer be responsible for his life, which was too precious to the nation for him to be allowed to risk it any longer. He gave way reluctantly, and a motor took him back to Antwerp along a highway crowded with terrified people fleeing the German tempest. The carillon of St. Rombaut was mute, and was to remain so despite every threat until the day of victory. As the fog was turning to a cold drizzle, the tired, heartbroken old man with a determined set to his jaw bumped past the challenge of the guards, over the *pavés*, back into panic-stricken Antwerp. But in Antwerp there was neither refuge nor strength. The redoubtable fortifications went down before the German artillery as if they were of cardboard instead of reinforced concrete. Belgian and British soldiers left, but Mercier stuck to his post. "I shall leave," he said, "only upon the formal order of my King." The two had come to the understanding that Albert would never order the shepherd to leave his flock. So the tall, lean, angry prelate, at bay, awaited the enemy. When they came, the head chaplain of the Navy called on Mercier, and the two soon came to terms on the basis of a prompt resumption of religious life throughout the country, and a guarantee of its unmolested continuance. The Bishops, too, were to have complete liberty of communication with their flocks. On this agreement, Mercier issued a circular letter to his clergy urging them to return to their work under the guarantee of normal ways of life and public safety. This letter contributed greatly to the re-establishment of normal conditions.

Normal, however, it was not and could not be in the path of advance of an enemy army, which has never in history been without cruelty, pillage, and rapine. The Germans believed, rightly or wrongly, that snipers fired at them from ambush. Their retaliation was terrible, for they sought to bring about abject submission by abject fear. After the Germans had conquered all of Belgium but a strip in the southwest, they set up a temporary government of characteristic Prussian efficiency. The measures it took were then and later outrageous to civilized ideas of right and justice, and from them there was no redress, for the courts were inquisitional bodies before whom the accused had no rights. Conditions were outrageous, and abroad they were greatly exaggerated. Mercier did what he could to ameliorate them. As soon as the new regime established itself, Mercier called on the military Governor, General von Huene, and succeeded in obtaining from him a promise that young Belgians remaining in the country would not be transported to Germany nor forced to work for the Germans in Belgium. This promise was of importance to Mercier later on.

Toward the end of October, Mercier contrived to return to his Archbishopric. There he found a doddering, near-sighted old gentleman, Field-Marshal General von der Goltz, installed as Governor General. He was not to remain long. Mercier as a matter of course exchanged courtesy calls with him, and tried to gain his influence to have priests and teachers returned to their charges, but nothing came of it, for von der Goltz was relieved and succeeded by Baron von Bissing early in December of 1914.

Meanwhile, Mercier turned his palace into a busy headquarters, organizing the duties of the clergy of all ranks to meet the emergency. The misery and suffering on every side were such that there must be no delay, and there were few to help the work along, for many a priest and many a teacher now cryingly needed at his post had been caught up by the advancing waves of war and dragged by the back-wash into Germany. Mercier wrote in the bitterness of his soul,

I have travelled through the devastated regions of the diocese. Despite my worst apprehension, what I have seen of ruins and cinders surpasses imagination. Many parishes have lost their pastors. . . . Thousands of Belgian citizens have been deported to German prisons; I know of thirteen priests or ecclesiastics in one parish alone who were put to death. We cannot count our dead, nor measure the extent of our ruins. . . . The last four months seem to me to have lasted a century.

Such was the devastation he had seen when he went to make his call on the new Governor General.

General-Oberst Moritz Ferdinand, Freiherr von Bissing, reminded one of some merciless bird of prey. Half a century of Prussian discipline, exercised in the campaigns of 1866 and 1870, had successfully removed from his face every vestige of kindliness or humor. His firm mouth shut tightly, and his shrewd blue-black eyes flashed pitilessly at any opposition to his will. He was said to have been sent to Belgium because he was "the right man" for the job of teaching the Belgians to obey. He had proved himself a great strategist in the East, and his age—he was past seventy—had not lessened his efficiency. His silver spurs and his sabre clanked against the stone of stair and courtyard as he marched with the briskness of a youth from his office to his motor, and his heavy mustache and weather-beaten features scarcely moved as he snapped out his orders to his subordinates. Beyond question he was "the right man in the right place." He perceived that the Cardinal was a tremendous force for law and order and peaceful government, and decided at once to try to initiate friendly relations. The contrasting concepts of the two as to the term "law" were to make this difficult. Von Bissing wrote to the German Cardinal Archbishop of Cologne, von Hartmann, requesting his good offices. Cardinal von Hartmann transmitted von Bissing's friendly advance to his brother Cardinal of Malines, saying that the new Governor General was "an intelligent, just, circumspect, and benevolent man who had it at heart to conform to the wishes of the Bishops." Mercier's reply to von Hartmann denounced the horrors to which he was a daily witness, which reminded him of the pagan persecutions of the first three centuries of the Roman Church. Von Bissing refused to forward this to Cologne. The Baron's first step advanced him not at all. He tried another. He informed the Cardinal that the German War Ministry had ordered the repatriation of all the Belgian priests detained in Germany, and declared his good intentions toward the Belgians. Mercier thanked him, but added that he could not forget the horrors perpetrated by the German soldiery, and von Bissing's second step left him where the first began. Mercier made his position quite clear in his next letter:

My esteem for Your Excellency personally, my gratitude for the interest you manifest in the welfare of my country, my desire not to augment, but rather, indeed, to lighten the burdens of your office and its incident responsibilities, are absolutely sincere. But I consider it the part of frankness to add that, whatever the personal inclinations of Baron von

Bissing may be, he represents among us, as Governor General, a hostile and usurping power, against which we assert our right to independence and the respect of our neutrality. Furthermore, speaking as the representative of the moral and religious interests of Belgium, I protest against the violent acts of injustice of which my fellow-countrymen have been innocent victims.

Those present when von Bissing received this have left no record of anything he said or thought of it, but coming from one of the subjugated Belgians in a tone to which he was utterly unused, these words must have dumbfounded him. In time he must have become more habituated to such shocks, for again and again, despite all threats of commanders and all vicissitudes of war, that eloquent and irrepressible voice was to remind him of the superiority of Right over Might.

The correspondence that went on through the invasion and occupation between Mercier on the one side and von Bissing and his political aide, Baron von der Lancken, on the other, will go down in history as among the most remarkable ever exchanged between captor and captive. It shows an astounding knowledge on Mercier's part of politics no less than of philosophy. His letters have in them not only a complete code of ethics, but the essential structure of all international law, a consistent correctness of basic principles, and an adroitness of logic which the two Germans never succeeded in parrying. Nor had they anything to oppose to the lucidity and precision of his style. How often must they have wished him at the bottom of the sea! If their hope was actually to silence him, they must have been devoid of all historical sense, and all feeling for human psychology, for it must have been apparent enough that he was all too eager for a martyr's crown. In fact they were too astute to grant him that. Nor could von Bissing very well imprison him, as he had Burgomaster Max, and many another, though at times, when feelings ran high in Germany and the Prophet's voice was at its loudest, strong pressure was put upon him to do so. But the feelings of Catholic neutrals had to be taken into account, and the feelings of Catholic Germany.

Mercier was, in fact, the most uncomfortable neighbor with whom von Bissing could possibly have been cursed. As a Belgian citizen he had to speak out. After mature deliberation he decided that the best way to make his voice heard was through pastoral letters. The Germans could not silence them because they could not know beforehand when they would be read; he could reach every one, and would be within his rights in his own churches. Thus he spoke, and to tremendous effect. It was largely owing to his pastoral letters that the people remained calm and refrained from excesses, particularly when the day came for the withdrawal of the German troops from the country. On Christmas Day, 1914, Mercier sent to the priests of his diocese the pastoral letter entitled "Patriotism and Endurance," which became the fundamental Charter of Rights and Duties of occupied Belgium, and was one of the greatest documents of the World War. Several motives impelled him to write this letter, and to publish it to the world. Certain neutral opinion, particularly in neighboring Holland, overflowing with Belgian refugees, condemned Belgium for not granting free passage to the invading Imperial armies. Mercier felt the necessity of stigmatizing the behavior of the Germans and of placing Belgium's heroic resistance before the world in its true perspective. This letter had a tonic effect on the ebbing morale of the Belgian people. Through secret channels it permeated the country, and news of it went secretly in advance. Socialists, Communists, and Freemasons flocked to the Catholic churches to hear it read. As if on the very winds it "went flying all abroad." It stirred Frenchmen of all classes deeply, and the Cardinals of France replied in a joint letter of thanks. Mercier's words were becoming the chief weapon of the Church. They made of him a figure of international importance, suddenly illuminated to all who had not known him. The letter is too long to be given in full text, but some of the words which placed Mercier in a position of leadership and protection comparable while it lasted to that of the King, are worthy of special notice:

Belgium has pledged her honor to defend her independence. She has kept her word. . . . Germany has broken her oath. I consider it to be an obligation of my pastoral charge to define your duties of conscience in face of the power that has invaded our soil and that has, for the time being, occupied the greater portion of it. This power is not a legitimate authority, and consequently at the bottom of your heart you owe it neither respect, attachment, nor obedience. The sole legitimate authority in Belgium is that which belongs to our King, to his Government, and to the representatives of the Nation. He alone has the right to the love of our hearts and our allegiance, he alone means authority to us.

The acts of public administration of the occupant would in themselves be without force, but legitimate authority tacitly ratifies such as are justified by public interest. Their whole judicial value rests upon this ratification. Let us respect regulations as long as they neither conflict with the

liberty of our conscience, nor with our patriotic duty. . . .
God will save Belgium, my brothers, you can have no
doubt of this. Let us rather say, "He is saving her." In
very truth, through the glare of flames and the vapor of
blood, do you not already catch a glimpse of the evidence of
His love for us? Is there a patriot who does not feel that
Belgium has grown greater? Who is there that does not
contemplate with pride the brightness of the glory of our
stricken land? When in her throes she brings forth heroes,
our Mother Country gives her own energy to the blood of
these sons of hers.

Each of us harbors a sentiment greater than mere personal interest, than ties of blood or the call of party, namely
the necessity, and consequently the will, to devote oneself to
the common interest, to what Rome called "the public thing,"
Res Publica. This sentiment is patriotism. The fatherland
is not an agglomeration of individuals or families living on
the same spot, having more or less intimate neighborly or
business relations, recalling the same happy or painful memories. No, it is an association of souls in the service of the
same social organization, which must be safeguarded and
defended at all costs, even with one's blood and under the
leadership of him or those who guard its destiny. Compatriots live because they are of one soul, springing from
traditions of a common life in the past as well as common
hopes and aspirations.

Patriotism, an internal principle of unity and order, an
organic bond of the members of a nation, was placed by the
first thinkers of ancient Greece and Rome at the head of
the natural virtues. Aristotle, the prince of pagan philosophers, deemed disinterestedness in the service of the city,
that is, of the state, to be the very ideal of human duty. The
religion of Christ made patriotism a law. There can be no
perfect Christian who is not a perfect patriot.

If the effect of this letter on the Belgian people was widespread and stirring, on the enemy it was no less. Mercier

sent with it a note enjoining his priests to read it to the faithful "without any omission or excision no matter what authority might give orders to the contrary." Orders to the contrary came promptly. Von Bissing sent to most of the Curés forbidding the reading, and tried to seize copies of the letter where they could be found. He searched the house of the printer, Monsieur Dessain of Malines, confiscated remaining copies of the letter, and fined Dessain. Mercier had, of course, foreseen this, and had suggested employing some other printer less likely to be suspected, but the printer was no less loyal than the Cardinal. "Is not Dessain official printer to the Archbishopric of Malines?" he replied.

Another printer, Warny, almost lost his life during the war because of his devotion to Mercier. It was in connection with a pamphlet called: *The German Army at Louvain and the White Book*, which Mercier had commissioned Professor Mayence to write in refutation of the German *White Book*, especially against the part dealing with the Louvain outrages. The whole thing had to be done in secrecy. Warny was printing it in the parlor of a private residence in an out-of-the-way part of Louvain. Several copies had already been printed and circulated before the German Intelligence Officer discovered it. He traced them to the printing establishment, which he raided, and discovered Warny hard at work printing more. He demanded to know where they originated and who was responsible. Warny would disclose nothing. He only said, "What can a poor printer's devil know of the original of the manuscript?" He was taken to St. Gilles prison in Brussels, but no threat nor bribe could induce him to speak. He would die rather than betray his Cardinal.

"PATRIOTISM AND ENDURANCE"

Von Bissing's next move was to send his aide, von der Lancken, to call on Mercier. The Baron von der Lancken was so finished a product of diplomacy as to be considered the envy of his colleagues in the *Wilhelmstrasse*. In looks, in dress, in manner, he was impeccable. The marriageable daughters of the Berlin aristocracy used to admire his handsome figure and smart-fitting uniform. His complexion was so fresh it might have been produced by British fogs. At home he had wide-spreading estates; behind him was an enviable foreign career. Ten years in the Paris Embassy had made his French as faultless as his society behavior. What is more, his mind was so truly well-trained that the foreign office felt that he might quite probably rise to the very top of its ladder, especially if he were to handle successfully the ticklish political problems of occupied Belgium. He worked well under von Bissing, not, indeed, for the first time, for he had served in the *Garde du Corps* regiment at Potsdam in the days when von Bissing, then a rising cavalry officer, was its Lieutenant Colonel. He has written himself into history as the man who would not lift a finger to stop the military execution of a British Army nurse on the ground that "the effect upon the civilized world of shooting Edith Cavell would be excellent." With no better judgment of the feelings of civilized men than that, he still prided himself on his erudition, and fancied himself an adept in dialectics. He looked forward to crossing swords in diplomatic discussion with the Cardinal. He did not underestimate Mercier's ability, but expected his feelings to throw him off his guard.

At half past six in the morning following the publication of the pastoral letter, von der Lancken with two attendant

147

officers called at the Archbishop's palace. It was still dark, but the Cardinal was just about to go to his chapel for early mass; if von der Lancken expected the advantage of surprise in the earliness of the hour, he mistook his man. Mercier had them shown into the big unheated reception room on the ground floor, and entered to them with the full effect of his imposing dignity. "To what," he asked, "do I owe the honor of a visit at so unusual an hour?"

The Baron declared his errand: to express the surprise of the Governor-General at the pastoral letter, and to call for an explanation, for the letter said infamous things about the Germans with the intention of stirring up the populace. More than that, the Cardinal must be fully aware of the regulations forbidding the publication of anything not passed by the German censor.

"If I have said disagreeable things," Mercier replied, "you have done them. Is it culpable to unmask crime? Re-read my letter, and you will see that on the contrary I invite the faithful to bear with your trying presence as a mark of their faith. I have spoken to the faithful members of my diocese as a father who has confidence in his sons. You question me as to my relations with my King and with the King of England; you wish to know why I have invited the members of my diocese to make the 3d day of January a day of prayer in accordance with the request of the King of England.[3] I am frankly surprised by your questions. If I am not mistaken, the acts of one's private life are not subject to government control. Do you claim the right to enter into my relations with my own, or foreign sovereigns? I have

[3] In this matter, Mercier had consulted his Government at le Havre.

Photograph by L. Bossut, Malines

Mercier in the processional blessing the people

no need of asking any censor's permission in the exercise of my pastoral duties. I am a Bishop. I am a Cardinal of the Holy Roman Church, and duly receive my orders from the Sovereign Pontiff. The preacher of the word of God would have failed in his mission if he did not understand that in the tragic times which we are traversing agonized consciences need guidance. Are we to accept and submit to occupation? Has the invader, unjust at the start, become a legitimate authority? If so, how are we to reconcile our respect for the oppressors with our fidelity to our King? Which will gain the upper hand, Might or Right?"

Though the Cardinal's smile may have been as sweet as the kiss of peace at the *Missa Fidelium*, his retort courteous was full of saintly venom. But it was more the courtesy than the venom that checked his adversary's first move. Von Bissing's next move was to forbid further publication of the letter, and to place sentinels around the Archbishop's palace. A day or two later his adjutant, Captain von Stempel, called at the palace with a letter demanding a reply, which, he declared, he would not leave without. Von Bissing's demand to which Mercier must give immediate reply was, "I am obliged to request Your Eminence to forbid your clergy at once to circulate the pastoral." Mercier left the room to prepare his reply. The situation was critical. Ready as he may have been for a martyr's crown, he could not win it at the expense of his plain duty. Imprisonment or death, whatever glory they might bring to him, would bring to his people suffering without leadership or comfort. The King was beyond the lines, but Mercier was as well assured of his approval and sympathy as if his endorsement of the pastoral

149

had been sent to him instead of necessarily to the Pope to whom King Albert had written:

"I express to the venerated head of the Roman Catholic Church my admiration of Cardinal Mercier's conduct. Following the example of the glorious prelates of the past, he has not feared to proclaim the truth in the face of error, and the unwritten, righteous cause of the universal conscience."

Mercier prepared his reply to von Bissing in his oratory rather than in his study. There he received strength and enlightenment to reply to von Bissing's demand by an unqualified refusal to withdraw his communication to his clergy. The German officers straightened their backs, clicked their heels, and bowed themselves away from a figure erect and defiant.

Von Bissing decided to arrest Mercier and intern him in Germany, and immediately sent the Cardinal telegraphic orders to remain in his palace. Von der Lancken decided on a slightly more diplomatic course, and informed the Spanish Minister, the Marquis de Villalobar, of what they intended to do. Villalobar was horrified. He warned them by word and by display of feeling of the wrath of Rome and the effect on public opinion and sympathy. It prompted them to second thoughts, and they consulted the German Chancellor. He took time to reflect. Meanwhile a rumor went abroad that Mercier had been placed under arrest. It reached Rome, and the Pope gave the German envoy to the Vatican a bad quarter of an hour over it, and telegraphed a protest to Berlin. Germany decided to move cautiously. Mercier went free. Von Bissing, however, attempted another sort of attack. He circulated what purported to be Mercier's reply to his demand of suppression, so distorted and perverted as to convey the impression that Mercier, in order to avoid difficulty, wished the clergy to refrain from further use of the pastoral letter. On behalf of the bewildered clergy, Mgr. Everard, Dean of Ste. Gudule in Brussels, applied to Mercier for official information. Mercier promptly informed all parish priests and rural deans that the "written German prohibition is deceptive and false."

He heard no more of that, but he soon had to raise his voice against another sort of propaganda. The German press circulated inflammatory stories of atrocities perpetrated by Belgians on Germans, many of whom were said to have been horribly mutilated in various parts of the country. The absurdity and injustice of these reports roused the Cardinal to action. He suggested to Colonel Wergersky, the Kreischef of Malines, that a commission be appointed, consisting of an equal number of Germans and Belgian magistrates presided over by a neutral, to sift the reports of the "atrocities." Naturally the invaders would not consider so equitable a suggestion.

Such difficulties as these rose and disappeared, and so long as the Cardinal believed, as so many did at the time, that the conflict would be swift and short, the evils of it were sufficient unto the day. But the check of the German armies in the fall of 1914 brought to him, as well as to the rest of the world, the realization that the war would be long drawn out, and Belgium herself understood that her captivity would be long to endure. To meet the food problem brought about by the situation, an American engineer living in London, named Herbert Hoover, devised a plan for feeding Belgian children in the hope of saving them, at least, from downright starvation. As soon as the Germans and the Allied and Associated Powers had approved the plan, a group of American idealists went into Belgium to feed the hungry and help to keep the peace. Meanwhile, Mercier suspended the Church regulations as to fasting and abstinence until the end of the war.

Mercier's next attack was against military reprisals and executions, which, the Germans declared, were brought about by the Belgian "free-shooters" or "snipers." Mercier, in the attempt to shed the light of truth on the German excuses for their wantonness, published a long letter to the Cardinals and Bishops of the Church in Germany, Bavaria, and Austria-Hungary, begging them to join the Belgian Bishops in an impartial mixed tribunal, as a counter suggestion to the all-German committee proposed by von Bissing. If Mercier believed that the German prelates would be as high-minded as himself in the matter, he was soon disillusioned. Neither they, nor Mgr. Mittendorf, the Chief Catholic Chaplain for the German Armies of the West, would consent to anything so impartial. He called on Mercier with a message from von Bissing and a manner of his own, a manner clearly dictated by a sense of military rather than ecclesiastical relationship. He began by trying to entrap the Cardinal by a sort of cross-examination which Mercier, unruffled by the flagrant discourtesy, baffled by his suave courtesy. Then Bishop Mittendorf formally read his rebuke from von Bissing, calling the Cardinal to account for having written to the Archbishop of Paris without submitting his letter to the German censor. Mercier replied with a home thrust so keen that Mittendorf hardly knew how deep it cut. "You Germans," said Mercier, "after many months of occupation, have not yet got to know the Belgians. Among you, a general commands, and automatically every one obeys. Here with us, good sense, regard for higher interests, interprets the order and dictates our conduct. External regulations are meant, no doubt, for every one; and it is in this sense that I have acknowledged them as the Governor-General reminds me in his letter. But every one applies them with a due regard for different contingencies, and the obligations which they entail." And in his written reply to von Bissing, he said,

Germans have assuredly their qualities, but they lack psychology. You believe the world can be governed by abstract formulas. You imagine that the method of domination which you may have employed successfully in Germany will also succeed here. You are entirely mistaken. I have spent my life teaching. I have learnt that to be able to educate a young man, you must know him before applying formulas to him. To pass laws and apply the legislation are two entirely different things. You seem to ignore these elementary truths.

Mercier's office was occupied with a ceaseless stream of correspondence, endless letters on a wide variety of subjects to and from friends and foes; to Hoover, the American food administrator, keeping before him the urgency of increasing the shipments of foodstuffs; to General Leman, the heroic defender of the fort of Loncin, on military topics; and the ceaseless vigorous controversy with the office of the Kreischef of Malines. The never-ending question there was the treatment of the Belgian clergy, particularly the release of those confined at Heidelberg. Beyond question, the Germans, stung by Mercier's incessant attacks, revenged themselves on his clergy, particularly the Jesuits. Such reprisals incited Mercier to greater activity. Whenever von Bissing accused his priests of disturbing public order by their exhortations to patriotism, Mercier retorted with the contention that there was only one way to assist the Belgian people in their suffering, and that was to show them that they were understood. This was, of course, the merest nonsense to the Prussian disciplinarians, who persecuted the priests by imprisonment and deportation to Germany on charges of inciting the people to attack and mistreat the German soldiery. Again and again Mercier tried to obtain mitigation of such sentences, or absolute release of the victims, and the fact that he seldom succeeded never lessened his ardor, or his energy in emphasizing the influence of the martyrs' example to their flocks. With no less energy he worked to gain von Bissing's permission to send chaplains to the Belgian Army and to the Belgian political prisoners. And his answers to von Bissing's complaints of the seditious nature of the sermons of his clergy were the daily grist of Mercier's industrious mill.

Mercier's true greatness throughout all this is the genuineness of his Christian attitude. His enmity was for wrong, his charity for the person who did it. There is no trace of personal enmity to von Bissing in all their correspondence. In one of his letters he speaks of and to him:

I do not cast any doubt on the sincerity of *Monsieur le Gouverneur*. When I had the honor of seeing him, he spoke in a tone of sincerity in which I had, and still have, faith. But there exists between us a fundamental misunderstanding. He would like to see us submissive, and we claim the right to remain unsubmissive in our heart and soul. We respect the regulations in so far as they are necessary to public order, but our obedience lies elsewhere. There is a difference between intentions and actions.

His Lenten pastoral of 1915, a dogmatic treatise on devotion to Christ and the Virgin Mary, brought no protest from von Bissing's office, but the pastoral letter of September, "A Call to Prayer," brought grave consequences. It invited all Catholics to pray that "the Prince of the Heavenly host cast down into hell Satan and the other wicked spirits who wander through the world for the ruin of souls." Von Bissing was so fatuous as to assume that this referred to him and his staff, and sent the chief of the "wicked spirits," von der Lancken, forthwith to the Archbishop's palace. The German was unruffled and suave, the Archbishop courteous and dignified, and neither minced his words. Mercier began by reminding the Chief of Staff that experience did not seem to open his eyes, that the Germans had used every expedient to provoke a rising of the people, and that only the obstinate calmness of the Belgians had prevented it.

"After a whole year's experience," he went on, "you do not grasp it. It is by giving our people the assurance that Belgium is, and will remain, a free country, that we are able to preach patience and to see that it is practised in spite of you. Your mistake begins when you believe that you can treat us as submissive children. This you cannot do; Belgium is not a conquered country which you have the right to treat as your own. It is a belligerent nation which has preserved and hopes still to preserve her independence and her King."

The uncomfortable German remarked that His Eminence's pastoral was in itself an "incentive to resistance."

"If by resistance you mean rebellion," retorted Mercier, "recourse to violent measures, or inciting others to have recourse to them, then you are within your rights in forbidding us to resist, and we assert, on our side, that in this sense, we abstain from resistance. But if by resistance you understand this assertion of our rights, recourse to prayer, whether public or private, to obtain God's protection of our country and the triumph of the sacred right of patriotism —then, Baron, I am obliged in conscience to tell you that I will continue to resist you without flinching."

This irresistible attack left his opponents defenseless, and behind it Mercier seems to have succeded throughout the war years in communicating practically at will with whomsoever he would. His private as well as his pastoral letters reached their destinations. The new Bishop of Tournai, Mgr. Crooy, tutor to the royal children before the war, was at times his Roman courier. Every time Belgian rights were violated, the Bishops defended them, and saw to it that the first copy of their protest came promptly to the Pope's desk in the Vatican. Moreover, Mercier wrote from time to time confidentially to the Pope himself acquainting him with the principal measures in his Malines administration. Never was there a word of criticism in any of the replies. The Pope's opinion of the correspondence he expressed afterwards when Mercier had laid down his pen forever: "Christian valor dictated the words Mercier wrote to raise the drooping spirits and stiffen the knees that were faltering."

The German authorities were quite right in believing that Mercier was in constant contact with the Government in le Havre. He and the Prime Minister, de Broqueville, exchanged letters repeatedly. To the Premier, Mercier was an important source of information on the state of mind of the population and its unity in resistance. At one time when he was suggesting a day of prayer for Belgium and England, he wrote, lest the Government should be misled by the tone of the Belgian press, "Do not forget that all the newspapers here are either inspired by the Germans or in their pay. Consequently, all articles reprinted from the so-called Belgian press are of German inspiration." "Never," he wrote later, "must the ministry give the least impression that there is the slightest weakening in our patriotic unity."

"Suffering accepted and vanquished . . . will give you a serenity which may well prove the most exquisite fruit of your life."—CARDINAL MERCIER.

CHAPTER VIII

TRIAL OF SOULS

THE time came when Pope Benedict summoned Mercier to Rome, wishing to have first-hand and absolutely trustworthy information as to the ceaseless turmoil in the little country. Reports of facts from Belgian and French churchmen on the one side and from German and Austrian on the other, were flatly contradictory. So the Holy Father once more obtained the requisite passport of free passage forth and back for the Cardinal, on the ground that he required his presence at the Vatican to assist in the contemplated reorganization of the Congregation of Studies. No sooner had Mercier left than the Germans circulated the rumor that he was bound for Rome, not only to participate in the extraordinary meeting of the Congregation of Seminaries and Universities, but also so as to suffer a reprimand from the Pope for his and his Bishops' political activities. There was no fear, so said the rumor, that he would ever be allowed to return. After the Cardinal's farewell visit to Ste. Gudule, a German officer remarked, sufficiently loudly to be overheard by one of Mercier's attendants: "Thank God,

158

that's the last time he'll cross the threshold of this cathedral."

The Vatican had taken every precaution for Mercier's safety on the journey. It had received telegraphic assurance from Berlin that he would not only be permitted to leave Belgium for Rome but also to return to his country. Just so as to obviate future trouble, Rome, being distrustful, further demanded and received the confirmation in writing, not only for Mercier to leave Belgium but also to re-enter. Even so, the German representative at the Vatican tried on the day before Mercier was to leave Rome to retract the permit to return. The Pope, however, stood sturdily on his assurances, and threatened that, if Cardinal Mercier's liberty were restricted, the Holy See would publish the entire correspondence on the subject. The threat effectively put an end to all talk of revoking the safe-conduct.

When Mercier got to Rome, he found his room banked high with flowers from his admirers. Callers came in throngs which made work impossible for him. There were not only the ordinary visits of courtesy or curiosity, but calls from distinguished men whose names filled page after page of his visitors' book, and took hour after hour of his time in conferences. They were all welcome, black Benedictines, brown Capuchins, black and white Dominicans, priests and princes, poilus and generals—he welcomed and chatted with all on easy terms. With a group of Belgian priests and soldiers, he fell into a discussion of the insults and outrages of the Hun that brought his indignation to the boiling point. At length, with a hearty bang of his fist on the table, he exploded:

"Il ne me plaît pas, sapristi, de baisser devant ces messieurs ma tête d'évêque et de Belge! Il ne me plaît pas!"

He trembled with indignation. The human outburst brought an instant response of sympathy from one of his humble compatriots.

"Your Eminence," burst out a corporal, "I just can't help telling you, you're—you're a 'chic' Cardinal."[1] Then, as he clumped out, surprised at his own audacity, he murmured to the Franciscan at his elbow,

"Cré nom, quel chic type!—Cré nom, quel, chic type!"[2]

The Pope, who was touchingly good, received Mercier with outstretched arms, and listened by the hour to the unburdening of his heart of his own and his people's afflictions. Benedict, when he had heard the whole of the sorrowful tale, embraced Mercier, and did his utmost to comfort him. He was steadfast, too, in withstanding the intrigues of Germans close to him who went to all lengths to bring about the retention of Mercier in Rome. They succeeded so far as to bring to Mercier the offer of work which would keep him in Rome, but naturally he scorned it. At the end of February, 1916, he set out on his journey homeward.

It was of the nature of a triumphant progress. Wherever the populace knew that his train would pass, it gathered to greet him with frantic enthusiasm. His gallant fight against such tremendous odds touched a responsive chord in the chivalrous Italian heart. Upon his arrival in Basel,

---

[1] It is impossible to give the exact flavor of the word *"chic,"* as here used, in translation; perhaps the American slang expression "swell" comes nearest to suggesting its associations.

[2] G. Ramaekers, *Le Grand Cardinal Belge.*

Swiss officers and soldiers received him as they would have welcomed a foreign sovereign, and the Belgian refugees who had assembled at the station for a glimpse of their Cardinal, knelt as he passed. At a hotel where he passed a night on his way through Switzerland, he is said to have received an involuntary reverence of special significance. As he entered the dining-room, a distinguished-looking gentleman quickly rose and bowed deeply. The act was spontaneous; it was not until he had reseated himself that Prince von Bülow realized that he had unconsciously paid a tribute which, coming from a late Chancellor of the German Empire, might be open to criticism.

In Malines, the German officers and soldiers received him as if he were an invading army. The guards were doubled, and the machine guns stood ready to sweep the *Grande Place*. In the face of all this, a tired, elderly traveller entered the city unexpectedly one morning, hurried to his church to pray, and then to his palace to bestow his blessing on a few old servants. Almost before Belgium could feel its deep relief at his return, he disappeared for a short retreat in a Benedictine Abbey near Louvain, from which he emerged to participate in a fervent *Te Deum* in St. Rombaut. Then he took up the defense of his people with a characteristic move of attack.

It was his Lenten pastoral letter, "On My Return from Rome," read in the churches on the 12th of March, 1916, in which he told his flock how kindly the Pope had received him, and expressed his feeling that the moral triumph had been definitely won. At it the German press burst into a flame of fury, demanding instant and condign punishment for the irrepressible Cardinal. No doubt von Bissing would have liked nothing better than to comply with the severest of the demands. No doubt he carefully considered precedent. There had been a case not unlike Mercier's, when the Kaiser's great-grandfather had acted with determination. Clemens August Droste zu Vischering, Archbishop of Cologne, had been taken away from his palace between two *gendarmes*, and shut up in a fortress whence no complaints could reach Rome. Of course, Gregory XVI had been incensed; "they had made a mockery of episcopal dignity," said he. Would Benedict XV be as completely outraged? There was precedent enough for refraining from the experiment; Mercier had been allowed to return to Belgium because Potsdam had learned from experience that the opinions of mankind commanded a decent respect. Von Bissing decided to withhold his hand in so far as the Cardinal himself was concerned, but he felt no such restraint in regard to less responsible actors. He imprisoned, tried, and deported the printer of the pastoral, the faithful Burgomaster of Malines, Charles Dessain, and four of his assistants.

Von Bissing withheld his hand from punishment of Mercier, but he could not refrain from an incautious gesture. In a letter of the 15th of March, 1916, he warned Mercier that he "would henceforth prosecute all political propaganda made under the cloak of religious worship, and every act tending to provoke hostile feeling toward the legitimate authority of the occupying Power, an authority recognized by international law." Further, the letter informed Mercier that he gave an example of insubordination to his clergy, and used his position to cause political agitation for which citizens and not he would have to suffer. Few of Mercier's letters to the Governor-General exhibit so exquisite a mingling of malicious courage and studied courtesy as does his reply to this. It was worthy of the best effort of Doctor Johnson or of Whistler, and must have enraged its recipient by its unanswerableness:

YOUR EXCELLENCY:

We are pleased to seize the opportunity afforded in acknowledging your letter to us, also to express our appreciation of the courtesy with which you mention the venerated head of our Church. As a faithful servant of Our Lord, Jesus Christ, we answered the summons of His representative here on earth.[3] But as Your Excellency is aware, we did not solicit the great honor of paying our respects to His Holiness. Though we may be struck with admiration at the warlike preparations surrounding you, and at the brilliant staff which, like King Saul, you have attached to your person, still you must permit us to retain complete liberty of judgment.

Mid the troubled hours which our country is passing through, we neither can nor will part with this liberty. In retaining it, we remain the faithful shepherd of the flock for which Our Lord gave his life. We shall remain obedient to the instructions of St. Peter's noble successor, His Holiness, Leo XIII.

In his encyclical, *Diuturnum Illud,* He has forbidden us to obey civil powers when these give orders which are manifestly contrary to the natural and divine right. "If any one," He says forcibly, "must choose between breaking the laws of God and those of the Prince, he must follow the precepts of Jesus Christ and answer as did the Apostles, 'It is better to obey God than man.'" In so acting, one does not merit the reproach of disobedience, for princes in opposing their will to that of divine laws, exceed their powers and

---

[3] *I.e.,* in going to Rome.

corrupt justice. In doing so, their authority is without force. Being unjust, it is non-existent.

Your Excellency, your authority can thus only be justly exercised. *Ecce in justitia regnabit rex.* As soon as the Prince deserts justice, we owe him neither obedience, respect, nor affection. Placed by the Grace of God on the Archepiscopal throne of Malines, we are only answerable to our conscience; and if we are obliged to raise our voice in the interests of our holy ministry, we believe we are following the teachings of our Divine Master: "Render unto Cæsar the things that are Cæsar's." While we pay you the silent homage due to Force, we retain closed to your attempts the sacred precincts of our conscience, the last refuge of oppressed Right.

Your Excellency may well believe that it is not without deep meditation that we have announced to the world the ills with which our brothers and sisters have been afflicted. Frightful ills, in truth, atrocious crimes, the tragic horror of which cold reason cannot grasp! If we had not done so, we should have been worthy neither of the inheritance of the apostles who evangelized Gallic Belgium, nor of being the spiritual son of those who by their labor have rendered illustrious the seat of Malines, whose Library at Louvain[4] was its purest jewel and inestimable, priceless treasure. *Alii laboraverunt et vim in labores eorum introistis.*

In the wellnigh mortal dejection of our people, we have spoken, and we have hoped that our thought might prove the object of your meditations. The Prince will have thoughts worthy of a Prince, and will preserve his authority over the leaders of the people.

As a Belgian, we have heard the anguished cries of our people; as a patriot, we have wished to dress the wounds of our country; as a Bishop, we have branded the crimes committed against our innocent priests.

I have the honor to remain,
   Your excellency's obedient servant,
      D. J. CARDINAL MERCIER.

[4] Burned by the Germans.

Again, in further rejoinder to the same complaint, Mercier wrote to von Bissing:

More than a month has passed since your Excellency felt obliged to inform public opinion that your dealings with the Belgian people and myself were beyond reproach, and that mine were reprehensible and seditious. . . .

Deep in my heart I am confident of the final success of our cause; my confidence is based upon motives of the natural order, that I refrained from developing in my pastoral, precisely so as not to appear a party to the plans of politicians and the calculations of Army Headquarters; my confidence is based, likewise, on supernatural motives, of which my conscience alone is judge. This confidence, I possess; it sustains my courage, and, because I love my flock, I want to share it with them.

Somewhat later he wrote to the Governor-General:

In spite of the military occupation of a great part of her provinces, our Belgian fatherland has not ceased to be of right, an autonomous, sovereign nation. Our respect and love for the soil and for our Belgian liberties are for all of us an honor and a duty. To realize this honor and to preach this duty forms a part of our clergy's social mission.

And again, still in defense of his preachers against von Bissing's complaints:

I have always found that the accused preacher has simply affirmed, without affront to the occupying power, that the Belgian fatherland is whole and united, and that the sole legitimate authority for the Belgian conscience is King Albert, his government, his magistracy, and his army. Were you willing, Excellency, to grasp this elementary truth of jurisprudence, the conflicts between us would come to an end.

These passages illustrate the unfailing courtesy and the unyielding directness of Mercier's flat refusals to limit his activities to purely religious matters. Mercier's adroitness and precision on points and phrases of international law, and his apt references to the Hague Tribunal, were probably furnished for the most part by his secretary, Dessain, brother of the printer, who had been an able practising lawyer before he took holy orders. We may guess that Mercier owed much of his immunity to these points of law which Dessain furnished to the correspondence, in so far as they kept constantly before the Governor-General the possible consequences of arousing the hostile opinion of other nations than those directly involved. Affairs of lesser scope von Bissing treated summarily. Mercier sent him a memorandum addressed to the Bishops of Germany on the subject of the inviolable religious liberty of apostolic teaching, just then denied to him, requesting that it be forwarded to those to whom it was addressed. It went into the filing cabinet of the Political Division, *spurlos versenkt*. The Berlin *Kladderadatsch* caricatured the situation in a cartoon which represented the Cardinal as a parrot which von Bissing was trying to silence. If von Bissing had been able to see the significance of the drawing, he might have read his lesson. And if the laugh really was at Mercier's expense, he could well afford it, for he had, as Chesterton said, "made a barbarian feel like a fool."

Mercier's courtesy toward a German was not always edged with irony; Leopold Heineman has told in the *Berliner Tageblatt* since Mercier's death of an instance in which it was warm with humanity. Mercier was in the cathedral one morning dressed without conspicuous insignia of his rank, accompanied by one of his priests. A young German lieutenant stood looking up at the Rubens altar piece with an expression that caught the attention of the Cardinal to whom boys were open books. Speaking in Latin, Mercier asked his companion what age he thought the lieutenant might be. To his surprise, the lad turned, and with deference replied:

"Diem natalem vicesimam hodie Mechliniae habeo" (I am celebrating my twentieth birthday here in Malines today).

Mercier's heart went out to him as he stood before the altar, his youth and innocence covered by the filth of the trenches. He wished him many happy returns of the day, chatted with him for a time in Latin, then took him back to his dinner table where he asked him about his home and all that meant much to the boy. At length, the Cardinal questioned him about his life in the trenches.

"Ego dormio, et cor meum vigilat," he replied in the words of the sage (I sleep—it is my heart that keeps me awake).

Mercier was so touched that tears came into his eyes, and, though the lad had told him he was not a Catholic, Mercier gave him his benediction, saying, "I give you my blessing, not as from an Archbishop of the Church, but as from an old man who has always tried to do his duty, and is eager to encourage a young man who is going out to do his. Go, under God's care, and may He protect you."

Shortly afterwards, when the lieutenant was clambering into the train which was to take him south to the front, an ecclesiastic handed him a package of goodies and a book, the

Carmina Horatii, with four lines underscored on a marked page. They read:

> *Virtus, recludens immeritis mori*
> *Coelum, negata tentat inter via*
> *Coetusque vulgares et udam*
> *Spernit humum fugiente penna.*[5]

July 21 is Belgium's Independence Day. As it approached in the summer of 1916, the Governor-General began to prepare for trouble. He forbade all forms of assembly and demonstration. He had patrols and armored cars rattling over the cobble-stones of Brussels, thus keeping the atmosphere in a ferment of excitement. Lieutenant-General Hurt, Governor of the City, added yeast to the ferment by a manifesto specifying penalties which the citizens might incur by any infractions of the orders. One of the orders was against the wearing of patriotic emblems, but there was nothing to prevent the citizens from wearing ivy leaves in their buttonholes, for the ivy, *le lierre,* was the emblem of fidelity; it says, *"je meurs où je m'attache,"*—"I die where I cling."

Despite portentous threats and frantic efforts on the part of the invaders, a small sheet called *La Libre Belgique, Bulletin de Propagande Patriotique* had been appearing "regularly at irregular intervals," as it said of itself. It boasted that it submitted to no censor, and insolently gave its telegraphic address as "Kommandantur" (Governor-

---

[5] "Virtue, to crown her favorites loves to try
Some new unbeaten passage to the sky,
Where Jove a seat among the Gods will give
To those who die for meriting to live."
            Horace, III, 2, 6; Dean Swift's translation.

General's Office), Brussels. Von Bissing and his staff went
to all lengths to discover its editors and its press; at length
they even offered seventy-five thousand marks to any one who
would denounce its editors. They kept hot on its trail, and
more than once their spies came just too late upon its deserted printing establishment; then before long, out it would
come again from another source, and each time impishly
make good its professed address by a fresh copy on the
Governor-General's desk in his private office. In vain did
the infuriated officer change his guards, and threaten them
with death; no one could account for the phenomenon, much
less prevent it. After February, 1917, when the hunt was
at its hottest, the Abbé van den Hout, since editor of *La
Revue Catholique des Idées et des Faits*, founded by Mercier in 1921, edited it in the Institut St. Louis. It was
printed in at least half a dozen different places in Brussels,
longest of all in an underground cellar, concealed from outside by a pile of old furniture. Whenever the presses were
discovered, the printers were arrested and brought before
a court martial, but the court could get little or nothing
from them. They professed ignorance of the identity of
their employers, and admitted nothing but that they were
well paid in gold. At times citizens were caught distributing the paper—the Redemptorist father, Verriest, was fined
four thousand marks for so doing—but the distributors
seemed to be as ignorant as the printers of "those higher up."
They could tell nothing except that they received the papers
for distribution at most irregular intervals from persons to
them unknown who paid them well. At times the copies
smelt unbearably of herring or Hervé cheese, but those

scents were too pervasive to lead the German sleuth-hounds to any specific locality.

One of the most successful of *La Libre Belgique's* many excellent cartoons was an adaptation of the one in *Kladderadatsch* which represented Mercier as a parrot. In the Belgian drawing, the parrot had seized the Governor-General's finger in his beak, and the legend was, "What Belgium holds, she holds firmly," echoing von Bissing's famous boast, "What we hold, we hold firmly."

Mercier guarded carefully his official ignorance of all this. Once when funds for publication were at low tide, van den Hout went to him for help. He refused it, saying that he could have nothing to do with the paper, and did not wish to know anything about it. Crestfallen, the Abbé was about to leave, when Mercier produced a handful of bills from his desk. "By the way," he said, with his enigmatic smile, "here is some money for your favorite charity."

Charity, indeed, it was; food for the Belgian spirit which the Germans were trying so systematically to destroy by starvation, for to many it brought the only news they could get of their King, of the efforts of the Allies, of victories, of the draining of Germany's strength, and of all else they so urgently craved to keep up the strength of their courage.[6]

The edition which appeared shortly before Independence Day, 1916, urged all Belgians, regardless of whether they were good Catholics or not, to go to Ste. Gudule's on July 21.

The Collegiate Church, called the Cathedral of Brussels, is popularly known as "Ste. Gudule" despite the fact that

[6] A complete file of *La Libre Belgique* was sent by Mercier to America to be sold for the benefit of his Children's Charities. It was presented to the Harvard College Library through the generosity of Thomas W. Lamont, of the Class of '92.

its mediæval baptismal name was "Saints Gudule and Michael."[7] It is a magnificent church, superbly located at almost the crest of the Brussels hill. Some of its loveliest parts were built under the great Margaret's regency in the early sixteenth century.

The word went round that Mercier would conduct solemn Mass for the souls of the fallen soldiers, and would preach a sermon in Ste. Gudule. All Belgians knew that his sympathy for them, his spirit no less militant than theirs in its opposition to the enemy, would find expression in words of patriotic inspiration for all his countrymen.

When the day came, the congregation packed the great

[7] If ever a woman was brought up in the odor of sanctity with no chance whatever of going astray, it was the little seventh-century girl, Gudula. Not only did her mother become a saint, but also her brother and sister. With the canonization of Gudula, herself, few mediæval families could hold their noses higher, at least if the Calendar of Saints was the standard of excellence.

Despite all this, however, her body was most shamefully neglected in the little church of St. Gery until the good Count of Louvain decided to transfer it, most honorably, for the salvation of his own and his relatives' souls, to the City of Brussels, and to erect over it a fitting shrine.

During her virtuous earthly existence, Gudula was so wise as to make a good friend of St. Michael, the powerful patron of the Town of Brussels. It stood her in good stead, particularly as she was so rash as frequently to repair to church before cock-crow, with a candle or lantern to light her way in the dark. The devil, who had been strangely attracted by Gudula's charms, felt reasonably certain of succeeding in his evil purpose of seizing her if he could first extinguish the light she was carrying.

As good luck would have it, the foggy night that the devil decided to carry out his foul plan and had actually blown out Gudula's light, St. Michael was also up and about early. As handy with Satan as with the Dragon, the warrior of the Cross spitted the fiend in the nick of time.

Having finally been laid to rest and sainted, one would have thought Gudula deserved peace. But no. Vandals in the shape of the *Gueux* dragged out her bones in the sixteenth century and scattered them in the mud of Brussels. The faithful *Bruxellois* still worship, however, in the lovely church dedicated to Gudule and Michael, and every fall, the flowers of the *"tremella deliquescens,"* also known as Ste. Gudule's little lamp, recall that the good Lord decreed that the Saint's lantern should be rekindled each year.

She and her champion stand all in gold, on each side of the crossing. In one hand, she has her church and in the other, her lantern, which an obliging little angel is watching to see that it remains lighted.

171

church to the very limits of its space. They listened to the Gospel, and to the noble and ancient strains of the *Dies Irae*. Then Mercier, with a shrewd sense of picturesque values, ascended the pulpit in cape and mitre, with crozier in hand, appearing as one of the line of his predecessors in the stained glass above, or companion to Saul of Tarsus on the pillar to the side. Those who stood nearest saw that he was somewhat paler than common, with the hard, determined expression of the mouth that came with the war years. A note of harshness in his voice, too, was new. His manner was incisive; his French was that of Paris rather than that of Belgium. His sermon, *Per Crucem ad Lucem*, took its text from the first chapter of the first book of the Maccabees, *Jerusalem facta est habitatio exteriorum; dies festi ejus conversi sunt in luctum*—"Jerusalem was made the habitation of strangers, her festival days were turned into mourning." He dwelt on the significance of the day, and its meaning in days to come when the country should be free:

Fourteen years hence, on this same day,[8] our restored cathedrals and our rebuilt churches will open wide their doors; crowds will fill them; our King Albert, standing on his throne, will bow his unconquered head freely before the majesty of the King of Kings; the Queen and the royal princes will be grouped around him; we shall hear again the joyous pealing of our bells from the Yser to the Meuse and from the La Panne to Arlon: under the vaults of the temples, the Belgians, hand in hand, will renew allegiance to their God, their sovereign and their liberties, while the Bishops and the priests, interpreters of the soul of the nation, will entone, in a united burst of joyous gratitude, a triumphal *Te Deum*. . . .

[8] July 21, 1930, centenary of Belgian independence. Mercier's prophecy was fulfilled on that date, but unfortunately he was not there to take part in the great celebration.

In spite of its horrors, war—I mean a just war—has much austere beauty. That is because it unites in unselfish enthusiasm a whole people which gives, or is prepared to give, its most precious possession, life itself, for the defense or the reclaiming of something which cannot be weighed, or counted, or monopolized: Right, Honor, Peace, Liberty.

Have you not felt during the last two years that the war —the ardent, sustained attention, which, even from your situation here, you lent it—purifies you, separates your higher natures from the dross, lifts you up and causes you to mount toward something better than yourselves?

It is toward the ideal of Justice and Honor that you are ascending. Its attraction sustains you. . . .

The hour of our deliverance draws near, but has not yet struck. Let us remain patient. Let not our courage give way. Let us leave to divine Providence the care of perfecting our national education.

The sermon caused patriotic fervor, excitement, ebullition, demonstration in the streets, but nothing that need have caused fear on the part of the German occupiers. They, however, took it seriously, as was to be expected. They suppressed it with the bayonet, and punished it with a heavy fine. Then, as so often before, von Bissing made the clumsy opening move which had so often led him into a stalemate. He sent von der Lancken to demand an explanation from Mercier. The well-known way; he might have followed it blindfold—past the nursemaids' park now closed to all but cavalrymen and their orderlies; past the rue de la Loi, now barred by sentries to all but the invaders; past royal Laeken, now inhabited by the sleeping monarchs only; beside the ribbon of the Senne, along the long rows of poplars, and the cattle growing leaner, over the winding Dyle, in through the mediæval gateway and portcullis and round the battered flanks of St. Rombaut. All that way, only to hear the Cardinal say that the text of the sermon handed him for verification was very faulty; that the officers who reported it should have been more attentive; that they should have known their French better; that he would, however, correct their work, and stand answerable for what he had said. "I spoke as the Bishop," he declared, "and I spoke only words of charity and comfort. You will have to seek the provocation elsewhere." Von Bissing knew too well where the real provocation lay to wish to bring it to the tribunal of the opinions of nations.

As if he were a mechanical toy, von Bissing seems to have repeated these motions every time Mercier wound him up. In the month of the Rosary, October, 1916, Mercier's pastoral letter on "the Voice of God" once more set von der Lancken off like an automaton past the nursemaids' park and all the other familiar landmarks to the flanks of St. Rombaut. He could have had no zest in it, for he must have known how little it served his purpose, or von Bissing's, or the Emperor's. But it served Mercier's purpose, for the correspondence in these successive cases has put on record for all time the case of Belgium against her aggressor.

A mental atmosphere has been produced in Germany in which legal matters are divorced from moral right. Kant, Hegel, Nietzsche, have spread this through all ranks of society. In this atmosphere, a militarist idea of things has been formed, and has gathered strength, according to which a nation has a right to live and to develop its life to any extent, without being answerable for its doings before that moral tribunal of the conscience which judges our every-day actions.

174

And again:

Religion degenerates into superstition when it does not permeate our moral consciousness. Morality misses the mark, partially at least, when it does not extend its dominion over all human activities, social as well as individual.

Once, at least, von der Lancken advanced into the Cardinal's own field, philosophy, armed with the thesis that if the conduct of the Germans at the beginning of the war be attributed to their study of the German philosophers, it is necessary to infer that the action of the English in coming to the defense of Belgium is the result of their familiarity with the conveniently utilitarian philosophies. To this the Cardinal replied:

Baron, it is unnecessary for me to scrutinize the intentions of others. I limit myself to facts. Germany caused us much pain in order to benefit thereby. England went to much pains in order that we might benefit by it. Germany attacked us when she was ready. England did not wait till she was ready in order to defend us. The inborn sense of justice in the English people triumphed over the local and superficial influence of a special school. The profound, worldly and widespread influence in Germany of Kant and his disciples perverted the public spirit.

By the time an episode had simmered down to such correspondence as this, it was hardly more than pastime for such a brain as Mercier's. His heart and his spirit were deeply occupied in 1916 with other and deeper concerns. The most infamous measure of the whole German occupation of Belgium was that of deportation. It disgraced humanity, and the Germans did not know it—or did not care. War does not sharpen sensibilities. The idea originated in the minds of the *Grossindustrie*, and particularly in those of Hugo

Stinnes and Walter Rathenau, both of whom left the stage so dramatically at a later date.

Verdun had been costly; the consumption of *Kanonenfutter* had been unbelievably great. The Fatherland needed more soldiers, a great many more. The Supreme Army Command demanded what amounted to the mobilization of every German male who could carry a rifle. This met with angry protests from whosoever could voice them with impunity. Why, asked the great industrialists, should those who were too old or too young, why should those who were profitably engaged in factories or at the plough, producing what was so cryingly needed for a starving people as well as for the army, be sent to the trenches when the conquered nations, Belgium and Poland, were swarming with healthy loafers of no value except as trouble-makers? To such voices the *Grosses Hauptquartier* lent a ready ear; it had long known of the existence of such supplies of labor, and had thought longingly of importing them if only such a breach of international law might not cause too much scandal throughout the civilized world.

Of such scandal, von Bissing had, as we have been, a wholesome fear, and so had the "political section" of his government. Both did all in their power to prevent the order for the deportations. The Governor-General went to the very verge of open quarrel with the Supreme Army Command, and then appealed directly to the Kaiser. When the Emperor denied his appeal, he requested permission to resign, but the Emperor denied that also. Then the Supreme Command instructed him to proceed with the collection and shipment of men from Belgium into Germany. Von Bissing had no recourse; he must obey.

He issued an ordinance informing the manhood of Belgium that it would find work in Germany. As many as four hundred thousand Belgians were idle, for the factories and workshops had been stripped of tools and machinery. Von Bissing declared that he was solicitous that all those who were idle should not become too great a charge on the charitable budget of the Belgian Committee of Help and Alimentation. He wished, he said, to save the many from the unemployment caused by the British blockade, and afford them opportunities to provide for their starving families. Belgium trembled, but bayonets met resistance wherever it occurred.

The King of the Belgians and his Government being outside the country, the citizens within it had formed a war committee for such internal administration as was requisite and permitted by the occupying force. Catholics, Liberals, and Socialists worked in perfect harmony as the so-called *Comité National*, which met every Thursday in the Board of Managers' room of the great Brussels bank, the *Société Générale*. The *Comité* president was the strong, self-willed banker, Emile Francqui, and its vice-president the talented, affable Emmanuel Janssen. As soon as the deportations began, these two leaders hurried to von der Lancken's office on the corner of the *rue Ducale*. Francqui never minced words, and this was no time to begin.

"You treat us like slaves," he bellowed, "and history will bear witness to it."

Suave and unruffled, the Prussian diplomat replied:

"No, you are mistaken, Monsieur. As we shall be the victors, it is *we* who will write history."

Leo XIII was quite right when he said, "The great events of history cannot be estimated by human calculations."

Slavery might be revolting, but Germany needed manpower. Every Belgian city and hamlet, every countryside, received its orders. All men between seventeen and fifty-five, priests, school-teachers, doctors, and lawyers excepted, were instructed to assemble for inspection. It was a debasing sight. The men were reviewed and passed on as if they were cattle. The strongest and best were herded into the trains which stood by with steam up. Those that were known to have disobeyed the order were torn from their homes, or driven into the pens at the point of the bayonet. The frantic sobbing women stood as near as they were allowed to come, but bristling guards stood always between them and their mates. The shrieks of the sirens mingled with the strains of the Belgian anthem, the *Brabançonne*, and the Flemish *Leeuw van Vlaanderen* (Lion of Flanders). These two songs sounded from the windows of the railway carriages so long as there were Belgian ears to hear. Then before long reports came back of the inhuman treatment of those who refused to sign the contracts offered them. Some had been forced to walk in freezing water and ice-cold mud for twelve hours at a time; others had been kept without food for twenty-four hours; others had been deprived of bed-clothes on winter nights—all so as to compel them to sign the "voluntary" contract to work.

At such news as this, Mercier's face turned paler than usual, set, rigid, the eyes alone denoting life as he listened to the tale. The American delegate to the Province of the Hainaut told him of eight thousand men of Mons marching

178

down their hill in the gray of dawn to meet the swaggering
Governor, von Haniel, and his staff. The sturdy Fulgence
Masson had marched at the head of the Belgians. He was,
at a later day, to be saluted on his return from his German
prison as Belgium's Minister of War. But now the drill-
sergeants were frantically busy, measuring arm and chest
with their eyes. The harvest was rich, for the miners of the
Borinage, the mining district of the Hainaut, were brawny.
A wife with child, infirm dependents, a large, hungry flock
—all excuses were brushed aside. Germany needed men.

The Cardinal's manhood rose up within him as he listened to the American's story. This was the degradation of
his race. The gentle, serene priest boiled with rage. He
sprang to work to put into operation every slender means at
his command. First he wrote to von Bissing and von der
Lancken. Had not their own Frederick the Great honored
individual liberty as if it were a dogma? Had not General
von Huene assured him, both in writing and by word of
mouth, that Belgium's young men need have no fear of
being carried off into Germany, either for enrolment in the
army, or there to be employed at compulsory work? Von der
Goltz had confirmed it. Was this also a scrap of paper? He
wrote von Bissing:

In the name of freedom of domicile and the freedom of
labor, in the name of the inviolability of family life, in the
name of morality which the policy of deportation would
gravely compromise, in the name of the pledges given by the
Governor of Antwerp and the Governor-General, the immediate representatives of the German Empire, I respectfully
ask Your Excellency to have the measures of compulsory
labor and deportation repealed, and to restore to their

hearths the Belgian workmen who have already been deported.

. . . The naked truth is that every deported workman means a soldier added to the German Army, for he will take the place of a German workman who will be made into a soldier. . . . Slavery and deportation are the hardest punishments in the penal code after death.—Has Belgium, which never did you any harm, merited such treatment from you, treatment which calls to Heaven for vengeance? . . . To-day, it is no longer war. It is cold calculation, deliberate destruction, the victory of Might over Right, the debasement of human nature, a challenge to humanity.

Mercier could not restrain the bitterness of his soul when he begged von der Lancken not to write, as he had, of "the necessity of lightening the burdens of public charity." In a letter of October 19, 1916, he asked him to refrain from such bitter irony. And as for the implication that the Belgian workman was prone to idleness, all his history bore testimony to the fact that he made a very religion of his labor. In the long struggle of economic life, the Belgian worker had for generations proved his qualities. It was only patriotic self-respect that made him scorn the wages held out to him by the occupying government. Von Bissing might well have respected Mercier's appeal if he had had the slightest freedom of action. As it was, he asked the parochial authorities to furnish him with the lists of their male parishioners so that none might be overlooked. Naturally, they scorned the request, and instead begged permission to accompany the deportees into Germany. Mercier boldly seconded the request:

A large number of my clergy have implored me to claim for them a place in the vanguard of the persecuted. I wish to place them on record, and proudly submit their request to you. . . . There is a barrier behind which Military force is held up, and behind which is intrenched inviolable right. On this side of the barrier, it is we, the representatives of moral authority, who speak as masters. We cannot and will not let the word of God be shackled.

Seeking desperately for help, Mercier appealed to public opinion throughout the world in his "Cry of Distress," of November 7, 1916, sent to every country where human dignity was respected. Then he turned to the American, Spanish, and Dutch legations, still in Brussels. He preached in Ste. Gudule on "Those in Captivity." He appealed to Rome. The Pope and several of the neutral nations, including the United States, protested. Ludendorff, with a cynicism and a psychology that the world was learning to think of as German, characterized Mercier's efforts as an "exhibition of a very childish judgment of the war."

The three legations, American, Spanish, and Dutch, were the only major ones left in Brussels, because they were those of the major nations then neutral. After Brand Whitlock and his courageous lieutenant, Hugh Gibson, had departed, the Marquis de Villalobar and Herr van Vollenhoven remained as the only influential intermediaries between the Belgians and the allied nations on the one side and the German authorities on the other. Villalobar was seasoned by a long diplomatic career, full of initiative, of indefatigable energy, and of such strength of mind that it overcame the staggering physical handicap of several mechanical limbs, for at birth he had little more than head and body. The Dutchman was fat, rosy, pleasure-loving, and self-indulgent. He finally left his country's diplomatic service after being called to account for speculating in the rapidly falling German mark and misusing the pouches in his transactions. A Spanish *Grandese* of the third degree consoled him for his lost honors. Both the Spanish minister and the Dutch *chargé des Affaires,* in order to accomplish anything, were naturally obliged to work discreetly and largely under cover. Under the inevitable limitations they did unquestionably their best, and American Relief workers, and Belgian sufferers no less, owed them much for the endless pains they took in trying to fight the battles of those so sorely in need of help.

The Marquis of Villalobar, after conferring with von Bissing, advised the Cardinal to organize a committee of all the leaders remaining in the country, and, over their joint signature, to lay before the Kaiser the injustice and degradation of the deportations. Mercier, much surprised, replied that he could not make such an appeal unless von der Lancken would assure him that it would not meet with refusal. The Chief of the Political Bureau went to work with characteristic method. He first assured himself as to what von Ludendorff and G. H. Q. would, after what had happened, report to the Emperor in the matter, and, having made certain that they at last realized the error and failure of the deportations, von der Lancken returned to Belgium and informed the Cardinal that his appeal would meet with a gracious reception. Acting on this assurance, Mercier made his appeal. The result was that von der Lancken received instructions to inform the Belgian Senate that His Majesty the Kaiser had ordered him to cease further enrolment and to return to Belgium such Belgian workmen as had been deported to find employment. The ill and emaciated men who returned were a sickening sight; their appearance nearly wrecked the relief work. Hoover wrote that "Belgium has passed through the worst of many troubles since the first agony." Mercier refers to the period of the deportations as "the most painful of my life, and the most agonized of my episcopal career."

It was a conspicuous victory, but it brought Mercier no respite in his righteous warfare. His tireless foes promptly attacked another weak spot, the point of union between Fleming and Walloon. Already German agents, working very quietly, had been persistent in fomenting trouble and sowing dissension. Ostensibly for the purpose of satisfying the Flemish party, von Bissing had, early in 1916, published a series of decrees ordering instruction in the Flemish language in the primary schools of the Flemish provinces. The real motive was to prepare the way for separate administration in the two parts of the country. Half a year later he came out with a new decree instituting a new system of certification of teachers in the primary and infant schools, so devised as to overthrow the entire system of normal school teaching in the Flemish provinces, to overthrow all Catholic influence over children, to overthrow the Belgian educational law, indeed, the very Constitution itself. It did not need the protests of his clergy to call Mercier to arms. He saw all Belgian culture threatened, and Belgium herself divided as with a sword. Again he sent out a ringing appeal to his countrymen and to the outside world.

In spite of him, the work of setting up the two governments in Belgium went relentlessly on throughout 1916.

Certain departments in the ministries were provided with two sets of functionaries, one Flemish and one Walloon, and separate teachers were appointed for the schools. Some of the government employees resigned, and were punished by deportation to Germany. To those who bowed to the German will, Mercier said, "Those who assist the attempts at rupturing our national unity are traitors." Among these were the Belgians who constituted the *Conseil des Flandres*, which had proved a willing tool. They had been pleased to go to Berlin to request the Chancellor to appoint a separate civil administration for the Flemish provinces. Von Bissing was glad to meet their wishes. A decree was issued erecting two separate administrative districts, one to be governed from Brussels, the other from Namur. Against this, all of Mercier's efforts were vain. The work of disintegration continued throughout the German occupation.

In a lesser matter he had greater success. The Germans, beginning systematically with a decree which made obligatory the declaration of all copper, tin, nickel, and bronze in the occupied territory, even including such things as lighting fixtures in private houses, had very nearly stripped the country of all these metals, such was their shortage of materials for shell casings and other military purposes. Now they proposed to take down the church bells to feed their munition works. Church bells meant more to Belgium than, possibly, to any other nation. They have for centuries been an important part of the life and the history of the people. Without them the silence of the cities inspired fear. Some of them have names, known in poetry and legend since the Middle Ages. They were consecrated, blessed with holy water by the Bishop before being sent aloft to ring their various messages down through the centuries. By virtue of their consecration, their object, their function, Mercier declared them sacred. Belgian burgomasters had gone into exile for refusing to have them rung in celebration of German victories—like other sacred things, they had their martyrs. Inasmuch as the new Chancellor, von Hertling, was a Catholic, a philosopher, and a Thomist, it did not take Mercier long to convince him that the seizure of the church bells would be sacrilege. The Pope threw the weight of his influence on Mercier's side, and von Bissing decreed immunity for the Belgian bells.

It was not the first time that His Holiness had lent a helping hand, but apparently not all of Belgium knew it. Many Belgians had expressed disappointment at lack of support from Rome, asking what the Pope thought of it all? Would he remain silent before all outrages merely because there were so many Roman Catholics among the Germans and Austrians? Had he forgotten that the Belgians were among the most devoted children of the Church of Rome? Such expressions of this feeling as he had heard had prompted Mercier to write his Lenten Pastoral of 1915. The Pope, too, declared his position:

May we be allowed in this assembly to make an appeal to the human sentiments of those who have carried the war into foreign territories? Let them spare those countries the devastation which their occupation by no means renders necessary; let them refrain from what would be a graver matter, from wounding to no purpose the feelings of the people in those matters which they prize above all—their churches, their priests, and the rights belonging to Religion and the Faith.

Possibly the skeletons of Rheims and Amiens were before the Holy Father's eyes. Of Belgium he spoke directly in a letter to Mercier:

While We are concerned with all Our authority to bring alleviation to the sufferings of so many of Our unfortunate sons, We have never ceased to exert Ourselves to bring about the restoration to your dear nation of her full political, military, and economic independence, as well as the reparation of losses she has sustained. We are fully persuaded that We have done for Belgium and her people all that it was possible for Us to do, and everything that the burning charity of Christ and the most tender paternal affection could suggest to Us.

Such expressions as these left no doubt in the minds of those whom they reached as to the Pope's position. They felt that he had met the issue squarely, and that knowledge comforted the hearts of Mercier and the Belgians. Once again he wrote to Mercier in reply to the lamentations of his people:

May sorrowing and afflicted souls find comfort and consolation in the assurances of the paternal tenderness which inspires Our prayer. May God have pity on the Belgian nation. May He heap the abundance of benefits upon her.

And he sent word by Cardinal Ceretti, "Say to Cardinal Mercier that he has saved the Church." These were strong words, coming from a temperate and guarded man.

The tumult and the shouting dies,
  The captains and the kings depart;
Still stands Thine ancient sacrifice,
  An humble and a contrite heart.
              —KIPLING, "The Recessional."

CHAPTER IX

FREE BELGIUM

NOT many more were the exchanges of protests and rejoinders between Mercier and von Bissing. Still to the end when the Cardinal preached a sermon or issued a pastoral, such as his "Voice of God" in October, 1916, or his "Courage, My Brethren," at Lent, 1917, von Bissing would receive them as if they were political dynamite, and leave the Cardinal and von der Lancken to bombard one another wth polemics. These exchanges give us some of Mercier's best writing, and if they embarrassed the Governor-General by the keen thrusts of their eloquence and philosophy, they charmed his sympathizers with their simplicity and form. In scope they covered the entire issue, illuminating all, and focussing all with inexorable cogency on the essential point. He was an idealist to the core, but he had a profound sense of reality, and nothing is more striking to thoughtful readers of his controversial letters

187

than their practical adaptation of content and method to their purpose. And often the most practical weapon he could use was the force of his passion. His pity, his indignation, his revolt, gave unlimited passionate force to his appeals for justice. His lifelong exercise of self-restraint gave irresistible power to his feeling when he released it.

One morning in April, 1917, an adjutant of Count Bismarck, then Kreischef of Malines, called at the palace and requested the honor of delivering a letter personally to the Cardinal. It informed him of the death of the Governor-General; the most ruthless of all captains had disarmed von Bissing, and stripped him of all authority. Mercier immediately went to his writing table. Taking, as was his habit, his pen between index and middle finger, he wrote to von der Lancken:

MONSIEUR LE BARON:

I appreciate deeply the thoughtful attention of your letter, and express my gratitude for it.

Baron von Bissing was a Christian. I remember his saying to me one day, in a tone that placed his sincerity beyond all doubt, "I am not a Catholic, but I believe in Christ." To the Christ, therefore, I shall pray, and very sincerely, for the repose of his soul.

Accept, Monsieur le Baron, the expression of my high regards.

On April 24, 1917, Baron von Falkenhausen succeeded von Bissing as Governor-General of Belgium.

The great drama was drawing to a close; Mercier was soon to exchange the sword for the crozier. Like the prophet of the earlier day, he had seen the handwriting on the wall, and never doubted that the German occupation could be more than temporary occupation. His unshakable confidence in the cause of justice was soon to be vindicated. Germany was breaking up from within as the Allies were at last forcing their way through the German lines. The disintegration was very evident from within Belgium. Mercier was kept well informed through the channels of the Church's widespread and complete organization. Moreover there was a nervousness among the occupiers not to be concealed from his penetrating eyes.

On October 10, 1918, the same two heads of the *Comité National* who had pleaded with von der Lancken to hinder the deportations were called to the German headquarters in the Place Royale. They could hardly believe their ears. Of course they knew the end would come before the winter was over, but at the time they did not expect such news. They received passports through all the lines to Holland, and a request from the Governor-General on behalf of the German Government to telephone to the Belgian Government in le Havre and to suggest an armistice on these terms: the *Comité National* to negotiate on behalf of Belgium; peace to be negotiated in Brussels; German, French, and Belgian troops to be withdrawn to their respective frontiers. The proposals were absurd, indicating either sheer effrontery or complete lack of psychological insight. They indicated the assumption on the part of the Germans that none but their own staff knew as yet that the big cannon had been removed from the Belgian coast, and that the German reserves behind the front were slowly being moved eastward. So long as these movements were secret, the Germans thought they

189

might be allowed to withdraw from Belgium at their own convenience.

Francqui and Janssen wasted no time in getting out of Brussels, but decided that they simply must stop at Malines to tell the Cardinal the staggering news. Trembling with excitement, Janssen tugged at the brass handle of the palace bell. Was the Cardinal in? Unfortunately, no, he had gone to administer comfort to an old lady who was dying. What a pity! Were any of the Vicars-general in, or perhaps the Cardinal's secretary? Certainly. They blurted out the news to whosoever happened to be there to hear it, and sped on their way. Indeed, it was a pity that the discreet Cardinal was not the sole hearer. The news ran like quicksilver all through the palace. Faster yet it ran all over Malines, and trickled into the office of the Kreischef, and from thence flashed over the wire to the Intelligence officer in Brussels. He telephoned to the military post by the electric wires on the Dutch frontier to stop and return to Brussels under military escort the two garrulous Belgians. But it was too late. They were already telephoning from The Hague to de Brogueville at Havre, who was replying that they were very gullible; it was all nonsense; why waste telephone charges? So the Cardinal had another month of hopeful patience.

Von Falkenhausen, like his predecessors, had appreciated the generosity and tolerance of the Cardinal's views. Wishing to please him, as well as to obliterate all traces of the vandalism, he now sent word that he should like to make good the damage to St. Rombaut. "We shall soon be asking for an accounting," Mercier replied to the emissary; "meanwhile, we shall accept no alms from the Germans." And to Baron von der Lancken he wrote on the same subject, "To speak frankly, Baron, we Belgians are touchy; we insist upon our rights, but we do not care for favors."

The German press, which had been indefatigable in its abuse of Mercier, became increasingly bitter and sharp as the drama progressed, and the Cardinal's greatness was increasingly recognized by the world. One of the German papers said of him:

Mercier's letters are pompous, political speeches, containing phrases that might have been written by d'Annunzio. The Churchman is too fond of his own rhetoric and *réclame*. He oversteps the limits of his office.

But when it was all over, after Mercier's death, von der Lancken said in the *Berliner Tageblatt* that Mercier had not been *"Deutschlands erbitterster Hasser:*

Certainly no one has fought the Germans with sharper weapons than did Mercier; certainly no one has done us more harm in Belgium and throughout the world, although he failed in accomplishing what was his greatest aim, namely, to cause a quarrel between us and Rome. But he had no bitter hatred for Germany. Apart from his religious duties, which he had very much at heart, he was far too intelligent to hate, and he would not have been so dangerous to us as he became, if his patriotism had been stimulated by the impulse of hatred. He fought us with invincible strength and pitiless dialectics, which he had acquired by the long discipline of his will, of his spirit, and of his whole personality. He was dangerous to us owing to the spiritual ascendency and the sovereign prestige which these characteristics gave him over his political adversaries in Belgium, yes, even over the anti-clerical liberals and socialist anti-nationalists.

During the Ruhr conflict, I was once asked, "Would we
be sure of success if we had a Mercier?" I am certain that,
owing to the absence of a personality similar to Mercier's,
our resistance, which began so well, ended partly in fatigue
and partly in fruitless *sabotage*. But would a man of the
Cardinal's measure have found among all classes here the
support which Mercier found among his countrymen in occupied Belgium? As a German, I am sorry to have to put
the question. One more question. What do we gain by be-
littling Mercier, as do our papers? Mercier's grandeur is
our grandeur. Is it not better to draw from Mercier's example the following lesson? Leading personalities can only
develop when above all parties, and inversely, such personalities cannot be disregarded owing simply to party reasons.
If this great figure which has become a part of history could
impress this truth upon us, would not the Cardinal dead have
done us more good than the living Cardinal harmed us?

Though von der Lancken was quite right in saying that
Mercier never hated the German people, Mercier was nevertheless thoroughly convinced of its guilt. He felt that its
mentality had long been poisoned by such leaders as Kant,
Fichte, Schelling, and Hegel. Its philosophy was irrecon-
cilable with the fundamental concepts of Christianity. German Catholic priests with whom he had talked much before
the war often dreamed of "the power of the State," rather
than the power of love and the Kingdom of Jesus Christ.
The idea of renunciation, which seemed to Mercier the basis
of true Christian thought, was, he believed, submerged in
the instincts of the German race. Its belief in *Deutschthum*
had smothered its sense of Christian brotherhood. Mercier
mistrusted the Germans intellectually, and disliked them in-
dividually. When the Kaiser visited Belgium in 1910, his

marked attentions were distasteful to Mercier, though of course the Kaiser got no inkling of the fact at the time. Six years later, the Kaiser suddenly announced his most unwelcome visit to the famous Benedictine Monastery of Maredsous. In the reception room where the All-Highest expected to be met by the Abbot and his assembled monks, he found only a dominating portrait of his prime Belgian enemy, Désiré Joseph, Cardinal Mercier. No one could ascertain whether the *farceur* of an Abbot had hung it particularly for the occasion.

Writing to Victor Giraud after the war, Mercier said:

Yes, God is great, and He acts greatly. The Prussian military caste has taken pleasure in defying a world of enemies, and now the magnificent creature is all alone,—alone at the feet of its conquerors, beaten, crouching, reduced to a nonentity!

The dreams of pangermanic domination have evaporated like an asphyxiating gas, dissipated by a breath of wind. Right alone is honored, the Right that avenges audacious iniquity. . . .

And in speaking to the French Institute, Mercier said that the catastrophe which had engulfed the world was a logical sequel to a dislocating and ruinous philosophy.

The end came at last. In October, 1918, Mercier wrote to the Belgian people:

The independence of our country is no longer doubted by any one. Let us bless the Lord for having assured us of its preservation. Let us bless Him for having saved for our affection, our King, the glory of the Belgian nation, our sweet and valiant Queen, and the royal children. Let us bless Him for having given us the patience to bear our long, hard trial without fear or trembling.

However unpleasant these words may have been for von der Lancken and von Falkenhausen to read, they knew that he was forgiving, that he was good, and they seem to have felt that he might not prove a bad friend at court. So von der Lancken wrote him on behalf of the Government in Berlin and the Governor-General:

In our eyes you are the living impersonation of occupied Belgium, which reveres you as its Pastor and heeds you as its Counsellor. It is to you, therefore, that the Governor-General and my Government have directed me to report that on our evacuation of your territory, we surrender to you, spontaneously and willingly, all Belgians who have been imprisoned or deported for resistance to our authority. They will be at liberty to return to their homes, some of them as early as next Monday, the 21st instant.

Since this announcement will, I am sure, bring you comfort, I esteem it a personal privilege to deliver it to you, all the more since I have been unable to live for four years among the Belgians without learning to esteem them and to appreciate their patriotism at its true value.

It was the last of the long series of messages, and these articles of unconditional capitulation were written in French. On the many occasions when von der Lancken had called on the Cardinal, Mercier had always received him standing, with frigid though unfailing courtesy, always tender of the dignity of his position. This time, when von der Lancken brought the lines of final surrender himself, and showed none of his customary eagerness for argument, the Cardinal, after he had read the message, offered von der Lancken his hand, and begged him to be seated.

Mercier lost no time in spreading the good tidings. A few days after he had read the message himself, it was read by the miners of the Hainaut and Limburg, by the woodsmen of the Luxemburg, by the smiths and factory hands of Liège and Namur, by the stevedores of Antwerp, by the farmers and laborers of Flanders and Brabant. Mercier had added the following admonition:

Continue to pray in unison.
Remain calm and dignified.
The definite hour of deliverance is nigh. Courage and confidence.
Sacred Heart of Jesus, I put my confidence in you.
Sacred Heart of Jesus, protect Belgium.
Our Lady of the Rosary, Mary Mediatrix, pray for us.

The American food dictator, Herbert Hoover, had no very high opinion of von der Lancken, and for that he had his reasons. Time and again, von der Lancken and his associate, Doctor Rieth, had all but wrecked the American Relief Commission's work by their foul dealing and their repudiation of the American-German contract. Hoover's justifiable complaints of the disappearance and diversion of supplies, and German obstruction of their orderly, well-planned distribution had been met by von der Lancken's bland or impudent denials. But now the shoe was on the other foot, and pinching badly. It was no longer poor, abused little Belgium that was the starving suppliant, but the Central Empires. Hoover's Rotterdam representative received a telegram from Berlin describing the frightful starvation in

Germany, and informing him that Baron von der Lancken and Doctor Rieth, who had been appointed representatives of the German Government, requested an immediate meeting with the American food dictator. Hoover felt a quick revulsion of disgust. True enough, with his usual foresight he had more than one cargo of food on the Atlantic for the relief of Germany, but he had no mind to entrust a biscuit of it to any such agents. His instructions to his devoted secretary, Strauss, for the reply to this suggestion were, "You can describe two and a half years of arrogance toward ourselves and cruelty to the Belgians in any language you may select, and tell the pair personally to go to hell, with my compliments. When we negotiate with the Germans, it will not be with that pair." How the good Cardinal's eyes would have sparkled to hear such a message for his opponent coming from so long-suffering a man as the future President of the United States!

On November 11 the Armistice was signed, and Mercier spoke to his people:

After four years of arrogance and injustice, cruelty and perfidy, the enemy lies prostrate! On Monday, the 11th of November, at three o'clock in the afternoon, the flag of our country unfurled above the tower of St. Rombaut, opened out its folds toward Termonde and Ghent, and beckoned back into our midst again, our King and his soldiers. Information has come to hand that on Tuesday next, the 19th of November, 1918, Albert the Magnanimous will return as conqueror to his capital. The triumph of justice is complete. The conscience of mankind is vindicated.

Glory be to God, beloved brethren! Glory be to His justice! May the people of Belgium, may the victors, may the vanquished be mindful of it forever.

196

FREE BELGIUM

And on the doors of his churches throughout the dioceses of Belgium he caused to be posted the following exhortation:

November 11, 1918.

MY WELL-BELOVED BRETHREN:

The hour of Belgium's delivery has struck.

Let us open our hearts to joy and gratitude.

Let us, however, await the return of our King and the army before giving vent to our most ardent expressions of patriotism. Your dignity and endurance have won you the admiration of the world.

Do not, at the last moment, compromise the glorious name of the Belgian people.

Remain calm, dignified masters of your feelings.

Long live Belgium, united, free, and independent.

D. J. CARD. MERCIER,
Arch. of Malines.

Many have reviewed Mercier's work during the war, but no one has summarized it more ably than his distinguished pupil, Maurice de Wulf, who wrote,

Why will his personality be enthusiastically remembered by the present generation and be even more appreciated by future ones? Because he showed, above all others, at a time when everything seemed crumbling, that Right, Honor, Duty, and Truth remain unalterable, in regions inaccessible to individuals and beyond the reach of the masses. They dominate the centuries. They are unaffected by time. During the darkest hours of the war, Mercier was the interpreter, the Doctor of that unwritten law which is graven upon the inmost recesses of the conscience, and evoked, time and again, down through history, by the prophets and great poets, by the masters of eloquence and philosophy, by Micah and Sophocles, by Cicero and St. Augustine and St. Thomas. He made humanity appreciate the most sacred part of its patrimony, and for that reason, he made it better.

197

The carillons of Belgium rang out once more, from Antwerp to Malines and to Brussels, from Bruges to Ghent, from Tournai to Mons, and from Namur to Liège. All over the Lowlands their glad song was heard.[1] Mercier opened his palace windows wide to listen to the

> *Carillons de tes cités antiques*
> *Oh, vieux pays, gardien de tes mœurs domestiques*
> *Noble Flandre, où le nord se rechauffe, engourdie*
> *Au soleil de Castille, et s'accouple au midi.*[2]

Belgium was free; Mercier was to sing the Te Deum in Ste. Gudule before his King who had returned at the head of his troops. In his sermon he spoke directly to the King:

Yesterday Belgium acclaimed the glory of her King and joined him in admiring and expressing her gratitude to the army and the population which have been the authors of the Victory both in the invaded and the free portions of the country.

But hearts must lift up higher.

Bravery, armaments, military strategy are insufficient to

---

[1] Since way back in the sixteenth century, the carillons in the Lowland steeples have rung out over town and field. Emperors and dukes have stood sponsors at the consecration of the bells, upon their arrival from the great foundries of Hemony, Van den Gheyn or Waghevens, and Cardinals and Bishops have baptized them before they were hoisted on high. There they have testified to the love of music of the industrious toilers beneath them. The art of the bell-ringer was brought to great perfection and held in high esteem. Jef Denyn was perhaps the greatest of them all, having inherited all of his father's art and skill, and added to them in virtuosity of expression and in the delicacy of the sustained tones which he knew how to draw from his forty-five big and little bells. The carillon of St. Rombaut played its quaint old tunes every hour and half and quarter; so it seemed to be almost continually ringing, up there on high, but well did Mercier know when Jef Denyn sat down at his keyboard on Monday evenings during the summer. If Mercier then could steal a few minutes to himself, he would walk out among his white and red geraniums and listen with a happy smile on his face to the prelude the Master was improvising on his bells before starting Benoit's Song of the Flemings or some old fifteenth-century dance music, or best of all, Schubert's "Ave Maria" followed by the *"Frühlingsglaube."*

[2] Victor Hugo.

insure Victory. The enemy possessed all of those qualities and yet has been vanquished.

An all-powerful hand governs men and events, and disposes of armies, thrones, and empires.

Peace and order rest upon Justice. Justice gives to each one his due. The first duty of a nation is to praise Him to Whom it owes everything.

Your Majesty has already proved your gratitude, yesterday, in this very temple, in silent prayer, but Your Majesty has wished to do so again, officially and beside the Queen, the Royal Princes, and representatives of the Government.

I am proud to be the minister at this ceremony.

The entire Nation will pray with the lips of Your Majesty, and will praise the grandeur, the wisdom, and the goodness of God, who has protected Belgium.

As soon as peace was restored, Mercier's thoughts turned instantly to the moral and social wounds to be healed. The peace of Versailles was not Cardinal Mercier's peace, for its terms were inspired by vengeance and hate, and its triumph was vindictive. The guarantees and reparations he desired were a respect for the harmony of a world which had been convulsed, and a submission to the divine plan which had been disturbed. He did not want a pacifists' peace, but that of men of peace, who take into account the reality of eternity.

The Belgian Cardinal was now loaded down with honors, the worldly honors which meant so little in his life.[3] As

---

[3] When he was laid to rest, his decorations were carried beside his hearse according to Continental custom. They were as numerous as those of a Prussian Field-Marshal. The citation read to the soldiers of his own country was:

Désiré Félicien François Joseph Mercier—In order to serve his country more effectively, armed himself with his dignity as a Prince of the Church and Primate of Belgium. In the words of the enemy: 'became the very spirit of occupied Belgium.' Preached patriotism and endurance by word of mouth and example, from the first to the last day of the war. Added to his titles of illustrious thinker and Bishop, that of a great citizen.

the Cardinal's love for France was second only to that for his own Belgium, and as their fates had been so inextricably interwoven during the war, he was especially gratified by the *Ordre du Jour* of the French Army, proclaimed before the altar of St. Rombaut conferring upon the fighting Cardinal the *Croix de Guerre* of France. Poincaré conferred it with these words:

In barbaric times, the Bishops of the Church were the defenders of our cities. That you have been in our times. Speaking from the eminence of your cathedral, you expressed the thoughts of oppressed Belgium in imperishable phrases. You did more than that, you spoke in the name of Justice itself, and your words resounded through the civilized world.

An humbler Belgian, the Abbé Lebbe, who had spent his life in Chinese missions, met Francis Dessain in Rome. Hearing that he was Mercier's secretary, Lebbe threw up his hands and exclaimed, *"Mercier! Voilà quelqu'un au moins, qui osa se mêler de choses qui ne lui regardaient pas!"* But no keener or simpler appreciation of the Cardinal was ever uttered than that of a laborer who, one day as the Cardinal passed, turned to a friend to remark, *"Ça, c'est un prêtre!"*

"Charity suffereth long, and is kind; charity envieth not; charity vaunteth not itself, is not puffed up."—FIRST EPISTLE OF PAUL TO THE CORINTHIANS, xiii, 4.

CHAPTER X

THE COMPANY OF THE SAINTS

AN old friend of Mercier's, Mgr. Cartuyvels, once said that at forty a man was responsible for his physiognomy. Mercier repeated the words, and pointed out that St. Paul had said that it was true of Jesus at the age of thirty, "the life of Jesus was made manifest in his mortal flesh." The Cardinal's own body, which had proved the servant of his great spirit, radiated the inner life of the man. One might have applied to him what he once wrote of St. Francis de Sales:

His face was always tranquil, free of all embarrassment, always gay, serene, and open, without, however, playfulness or indiscreet badinage. . . . When he prayed, he was motionless as a column.

He stooped perceptibly now. The war had left its mark on him. But the moulding of the broad forehead was magnificent above the watchful, intelligent blue eyes which expressed both kindness and energy. His long arms and big hands were always willing to bless the faithful. Their fingers were not unlike those of Erasmus, so sensitively rendered by Holbein in his arresting portrait in the Louvre. His mouth had the firmness of renunciation, with lines showing pain accepted and conquered, the bitter but comforting savor of self-denial. Both mouth and eyes were constantly smiling. His nose was long and thin, exquisitely modelled, its aristocratic sensitiveness emphasized by the pince-nez loosely trembling on the bridge. All the ascetic features of the small, bony head reflected quickly the thoughts and impulses of the mediæval saint. The face had grown more beautiful with age. The principal impression made by his personality was one of genuine majesty, and by his speech, indisputable authority. One who knew him well, even to his humble origin, said of him, *"On dirait qu'il est né sur les marches d'un trône."*

He felt unconsciously the greatness of his office and its task. Whether mitred on his cathedral throne or wrapped in his old cape on some errand of charity, he bore himself with a poise which commanded immediate respect and admiration. He looked every inch a Prince of the Church, one who had consummate grace coupled with perfect dignity. All felt his unquestionable authority the moment he entered a room. Even if ignorant of his rank and identity, one sensed somehow that a great personage had come in, dominating his surroundings, and those present felt their own insignificance. As soon as he addressed one in his elegant and captivating manner, the intimate perfection of his life radiated from him.

That consummate artist, Saint-Simon, drew a picture of Fénelon so like Mercier that one might take it as readily for the Belgian as for the French Archbishop:

This prelate was a tall man, lean, well-made, pale, with large nose, and with eyes from which fire and intelligence poured like a torrent, a face such that I have never seen another like it and that you could not forget when you had seen it once, and in it contraries did not conflict with each other. There were gravity and gallantry, there were seriousness and gaiety, there were at once the scholar, the bishop and the grand gentleman. What predominated in it, as in his person, was subtlety, wit, grace, good taste, and above all a certain nobleness. It required an effort to turn your gaze away.

A friend said of Mercier that his constant contact with the Church Fathers and with St. Paul made of him an apostle of Jesus Christ rather than a specialist in the sacred sciences. They were his daily spiritual companions; all of them, Fathers Dionysus, Augustine—the most human of them all—Ambrose, Jerome, John Chrysostom, Basil, Gregory the Great, Aquinas, Cajetan, the whole glorious company, Greek, Roman, and mediæval, were his familiar spirits. But it was with St. Paul that Mercier had most in common; both had the same contempt for the shallowness of the verbal "show of wisdom" which marked in the view of each the philosophic rhetoric of his time; the same eagerness for learning and audacity, the same width of vision. Both examined everything with open mind so as to retain only what was good, both had inflexible courage in defense of vital principles, both were supremely concerned with living a life worthy of their Master's example, and both had that universal sympathy which Newman considered St. Paul's salient characteristic. Each was witness in the cause of liberty against what seemed unjustifiable authority. Mercier said:

St. Paul was the most vigorous artisan of our Christian civilization. It has been said, and I am inclined to believe it true, that the Epistle to the Hebrews, owing to the sublimity of its subject, its breadth, and its eloquence, is the masterpiece of this extraordinary man whose fourteen letters and speeches are the richest dogmatic treasure of the New Testament.

In his sermons, in his pastoral letters, and in his conversation, Mercier quoted St. Paul more frequently than he did any one else, and always with boundless admiration.

With St. Francis of Assisi, too, Mercier had much in common. Both had the richness and depth of spiritual life that made them sources of inspiration to so many of those with whom they came in contact. Both when hard beset found new strength and consolation in withdrawal for solitary contemplation and prayer. The essence of both was action, to be up and doing something for God or for their fellow men. The windswept sky, the fleeting clouds, the woodland scent and colors of Umbria were as beloved by the Saint of Assisi as were those of the Province of Antwerp by him of Malines. Both received from the same source joyousness as a cradle gift, held it into manhood, and professed it as an essential of Christianity. "What," said St. Francis, "are the servants of God but as it were merry-makers who should stir the hearts of men and impel them to spiritual joy?" To Mercier, as to St. Paul and St. Francis, conversion was a radical and complete change and submission to divine authority, which left the mind in a state of tranquillity and joy.

It is not wholly impertinent to place him in the company of the saints. To Belgium and to the entire civilized world he had become a living saint, and his name was a symbol of fearlessness, integrity, and righteousness. But the halo which in the view of the whole world now surely rested on his kindly and commanding head did not stiffen his movements in simple sincere tasks or make him less easily approachable by any who had burdens which he might share. Although he was a world figure and after the war had every temptation to be in the spot-light, Mercier preferred to carry on the humble work with his flock rather than to be the idol of strange multitudes. Display and demonstration were always a little bit shocking to his sensibilities. What he loved most was personal contact with those whom he might benefit, and so now after the war when public duty was more often a demand for the acknowledgment of the tributes which were flowing in from every side than a clear call of pressing service to Belgium and to humanity, he turned again with earnestness and pleasure to his pastoral care.

Children were among the passions of Mercier's life. He said of them:

I know no zealous work which surpasses that of placing Christ in the soul of a child. . . . The soul of a child is virgin, pliable as wax, ready to receive impressions of truth, of love, of God. The child is so flexible. Can you not read his spontaneous confidence in his limpid look?

Be patient in your work with children; bear with their frivolity and take them back to your heart without rancor. I never scold them. I try to teach them by example.

Children need much tenderness. That is the sunshine which opens hearts.

He loved to be with them. If submitting to a photographer, he wanted to be photographed with them. He loved to bless them above all others. His favorite charities were always those that were to benefit the young. That is partly why he took so vital an interest in Mr. Hoover's work, and that of the Commission for Relief in Belgium. It was the children's plight which wrung his heart. After the nightmare of starving Belgian children had passed, Hungarian, Polish, and Russian children became the concern of his heart. If little girls came to see him, he met them with open arms, and left them with a wave of the hand. The long, bony fingers loved to feel tiny, soft palms close confidently round them. If he happened to be near his garden, he gave them a posy as a remembrance. If they were sick, he selected just the little gifts they were likely to cherish most. He never talked over their heads, for their philosophy was also his; when he was with children, he was one of them. "Genius," says Baudelaire, "is childhood refound at will."

One day, when he was visiting a little sick boy, Mercier asked him what he wanted most of all.

"A fine horse on wheels," was the instant reply.

When the horse arrived the next day, the boy remarked, "You can't fool me, I knew very well that was Santa Claus who came to see me, so I was all ready for him."

He always welcomed little children, for he knew that theirs was the kingdom to which he devoted his all.

He was eager also for girls to be guided wisely as the responsibilities of maturity came to them. He was concerned about the new aspects of life that the war seemed to have brought before them.

The young girls buy luxurious and suggestive toilets and some of them turn to open profligacy. Complaisant or too feeble parents have no longer the reins of the family in their

Photograph by L. Bossut, Malines

Mercier in the streets of Malines blessing the children

hands. Some of them smile, others let their children do as they please. The young people fritter away their excessive earnings at gambling, or spend in mad pleasure the money they have quickly gained and pocketed without effort.

The orphan girls cared for by the Redemptorist nuns of Malines were his special pets, and never if he could help it would he miss one of their little celebrations. During the war, he constantly worried lest they should be insufficiently fed. One day when he was at his busiest, he suddenly pushed aside the papers before him on his desk, and wrote:

My dear daughters: In the liturgy of the Mass which I have said for you in order that we should have the same heart and soul, we repeat, *Si vales et ipse benefac;* "Do good if you have the means." I have a small reserve of chocolate, and I have hens. Won't you have a little chocolate party and accept some of the eggs of my hens? I wish I had time to come and celebrate the occasion with you, but I shall be there in spirit. And would you put some roses from my garden before the statue of your patron saint? All this is not much, but it is meant as an expression of my good will.

His success in the years of his teaching at the seminaries and the university was both the result and the cause of his extraordinary ability as a leader of youth. He considered that the Christian education consisted in studying the child's physical, intellectual, moral, and Christian characteristics, and developing them with a full understanding of their nature. He believed that to educate was to study the child's capacities for good, and to place them at the service of God. Education to him was the process of imparting a true appreciation of the relative values in life. With this idea of education he made a significant distinction between education and instruction. Instruction, he believed, was the means; education was the aim. Instruction was directed to the memory and the intelligence. Education should influence the will. Instruction produced capable men. Education formed character, and included virtue.

"Give me young men," he exclaimed one day, his eyes sparkling with enthusiasm, "who from their home to their school and from school to public life, breathe an atmosphere permeated with the sunshine of truth and the warmth of charity." Charity was in very truth to him the greatest of the virtues, invariably *caritas*, in all he did and in all he counselled. Every act of his own life was filled with its healing blessing. It was the foundation of his optimism and his courage, which, in turn, were the wellspring of the many profoundly wise and encouraging things he said to his pupils in his efforts to guide them in spiritual life:

The complete and harmonious development of all one's energies—that is the ideal of human nature. The law of the world is the law of progress. Man's march is constantly upwards, towards something better. That being so, the general theory of the universe should be optimism. Are not the noblest souls those who have the highest ideals?

However troubled a situation may be, or however near it may seem to disaster and despair, we must always keep our heads up and retain a stout heart. Discouragement never created energy, and only energy can prepare triumph.

Marshal Foch in his *War Lessons* asks who is the victor in armed conflicts. He answers, "The strongest will, which makes the lesser flinch."

Again and again Mercier repeated as his profound conviction that to teach was to affirm. Detesting pettiness and mediocrity, he said that to be neutral was to resign oneself to being a nonentity, to declare neither for nor against, to vote neither yes nor no—in fact, to abstain and wash one's hands as did Pontius Pilate. "Love activity," he advised the young, "and love life. Suffering accepted and vanquished will give you a security which may become the most exquisite fruit of your life." He had lived his whole life with boys; naturally he knew them through and through, and loved them as well as he knew them. "My dear seminarists," he said, "love me with filial affection. When I see them, when I speak to them and shake their hands, I feel that they are the very core of my heart. The thought of them pursues me everywhere." His work with girls was less in duration and extent, but sympathy and observation made it no less complete in understanding. "What young girl," he says, "of sixteen or eighteen, when virtue seems austere and duty tiresome, does not imagine that she is the heroine of a romance which fills her imagination?" No less are his sympathy and understanding when he talks to them of dress or vanity, or, for the matter of that, when he goes deeper and speaks of motherhood or home.

We have glimpses of the joy he had in teaching from such passages as this:

But it is you, above all students of today, whom I see before me, with your innate sensibility, with such cordial and generous spontaneity, with such impatient fervor, such strength in action, such nobility of disinterested intentions, such gay and playful fancies and the divine gift of enthusiasm, which all combine to make something inimitable and lovely, meaning to me the soul of Catholic youth.

Such lines as these round out in our minds the idea of the essential joyousness of religion, and the unity of religion and education. In religion no less than in education, the feeling he strove to inculcate was one of joyousness, the antithesis of Jansenism, of Calvinism, of the doctrine of fear of an angry Jehovah constantly abroad to avenge and punish. The world was not a vale of woe to Mercier, but a valley of glad service. The soaring glory of the Gothic cathedral, the luscious color-riot of its windows, the exultant tones of its organ, all praising the Lord God of inspiration—these were the harmonics of Mercier's religion, and his religion was the subject matter of his teaching. The world was a better place for the sojourn in it of such a spirit.

No keener or truer characterization has been made of Mercier than this of Professor de Wulf, who knew him to the core:

Mercier's personality was without deficiency or violent contrast. It was complete and harmonious. He possessed, in a remarkable degree, the logic which convinces, the charity which renders truth easily accessible to the intelligence, the prudence which gives a feeling of security, the firmness which compels followers, the authority which overawes, and that infinitely nice sense of duty—whether commonplace or heroic, which results in the most sacred form of action, and he possessed above all, the goodness, the radiance of which is irresistible—*bonus est diffusivum sui.*

Saintliness is beyond the understanding of most men, even beyond average appreciation. Francis of Assisi would have been a saint before the Lord had he never been canonized, and so would St. Ignatius and St. Francis Xavier and St. Jerome, and Father Damien too, now immortalized in the statue in one of the squares of his native Malines where he is shown stretching his hand over the leper. A very few are born saintly, but most of those who achieve saintliness do so through sacrifice, renunciation, and suffering, by living for their fellow men. To this glorious company belonged Désiré Mercier.

"You turned upon physical danger, upon brutal malice, and upon inhuman outrage of every kind the proud contempt of a pure and lofty spirit and a sublime Christian faith. Military power, until then unmatched in history, quailed before your burning words of exhortation and defiance. Your pen was mightier than the sword of the German armies. The heart of all America goes out to you and hails you as a worthy Prince of the Christian Church and a captain of the human spirit."—PRESIDENT NICHOLAS MURRAY BUTLER of Columbia University.

CHAPTER XI

THE AMERICAN TOUR

MERCIER had been showered with honors and with invitations from abroad since the war, and one of these invitations became so cordial and so insistent that he could no longer resist, probably because he was already predisposed to accept it. Early in the spring of 1919, a group of American journalists came to the Archbishop's palace, and insisted on an interview with Cardinal Mercier. He received them, and answered their long list of personal and impersonal questions with his unfailing good-nature. From them he received an invitation to visit America, and probably did not surprise them by his reply that he very much wished to do so. He told them that ever since the days of the Commission for Relief in Belgium, he had been eager personally to express to their compatriots his gratitude for their generous aid to his country.

212

THE AMERICAN TOUR

Many of the young Americans who had worked with the Cardinal during the war came to pay their respects to him after it was over. Of these, one and all added their invitations to those of the journalists. Always Mercier said that he wished to go to thank the Americans for their care of his children; just thanking *Monsieur le Ministre* Whitlock was not enough. Then President Wilson arrived, and invited him cordially. So did Cardinal Gibbons; so did the Knights of Columbus. So did each and every distinguished American who visited Belgium after the Armistice. But it did not need such a weight of insistence as this to tip the scale, with the Cardinal's inclinations already on the American side.

Mercier had always been fond of travelling when vacation time and summer came round, particularly if he might thereby assist his work and charities at home. He enjoyed the shifting scenes, the differences in customs and manners and above all, exchanging ideas with men of intellectual value. It satisfied his mental curiosity and stimulated his ideas. From his extensive reading he was more or less at home in much of the intellectual life of the country for which he was bound. Then, too, there was always enough of the boy left in him for adventure to be lurking around the corner wherever he was going.

He began to look on the American trip as a lark, and asked to cross on a transport full of home-going American doughboys. His advisers warned him that he would have from them a rough foretaste of what he might expect in the United States. They, like their fellow-citizens, would shout him to death and smother him with kindness in a well-meant effort toward hospitality which he would find inconsider-

213

ately, mercilessly tiring. But this, it appeared, was the very thing he wished to observe in its full strength and on its own ground.

He had seen it, even among his advisers themselves. Mr. McClure had called on him, and Virginie, the cook, and Franz, the butler, had done their best to make the dinner a success. Then Mr. McClure explained his idea of making the Cardinal's visit to the United States a "go." It was to be a course of lectures under his management. He dwelt on the crowded auditoriums, frenzied, cheering mobs, and money, pouring in endless streams into the coffers. He went so far as to show sample posters, appropriately blazing with cardinal red! Gently and firmly the Cardinal steered the conversation into safer channels. Like many another foreigner, Mercier did not know what to make of all this, but in spite of all in it that was antithetical to his very nature, it attracted him, for he felt in it the quality of youth, whose faults are glaring, whose virtues are endearing.

There was an air of excitement throughout the episcopal palace, of happy anticipation, such as seldom passed through its solemn corridors except when King Albert was expected at some great fête or other in St. Rombaut. Franz, the valet, could scarcely be held in check, for he was to go too, and he chattered incessantly as he aided his master with dress or food. He all but forgot his knock when entering the offices of the higher prelates, and greeted the ring of all callers with a broad grin on his rosy Flemish face. There was considerable suppressed speculation in the Vicariat as to who would and who would not be selected to accompany the Cardinal on his triumphal American tour. Invitations already crowded the new American "dossiers," and telegraph messengers rang the huge doorbell as if His Holiness had suddenly passed away. Fortunately, Dessain was as much at home in English as in French, so he could cope with the phraseology of the more difficult and important replies.

The small party sailed on the *Northern Pacific*, September 3, 1919. Mercier proved to be a miserable sailor, but his holiday spirit prevailed over his discomforts. One of his companions was a little round ball of a man, Father Nash. The Cardinal had begged to be left alone in the misery of his steamer chair. Nash came bouncing by, up and down the deck before him, smoking an enormous pipe. He caught the eye of his sick master. It twinkled. Nash stopped bouncing.

"Big pipe," asked Mercier, "where are you going with that little man, this stormy day?"

The Belgians found novelty in the American food. Nash liked the corn on the cob, and kept calling for more, so that his chief "might see him play the flute again."

Mercier proposed that on Sunday he should say Mass for the noisy doughboys instead of for the officers, but his staff feared that this might be misunderstood. So he merely spoke informally to the five hundred soldiers, pressing eagerly round him on the afterdeck, the Catholic among them kneeling with folded hands. The eager joy of life and admiration in their faces touched Mercier. In spite of his extensive English reading, it was difficult for him, now that he was out of practice, to speak in English; Spanish or German would have been much easier, or even Greek. But their admiring attention took him out of himself, and fluency came. "They who have been brave in battle," he told them, "must now have the generosity of which only the strong are capable. They must scorn anything less than the truth, and know that evil is scalding to the touch." The personal magnetism which sprang from his transparent sincerity held them captive. Protestant and Catholic alike knelt for the prayer, and remained on their knees till the last flutter of the Cardinal's cassock disappeared down the hatchway.

The wireless kept busy with messages to Mercier from the New World. Hundreds of cities and mayors to him unknown insisted on visits from him. The press of the country wished for his greeting. Mercier turned to those about him for suggestions and advice with the unconscious modesty that made his associates forget his mental powers and his high rank.[1]

With such a humble spirit as this, he could not have been less than surprised and bewildered when he came to the

---

[1] This was thoroughly characteristic of him, and could be illustrated by countless anecdotes. When the Frenchman, Victor Geraud, had written truthfully but very flatteringly of him, Mercier penned a friendly remonstrance. "As for what you say . . . ," he wrote, "I think I can forgive you for it, since I know that your intentions were of the kindliest, but I must tell you that as I read it, my guardian angel was constrained to whisper a prayer in my ear: 'O Lord, lead us not into temptation.'" Again, when His Imperial Highness, Prince Hirohito, not long before he came to the throne as the one hundred and twenty-third of his line, was going to pay a courtesy call to his late ally, the King of the Belgians, he learned that his way was through Malines, and he sent word that he would value highly a word with the Cardinal while waiting at the station.

"What on earth does he want to see me for?" asked Mercier of the priest who happened to be by him when the message came. "Surely it is only a courteous gesture." The priest realized to his amazement that Mercier did not understand that any one could wish to see him merely for the honor or the pleasure of it. After considerable prodding, Mercier was finally prevailed upon to go, and he was so charmed with the Japanese Prince that he accompanied him to Louvain and showed him the Institute. On his return, the Cardinal's first act was to send for the priest and thank him for the pleasure he had insisted on giving him.

end of his transatlantic voyage. New York—sirens—Irish Catholics—*Monsieur le Bourgmestre* Hylan—shrieking motorcycles! The strident voices seemed kindly, and the *sergeants-de-ville* smiled with the crowds pushing and shouting for his blessing. Wa-na-ma-ker, was it? *Quel nom!* The gentleman's French was even more difficult. Possibly it would go better if he himself tried English; the soldiers had seemed to understand it. It was a shame to take so much of *Monsieur le Bourgmestre's* time from the *Conseil Municipal.*

" 'At's all right," said Hylan.

"*C'est fort bien,*" whispered the Ambassador.

The moment he stepped ashore, the reporters asked him what were his impressions of America.

"Have pity," he replied, "and give me time to breathe."

Surely he would find relief at the Episcopal Palace of His Brother, Archbishop Hayes! *He* at least would have something of the spirit of contemplation so foreign to these noisy crowds! There the faithful Dessain would be able to protect him for his hour of peace and rest after the *dejeuner.* So much he demanded, a little rest in the middle of the day, and plenty of time for his prayers, and that was all the time he had to himself. But because of his rare capacity for conserving his mental and physical resources, this proved enough to carry him through all the demands on his time and energy. For even so little as this, however, Dessain had at times to use all his ingenuity. A Papal Countess called, an unfailing friend and helper of the Archbishop's. She must see the Cardinal; it was most important. Dessain was so hard-pressed that the Archbishop himself came to his aid.

Ah, it was a question of an autograph. Yes, of course, that could be arranged. The good Cardinal's favorite charity was his Malines orphanage. All she had to do was to sit down and with the Archbishop's own fountain pen to make out a cheque for five thousand dollars. The name of "D. J. Mercier, Archbishop of Malines," would inevitably appear on the back of it when it came back to her. She wrote the cheque, and afterwards many another, for Americans, as the Cardinal learned, had that virtue of the young, boundless generosity.

It was a circle of busy cities in a cycle of crowded days—Philadelphia, Washington, Baltimore, Richmond, St. Louis, Cleveland, Pittsburgh, Boston, Springfield, and almost as many more in Canada. Serene and smiling, the Cardinal took all as it came, banquets and speeches, delegations and committees, luncheons, teas, and receptions. Many, too, were the academic convocations, for he sought out every Catholic institution within the range of his travels, and every Protestant one sought him. Honorary degrees fell on him like rain. At Princeton, Dean West used Latin in presenting him for the degree; the rest of the ceremonies were in English. Mercier jokingly thanked him for having used a little Latin, "for," said he, "that was what I could follow most intelligently." Harvard,[2] too, conferred its highest honor on Mercier, and a few years later his own university, Louvain, requested Harvard's representative to take his place at

[2] Gossip said there was some hokus-pokus before President Lowell was able definitely to fix the date on which Harvard was to honor the Cardinal by conferring upon him an honorary degree. Evil tongues whispered that Cardinal O'Connell, who had never received one, had attempted to belittle in his Belgian brother's estimation, the distinction of America's great and oldest university. But as usual Mercier judged for himself.

the head of America's many delegates at the inauguration of the new library at Louvain (July 4, 1928).

Having given so much of his life to the instruction of boys of all ages at St. Rombaut's, at the seminaries, and at Louvain University, Mercier had frequently questioned his American friends about American boys. Now that he was in the United States, he was eager to talk to them himself whenever there was the slightest chance of escaping the limelight. But he was not always well impressed with what he was told of the American youth. A quizzical smile that said nothing but meant much spread over his face when he heard that the average time an American student gave to his daily work was about six hours.

"I mean students—university students," he reiterated.

"Yes, Your Eminence," replied his informer, "we think possibly overmuch of a sound mind in a sound body, and our well-to-do student takes fast motors and polo ponies far more for granted than an acquaintance with John Stuart Mill or Virgil."

The Cardinal was not to be outdone. With the delightful twinkle that was so often to be seen in his eyes, he retorted, "Oh, I quite understand. And I have also read that your youth takes the education of its parents very seriously, and insists on a proper chance to express itself."

In Washington, he was especially interested in the Catholic University, because it marked the beginning of his personal interest in the United States. When he was young, and his fame as a teacher was spreading, it had offered him a professorship. The offer had attracted him, but it was out of the question to accept it, for he knew that he could never be wholly happy and at ease anywhere but in Belgium. In Baltimore he was glad to visit the eighty-five-year-old Cardinal Gibbons, for he had always admired him profoundly, and wished to talk with him about the Vatican Council of 1870 in which Gibbons had participated. When he first became Archbishop, Mercier had looked upon Gibbons as the figure of his own time whom he most wished to emulate, especially in his enlightened and vigorous efforts so to place the acts of the apostles before the generations of his day that they would and could go and do likewise.

Sensitive to exterior impressions, Mercier eagerly observed what surrounded him in the vast new country where he seemed to be every one's guest and everybody's property.

The high spirits and optimism, the venturesome initiative, the unrestrained and often thoughtless speech and action of those with whom he came in contact, the generous response in giving to what Dessain or others had said were his favorite charities—all struck him as so different from the moods of the tired, ruined folk of Belgium and France whom he had endeavored to uplift after the artificial enthusiasm of war and victory had been quenched by the ashes of disillusion. Hope and courage seemed in the New World to have supplanted the dejection and despair of the Old.

And the tolerance in religious and political matters! How different it seemed from the strife and discord tearing at the vitals of his own little Belgium. Difference in political faith seemed to make no difference whatever in the relationship of one man to another; strange to say, very generally few knew what actually *was* the other's political views. Catholics seemed to have their parochial schools and seminaries side by side with those of other faiths. Protestant and Catholic children of the upper classes even went to one and the same school without any *"question scolaire"* seeming to rend the country. He questioned those in authority, Gibbons, Hayes, Mundelein, and O'Connell, and their answer was always the same: "We are content to tender our own flocks." And not infrequently, leaders of all denominations found the common good could best be attained by united conference or appeal. Protestants of all classes bowed their heads in the prayers which he was urged by them to offer, and Protestant mothers brought their children to him for his blessing. That could not have happened at home. And he never sat down to break bread with them either in public or private without being asked to say Grace and give a blessing.

He would have liked more time with the scholars and particularly with those whose teachings had been similar to his own—he wanted quiet evenings of thought and contemplation with some of them, but that was of course out of the question with every quarter hour of the day parcelled out to travel, banquets, visits, photographers, and receptions. He would have liked to have a few quiet hours with President Wilson and to return his courteous call at Malines, but that was out of the question now, for the President was too ill, and the Washington arrangements had perforce been altered. His own Ambassador, the good Cartier de Marchienne, had arranged all for the best and he would work hard to fulfil the seemingly endless engagements of each exacting day. He mustn't disappoint any one, and least of all, the Catholic institutions.

Mercier and his suite reached London on their way home on the first anniversary of the Armistice (November 11, 1919), and the Cardinal celebrated pontifical Mass in the Cathedral of Westminster, while his Father Confessor, Dom Columba Marmion, preached the sermon. English friends urged Mercier to stay, but as usual, when he had completed what he had set himself to do, he longed to return home as soon as possible.

Back in Malines, the Cardinal rejoiced at the greeting of his smiling household. There they were, all crowding around the doorway. Virginie, the cook, Oswald, the chauffeur, and Brother Hubert Egide, who managed the housekeeping.[3]

---

[3] Besides his Auxiliary Bishop, Mgr. de Wachter, and his secretary, Dessain, Mercier had taken his faithful valet, Franz, along with him on the great American adventure. His master had taught him punctuality. He practised it until they reached the hospitable home of Archbishop Mundelein in Chicago. Then, the Cardinal noticed unusual irregularities in Franz's conduct. He was reported in the servants' hall when his duties lay elsewhere. At last, the kindly master had to reprove him. Franz confessed. He had fallen in love with one of the maids. Believing the infatuation a temporary one, as well as possibly embarrassing to their host, Mercier merely smiled. Upon their return home, the Cardinal noticed, however, undue pensiveness on the part of Franz, and particularly on the receipt of American-stamped letters. Franz readily owned up that Betsy in Chicago and himself in Malines merely spelled misery to them both.

"Send for her at once," replied Mercier. So Betsy was sent for and was taken home from the station in state by the Cardinal's own car; and brought the radiant Franz in the next few years four sons in rapid succession.

Today Franz is still in the Episcopal Palace of Malines, but Betsy has followed her master to another world.

"O, I see the crescent promise of my spirit hath not set;
Ancient founts of inspiration well through all my fancy yet."
—TENNYSON, "Locksley Hall."

CHAPTER XII

THE TIRELESS LABORER

AFTER returning from his American trip, Mercier plunged again into the numberless activities which filled his days with the rich pleasure of being occupied fruitfully in the service of others. Though he was approaching a veteran old age when most men are content to relax a bit in the belief that the world no longer expects so much of them, he was not satisfied to do just the routine work of the diocese. His tremendous energy overflowed in many directions. Some of his interests dated from long before the war, but he was always aware of the contemporary world and its problems and he never shrank from the challenge of modern thought. He carried his activities as spiritual and social guide into every important sphere. The variety and genuine catholicity of his interests it is difficult to imagine. His mind was always ateem with ideas theoretical and practical, and mostly they were grounded in intellectual understanding and sound common sense.

Mercier's enterprise led him constantly into new undertakings, so many that, though his labors were tireless, some

tasks must needs be left unfinished. At the beginning of the
war he had promised God two things, hoping that the effort
to accomplish them might be acceptable, and that in pleas-
ing God, he might serve his suffering people. In so far as
his promises were to do all in his power, they were fulfilled,
but the works themselves remained unfinished at the end of
his life. One was to get the Vatican to authorize as dogma
the principle of the meditation of the Virgin Mary. Toward
this goal, however, he made no progress that was to him
satisfactory. The second promise was that he would do all
he could for the advancement of the building construction
of the great basilica of *Sacré Cœur.* King Leopold had
laid the corner-stone ten years before the war on the heights
of Kokelsberg overlooking Brussels. Since then work had
slowed down as enthusiasm waned. So far as it had progressed, it was an atrocity of yellow-pinkish brick with ochre
stone trimmings, designed with all that is worst in modern
architecture. For its faults, Mercier strangely seemed to
have no eye; he saw only that faith and funds were needed
to raise its walls to the glory of God. In 1930, Belgium was
to celebrate the centenary of her national independence,
and to complete the church for that occasion, the Cardinal
wished to collect at least six or seven million francs as a
thank offering to the Sacred Heart of Jesus for the liberation of Belgium. He worked hard to form committees
and a subscription organization, and, as a climax to the
whole, arranged for a "national pilgrimage" to the church
in 1919. King Albert, and the leaders of various national
activities and departments, came to listen and to respond to
Mercier's fervent appeal, which did succeed in rearousing

enthusiasm for the project and giving a new impetus to the building operations.

He had so many irons in the fire that the fire must be intense to heat them all at once. His energy seemed always enough to serve all his purposes because he knew how to direct it without waste. "Man was made to work," he said, "as the bird to fly." He wasted no time, but made every moment of the day serve him, most of them directly for his work, some indirectly for the restoration of his bodily energy. There was order in his daily tasks as in his mind, and as in God's universe as he conceived it. Without order the amount of his accomplishment would have been impossible for him to achieve. He defined peace as "security in order, order itself being the expression of justice. Order, peace, justice—all of them are names behind which reason discovers God." He was a thinker in his philosophical work, a man of action in his philanthropic work, a statesman in his political work and correspondence, a man complete. In the building up of this achievement he allowed himself necessary relaxation of effort but no cessation. He continued his work until his last breath with the contagious fire of youth.

The most important of his ideas are to be found in his Pastoral Letters. They touch upon all sides of Belgian life, dealing not only with such ecclesiastical matters as the liturgy, religious art, the formation of the clergy, mystic contemplation, and the organization of the church, but also with social questions such as economic problems of the day, the political and social crisis, family morals, education, Belgian colonial expansion and temperance and workingmen's unions.

He spoke almost as much as he wrote. He spoke everywhere, to soldiers, priests, workmen, and at the academy. His topics were so varied that it is almost impossible to judge of the relative merit of his speeches. Each one had its own unique appeal. Possibly the two greatest were the one delivered before the young Antwerp barristers in 1908 on "The Modern Conscience" and the one given when he was president of the Royal Belgian Academy, in 1913, on "Unity." Concerning unity he said, "Unity of spirit is not only, from an æsthetic point of view, the seal of greatness, and the revealing indication of order, it is a condition of human stability, the essential law of equilibrium and of durability." He spoke in London, in Paris, in Maux, in Vienna, in Rome, and where time or strength prevented him from speaking, as it did at the academy in Madrid and the Montalembert celebration in Paris, he wrote gracious and thoughtful epistles to take the place of his presence.

His most enthusiastic and perhaps his most distinguished speech on a literary subject was that which he delivered before the Royal Belgian Academy on June 6, 1921, on "The Poetic Genius of Dante."[1] Never were his words more felicitous. It was the seventh centenary of Italy's great poet, and he was being honored throughout the world, though his interpreters frequently did not understand him. But Mercier's tribute was more than perfunctory, for he saw in Dante his own views and attitudes most finely reflected. The divine poet embodied everything that Mercier loved:

[1] Mercier, who had, as a philosopher, been elected a corresponding member of the Academy in 1899 and a *"membre effectiff"* in 1902, became its president in 1913. It was considered a great treat whenever he rose to speak before that group.

he was a searcher after truth, with a regard for such science as his day knew; he was a philosopher who had worked such a synthesis as Mercier had dreamed of in his early philosophical gropings; he was a believer and a theologian who knew the bounds of knowledge and the extent of faith; he was a man of action and was concerned with making the truth prevail, for he had a deep regard for the moral consequences of his philosophy; he was a poet "altissime" who with his burning words unsealed the secrets of Christian hope.

As he spoke those who knew him best must have seen the clear reflection of Mercier's own sincerest qualities in all that he most admired in Dante, that savant with a passion for knowledge of everything known to his age, with that doubt which becomes a blessing when it stimulates the love for truth.

He began his lecture by saying that to judge is to compare, but there was nothing which he had found in contemporary or modern literature that might justly be compared to the work of Dante.

Today, the idea of a poem suggests immediately that of a creation wherein the imagination and the sensibilities play the first rôles. In the epic of Dante, those are of secondary consideration; thought, philosophical and theological, there is dominant.

The author of the Divine Comedy is a man of science, a searcher after truth; he is a philosopher; he is a believer and a theologian. But he is also a man of action; he takes upon himself the propagation of his beliefs; his work is animated with the breath of the apostle.

The profound unity of that synthesis of intelligence and of life gives to the sacred poem of Dante Alighieri an accent of sincerity, a force of penetration which makes of it a masterpiece apart in the gallery of literary history.

Mercier spoke almost exultingly of Dante's passion for knowledge and of the fact that, in his poem, it is the *idea* which rules:

Of first importance in the Italian poem stands the idea, meditated, entrenched, ordered: it issues commands to the imagination, to the passions; it imposes the shapes of the symbols, lends rhythm to the sonorousness, gives proportion to each of the parts, to each of the details of the work, gives harmony to the combination, and equilibrium to the integral structure.

Dante was, because he wished to be, a *savant*.

"Fools," said he, "those who, devoid of science and of art, confident in their own sufficiency, dare to risk singing of the sublime reality! Let those foolhardy ones draw back! Lazy as geese, how can they hope to escort the eagle, to soar with him to the conquest of the heavens!"

He has the passion for knowing, this glowing spirit; he was master of all that was known in his time.

Moreover he has a thirst for discovery.

He exults when, approaching the antarctic pole, he perceives four stars which must have been seen before only by our first parents in the terrestrial Eden.

Like the heroes of ancient Greece who departed on the ship *Argo* for the conquest of the Golden Fleece, Dante lifted the anchor in his search for unexplored worlds. Neptune, astonished, saw the *Argo* cast its shadow on the waters of the ocean; Dante trembles at the idea that he is the first to project his on the inviolate heavens; he plunges, to the very point of losing consciousness of himself, into the infinite depths of truth; he writes on this subject one of those untranslatable stanzas, wherein he condenses into three lines the riches of mythological memories, of history, of psychology, of exalted metaphysics:

THE TIRELESS LABORER

My soul, he says, has experienced in an instant a force of rapture more moving and powerful than all the admiration devoted by twenty-five centuries of literary history to the expedition of the Argonauts: I contemplated the Absolute, the Value without limits, *il Valore infinito* and my thought, absorbed and in suspense, looked upon it with a fixed gaze, motionless, captivated, and the more it looked, the more ardently there burned in it the passion to look.

Doubt itself the poet considers a good, for he sees in it a stimulus to the search for Truth.

Mercier must have been thinking of his own ardent attempts to synthesize modern science and Thomistic philosophy in his early days at the *Institut Supérieur de Philosophie* when he spoke of the philosophy of Dante:

Doubt, research, science, are the steps the ascent of which enlarges the field of vision of the poet, and they aid him to embrace, in a single view, nature, the soul, history.

Dante has a capacity for synthesis which few geniuses have surpassed or equalled.

Mercier contrasted the Hegelian idealism which delved into the indefinite domain of the abstract, and the substantial foundation of reality in Dante.

Dante, whether he observes, describes, or analyzes, whether he combines, puts in order, or synthesizes, is always the loyal servant of the object.

The Beautiful, when it detaches itself from his work, is the resplendency of the order which the genius of the poet has perceived for us in the real, and has aided us to seize, to contemplate.

And so he examined the whole thought and significance of Dante, while his rich imaginative language revealed the poetic soul in Mercier himself.

Mercier's culture was French. His clarity and logic were thoroughly Latin. So was his whole mentality. To understand him thoroughly, one must not only know French, one must think in French. Then only can one reach the roots of the ideas and feelings which were his delight. That great Frenchman, Marshal Foch, said of him once in these last years that he was the greatest figure of his time, and Foch spoke for France.

Of the interests which he had acquired long before the war and which concerned him deeply in these last years, several are worthy of special mention. He had for many years turned his attention to the questions of matrimony and the relations of the sexes, and the moral laxity of the years of disillusionment following the war troubled him considerably. Even in Victorian days when sexual relations were not supposed to be mentioned in public he had been outspoken, and his talks were the first that the little country had heard on the subject from the pulpit. His denunciation of neo-Malthusian birth-control caused quite a furor.

On Patriotism he wrote and preached all his life long. It was one of the profoundest and most fiery passions of his life. He often called it "patriotic piety," for it was a form of piety to him, something consuming and purifying. The great epic of his patriotic feeling was of course the famous pastoral letter, written during the war. And long before the German invasion had roused the sentiment in every one of his countrymen's hearts, Mercier had stirred them with his patriotic appeals. He said:

Patriotism is not merely a sentiment born of a community of recollections and aspirations of citizens of one and the same country. Patriotism is a virtue. One's country is one's enlarged family. The citizen owes his security to it and at least, in part, the free development of his faculties. He thus owes it the same feelings as he owes his family. Priests, laymen, all faithful citizens, let us unite in this tie of patriotism, in the heart of the great Belgian family, despite all differences of faith or opinion, and close around the Sovereign in whose hands lies our destiny!

To Mercier patriotism was founded on something loftier than man. It was another name for law, order, and justice, "various names behind which reason discovers God." It was an ideal to which unlimited devotion was due. He believed in patriotism because to him it was the outgrowth of the fundamental virtue, charity.

He entered vigorously into the temperance movement both in letters and in discourses. In 1912 the Pope realized the dreadful havoc created throughout the world by alcohol, and since Mercier had already shown himself champion in the defence against its ravages Pius X appointed him the protector of temperance work throughout the world. Mercier at once undertook an immense campaign of conferences, public and private meetings, and letter writing. He pitched into the thick of the conflict beside the Abbé Lemmens, the Curé of St. Foy, and spoke at Liège and again at the Congress of Brussels. The conservative Catholics didn't approve of his joining forces with the anti-clerical and liberal leader, Paul Janson. But the two worked together harmoniously, both being ardent temperance leaders. Mercier even published a letter in one of the newspapers heartily endorsing what Janson had said, and adding that he hoped every working man would take his golden words to heart.

Mercier's practical social works were just as extensive as his ideas which he put forth in writing and speaking. He founded the *Association de la Jeunesse Catholique* and its offshoot, the *Jeunesse Catholique Ouvrière*. He also organized the *Union Internationale d'Études Sociales*. The *Union* furthered the study of social problems in the light of Catholic morality, and communicated to the public, particularly social workers, its plans and resolutions, and founded an office for social advice. It spread thousands of its publications throughout the world. It met once a year at Malines with Mercier presiding. Its driving force was the leader of the Christian socialist party, the tireless, virile Dominican friar, Father Rutten. On the one hand the conservative and bourgeoisie Catholics criticized the Cardinal and stood aloof from the Union, while the workmen were still afraid of the intellectuals. Rutten had doffed his white cape to live with the workmen in their mines and hovels, and having followed the spread of the Socialist movement in Belgium, knew it was far better to keep the Socialists within the Church than allow them to leave it. Mercier saw the solution of this difficulty in a Christian-Socialist Party, which would give a voice to socialist opinion within the fold. Rutten now represents this party in the Senate.

Though Mercier was intellectually a great aristocrat, in his tastes and habits he was essentially democratic, for he enjoyed the society of the humble and disinherited of this earth, and detested a pharisaical spirit. His sane logic as well as his vision enabled him to read the signs of his time and see the danger signals flashing ahead. He was socially conscious as were few men of his time. Charity might go a long way, but it did little to relieve the hardships of the masses of people. The issue seemed to him to be a choice of Christ or Marx, the Church or Communism. What was the Church going to do about it he asked. Those of the lower classes who read and thought were sure they were not receiving what Leo XIII and Pius XI had in their Encyclicals insisted was their due. Mercier was in thorough sympathy with the lower classes. But he did not go to the extreme of Socialism or Communism. So deep did this love of the lower classes go that it manifested itself in many ways. When he became Archbishop he washed and kissed the feet of twelve poor on Maundy-Thursday according to time-honored custom in imitation of the Saviour. "The poor are our Master's," he said. "They teach us how to give, how to pray, how to love Christ." He believed, like Bossuet, in "the eminent dignity of the poor of our church." Among the artisans he was anxious to reawaken the mediæval *"Fierté d'artisan."* When he spoke to *"La femme de la classe qui peine,"* he shows all his intensest sympathy for the crushed working woman. He despised cast spirit, and over and over again preached the brotherhood of men, both in sermon and by example.

Forget today your religious, political, social, and professional preferences, and remember only that you are my brothers as I am yours.

The real superiority belongs to him alone who possesses the greatest nobility of heart, who is the most virtuous, most unselfish, most entirely at the service of others.

The workingman's language, his ready tongue ignores artifice. No one helps you better than he to read the hidden secrets of the soul.

Through his constant association with working people, he acquired a deep understanding of their difficulties and aspirations, which often exceeded that of the labor leaders. This was very natural, for only affection prompted Mercier's feelings. Moreover he remembered that many a great spirit of the Church has come from among the ranks of the working class. Gregory the Great had like his Master been the son of a carpenter; John XXII had been the son of a shoemaker; and Sextus V had been a shepherd. "I, for my part," he said, "expect the pleasant surprise to see in heaven the most gorgeous thrones occupied by the Christian workmen."

Though capitalism was not then as sick as it is today, Mercier heard the cracking of its economic structure from afar. He knew that unless he as the head of the Catholic Church in his own country took a far more courageous and definite stand than his predecessors ever had taken, there would be trouble ahead for the Church. Belgium had gone through a great social evolution during the period of 1880–1895. Mercier had followed every step in this with interest, for he saw that class warfare could only be escaped by the most intense efforts at class co-operation. He perceived clearly three great needs: the necessity of restoring the Christian notion of authority, the avoidance of the danger of class antagonism, and the need of an ideal of universal peace. But his vision did not stop there. Peace, he thought, was impossible without order, and order must rest upon Justice and Charity. *Ordo ducit ad Deum.* Trade unions had made little headway towards bettering the miserable conditions of their members. Social, political, and denominational isolation of the individual unions, their financial weakness, the low standard of education, the temperament of the workers, had all retarded progress.

What was then the way out? Certainly not Socialism. He never advocated the redistribution of wealth and reorganization of society on socialistic lines. He respected the workingman too much to flatter him as the Socialist and Communist did by talking only of his rights without also mentioning his duties. Labor must realize its duties and responsibilities as well as its rights, he felt. But this did not mean that he didn't feel that the Church was wrong to bolster up a social system which had rotten foundations of injustice and selfishness that must be changed into something more just. On the contrary, he felt strongly that the Church had a grave responsibility to help the situation. But he saw that Socialism was a menace to Catholicism. In order to overcome this menace, he wished all Catholics to join him in a tolerant attitude towards Socialism which would encourage Socialist workmen to join them. Mercier felt that they were merely bewildered. He did his best to help them by organizing Catholic associations for the workmen. Deploige, his successor as president of the Institute, and Defourny, a former pupil, now professor at Louvain, helped him in this work. He also aided vocational training, domestic science, educational clubs, Catholic labor leagues and syndicates, mutual-benefit associations, farmer and trade associations. He continually urged the workingmen to organize and join Christian professional unions. He felt certain that the urgent social problems could only be solved by a better understanding between employer and employees, and the mutual respect of capital and labor for each other's rights. Social peace was not "static immobility" but the harmony of dynamic equilibrium. Therefore he continually tried to establish understanding and tolerance between labor and capital without swinging either to the socialistic or the capitalistic extreme. He did all he could to raise the physical and intellectual standards of the workingman. It was a religious and moral problem as well as an economic one to Mercier.

He was aware that the war had not solved the most pressing social problems, though it had diverted attention from them temporarily. In the post-war years Mercier continued to speak and write both to and on behalf of the working classes. His appeal for social justice and his comments on the labor question were tempered by sanity and wisdom:

The spirit of solidarity which animates the working class deserves encouragement, but it needs to be wisely directed.

While the Socialists offer to unite the workmen in order to excite them against the capitalists, our patriotism and our faith make it our duty to unite them so as best to harmonize the interests of all.

The people are obviously deceived by those who, on the pretext of pacifying the bitterness of their souls, merely foment class hatred. That is pouring oil on the flame in order to put it out.

The possession of capital entails social responsibilities. Property is, not more than work, purely and simply a right. It imposes on the owner a certain duty in the universal organization. The right to abuse riches is a pagan conception, while the right to employ them for the good of oneself and others is the fundamental idea of justice enlightened by Christian morality.

Though Mercier championed the cause of labor indefatigably, he was misunderstood and attacked like so many other leaders who harmonize extremes and therefore satisfy neither wing. The socialist paper *Le Peuple*, which should have given him its heartiest support, attacked him for using an automobile. Mercier replied:

Why do you once more in the article in which you wish to be correct, repeat stupid words by which you hope to make me detested by the poor people of the working class? You say: "Monseigneur arrived in an auto—probably to remind us of the arrival of Jesus in Jerusalem, riding upon an ass's back." If I travelled on an ass's back, you would reproach me for being twenty centuries behind the times. I travel in an auto because it is the only means of locomotion enabling me to talk to workmen at Antwerp at noon and to visit an old people's home in the Stabroeck polders at four o'clock in the afternoon. Is there anything wrong in that?

I have not the honor of your acquaintance, Mr. Dewinne, but I am sure you travel by train, and even second class. Should I from my side accuse you of rising above the level of your "comrades," who travel third class, and above the level of the farm-hand, who tired out and spent, out of economy, covers the road either on foot or by the traditional dog-cart? For the good of the cause, I shan't insist upon doing so. Is not truth a duty, and the first duty towards him whom one considers one's adversary?

A personal letter of Mr. Georges Heupgen, *Vice-Président au Tribunal de première instance*, Mons, affords an interesting commentary upon Mercier's political activities:

After the war of 1870–71, Belgian industrial development assumed extraordinary proportions. Fortunes, other than those based on landed property, were amassed. The leaders acquired a clearer perception of facts, and scientific research made monumental strides.

Lying between two great suffrage nations, the Belgian working class began to study the London socialist manifesto of 1867, formulated by Bebel and Engels. Labor woke up from its long stupor. The young bourgeoisie, which before 1870 had listened to the French exiles of the Second Empire, and after 1871, to the refugees of the Commune, began to think thoughts of its own. Decoster wrote his exquisite epic of Flanders, and Camille Lemonnier published, in French, his masterpiece *Un Mâle*. The young people of young Belgium threw the bombs of their audacity among the sleeping bourgeoisie. The Liberal Party split into Conservatives and Radicals. The first traces of the Christian-Democratic party became discernible, and though the Socialist party was not as yet born, its conception seemed probable. The electorate based upon property holdings, did not exceed 200,000. A period of demolition was followed by one of reconstruction, a Renaissance filled with philosophic, religious, scientific, æsthetic, and technical questions.

This reconstruction period was admirably fitted to receive the lofty, self-contained, and powerful thought of a man as richly endowed in heart and mind as Cardinal Désiré Mercier.

Since the Great Cardinal fought the good fight in antebellum days, conditions have changed profoundly. Much, long-agitated social legislation has struggled its thorny path through the Chamber. The State has in fact been burdened with such a load of social care that the Belgian proletariat is today more fortunately situated than is the proletariat in any other European country, but should unemployment increase, the State's shoulders could no longer carry what has been placed upon them.

Salaries have gone up, while food, clothing, and rents have all gone down in the industrial centres. In the Hainaut, where the spirit of independence is the greatest, thousands of workmen have profited and built homes of their own, and with them, gained a consciousness of freedom, which has developed most admirably their sense of responsibility.

Material conditions, and with them the moral level of the

Belgian working classes, has been considerably raised. This has, in turn, given birth to a feeling of personal dignity which would cause the workingman's great friend to rejoice were he here to observe it.

Mercier's social activities as Archbishop were twofold, he engaged in intellectual work which dealt with ideas, and in the practical work of organization. The first consisted in writing and speaking. He wrote a great deal on social topics. His *Rerum Novarum* dealt with the moral education of the people, the professional education of the working-men and social legislation necessary for the protection of the weak. In *Peace and Fraternity* and *Socialism and Liberation* he strove to combat all the long hatred and bitterness which had grown out of decades of labor disputes.

"Et alias oves habeo, quae non sunt ex hoc ovili et illas oportet me adducere, et vocem meam audient, et fiet unum ovile et unus pastor."—St. John x, 16.

Chapter XIII

PASTORAL

FROM the time of his return from the American visit through the remaining years of his life, Mercier stood before the world as the sponsor of a series of conferences looking to the re-establishment of the unity of the Church, particularly of the Anglican and the Roman Catholic Churches.

Since their separation, there has hardly been a time when some one has not been working for their reunion. In the seventeenth century, the good Bossuet was greatly disturbed by the curses hurled back and forth between Catholic and Protestant or Huguenot. His most earnest wish was to reconcile the Protestants to the Roman Catholic Church, and to bring that reconciliation to pass he labored earnestly with Leibnitz and with the leaders of the French Huguenots to draw the factions into agreement and make Church unity once more a fact. The quarrel, however, was a many-sided one, too much for one man to compose. It would have been simpler had France become a Protestant kingdom, as it almost did, under the last of the Valois.

The phase of the movement with which Mercier was concerned begins with a Catholic priest, Abbé Portal, a member

240

of the Congregation of Missions, who worked many years for church unity. Cardinal Rampolla encouraged him. Leo XIII discussed with him the possibility of a conference between Anglicans and Roman Catholics, and approved of his undertaking. Portal attempted without success to push the project in 1896. He understood clearly that although the Anglican Church was in principle Protestant, it had still to a large extent retained Roman Catholic forms and ritual. Cardinals Manning and Newman had gone over to Catholicism, as had some twelve thousand Anglicans annually. Portal looked back to Newman's time, and the years, 1833–41, of the Oxford Movement, the Oxford declaration of war upon liberalism, political and religious. The action of the Oxford reformers was made possible by conditions of the time, brought about mainly by the Napoleonic wars which isolated England culturally from the currents of continental thought. This led indirectly to increasing emphasis on Catholic forms, and established by 1850 the Catholic hierarchy in the person of Cardinal Wiseman.

A devout English nobleman named Halifax became deeply concerned in the question. He came of energetic stock. His father had been prime minister under William IV, and his son was to become viceroy of India. He had been interested in church matters since youth; at twenty-eight he had been elected president of the Church Union. Halifax and Portal met by chance on their travels, in Madeira, and kindled one from the other new fire for the project both had so nearly at heart. They worked together to shape it into practical form. Unsolicited encouragement came from Rome. In the spring of 1895, Leo XIII, who had already formed an association which was to pray for church unity, wrote a letter, *Ad Anglos*, entitled *Amantissimae Voluntatis*, filled with affectionate expressions of good will for the brethren who had left the Church. To Halifax and Portal this seemed an opportunity. Halifax set out immediately for Rome, and returned home marvelling at the Holy Father's breadth of vision. He saw, however, that the project was one which could not be hurried, and set to work to build broadly and firmly. For years they labored to make a practicable plan. In 1910 came a gesture of encouragement from overseas. The Episcopal Church of the United States held a general convention which accepted the idea of Christian unity, and appointed a commission to call a conference for the examination of questions relating to "Faith and Order." With such periodic encouragements, Halifax and Portal worked out their plan. In 1913, Portal took it to Rome, but the war blocked it for the time.

The war having failed in everything except misery, the Church bethought itself of what might be done to encourage disillusioned civilization. This time the Church of England spoke the first word: "We think the time has come when all the separated groups of Christianity should agree to forget the past and reach out towards the ideal of a reconciled Catholic Church." Thus called to council at Lambeth, the Bishops agreed on the ideal, but saw no way to bring it to reality. Once again Halifax and Portal met for conference, this time in Paris, which was still filled with the soldiers of the victorious allies. Halifax was by that time past three score and ten, but still as enthusiastic as any of the returned warriors shouting on the sidewalks outside. He and Portal decided (and Rome was of the opinion) that there was only one man who could give assurance of success if they could enlist him in their cause, the noblest and most liberal of them all, Désiré, Cardinal Mercier. The Pope on the one side, and Thomas Randall Davidson on the other, were kept informed of proceedings, and from both Rome and Lambeth came blessings for the good work and the suggestion that it were well to keep out of print until there was something concrete to show.

The world accordingly heard nothing of their work until late in 1921. Then Halifax was proud to go to Malines in the distinguished company of Bishop Gore, the Dean of Wells, the future Bishop of Truro, and Doctor Kidd of Keble College, Oxford. It took no persuasion to enlist Mercier in a work which he had long wished to enter upon. There in the Archbishop's palace they met with van Roey, the Vicar General, Mgr. Battifol, and the Abbé Hemnen. Their host, the Cardinal, brought them not only his acute mind and benign presence, but the tacit approval of His Holiness Pius IX, and that of His Eminence Cardinal Gasparri. The British delegates brought with them that of his Grace the Archbishop of Canterbury. This meeting, in December, 1921, was the first of a series of conferences of the choicest minds of the two churches, which were afterwards known as the Conversations of Malines. The later meetings were in March, 1923, and May, 1925. In 1922 the matter came out with the publication of Lord Halifax's *A Call to Reunion*, and Mercier's letter, *Catholic Unity*. The press took it up, and the world spoke its mind. Anglican opinion was doubtful and on the whole disapproving. Catholic opinion was

that there was but one Church; never since the days of St.
Peter had there been but one. The Anglicans were either
willing or unwilling to return to it. The world's most powerful organization, based on the firm rock of tradition, certainly would not condescend to bargain with its erring children. The mental attitude and illogical doctrine resulting
from free Protestant study rendered inconceivable any immediate union of the Anglican Church and its submission to
Roman dogmatic control and the disciplinary consequences.
The Anglican Creed, thanks to the Protestant principle of
free thinking, was subject to all the vacillations of a doctrine
lacking the most important principle of authority. So
thought many a well-meaning Abbé.

British opinion was hardly more tolerant. *The Times*
published, as might be expected, vehement expressions from
laymen and clergymen. Many English Catholics, including
Cardinals Bourne and Gasquet, were irate. "Why, I might
as well go to Belgium and tell Mercier how to solve the
Flemish question," said Gasquet. If there were to be any
approach by the Anglicans, why did they not attempt it at
home rather than on the continent? Mercier was poaching
on his brother Bourne's preserves! And in the Anglican
hive the buzzing portended more sting than honey.

Mercier was too wise to be surprised at such reactions,
and too well-poised to be disturbed. To him the value of the
conversations lay in their moral significance. It was probably the first time in centuries that Protestants and Catholics had been able to sit together and discuss dispassionately
the vital questions that separated them. In frank friendli-
ness, the churchmen who met in Malines dwelt upon the
gravest matters dividing them spiritually and intellectually,

and at the close of each day's session knelt side by side while their leader prayed with straightforward simplicity for guidance to the Saviour who died for them all. "We must all remember," said Mercier, "that the intentions of the heart are often the best guides by which to arrive at a conclusion." It followed that for accomplishment the conferees must try to enter into one another's minds with understanding, into one another's hearts with sympathy, and into their motives with charity. In such spirit, words were of less moment than personalities. He said of their work:

Our first thought was not to examine in a given space of time certain theological, historical, or exegetical questions, in the hope of adding a chapter of apologetics or of controversy to the scientific-religious work of our predecessors. No, we faced each other, men of good will, sincere believers, appalled by the confusion of ideas, the division in the spirit of contemporary society, and saddened by the resulting progress of religious indifference and materialistic conceptions of life. As against all this, we thought of our Divine Saviour's supreme desire for union, for unity. *Ut unum sint!* Oh, if they could all only act as one! So we went to work without knowing how or when the union desired by Christ might best be realized, but persuaded that it was realizable, as the Christ wished it, and we had something to offer towards bringing it about. To bring about union is not, possibly will not be, our work, but it is in our power, and consequently it is our duty, to prepare for it and to befriend it.

The doubters asked insistently whether Mercier had any real starting point for his impossible undertaking. To this question he replied,

Now that the unity of the Christian faiths is shattered, it is so rare to meet, on the ground of cordial understanding with those who either do not believe or no longer have the same faith.

I feel confident that unity will some day be brought about. I know neither when nor how, but to judge from the universality of interest manifested for the lower classes, it seems to me that its point of departure might be the feeling of mercy for human suffering and the common desire to relieve it.

We thought that by speaking openly and with the persuasiveness of intimacy, we might possibly come to see that all the mistakes in a vast historic conflict which has lasted for centuries were not on one side only; that by defining the terms of certain questions in dispute, we might cause certain prejudices and matters of distrust to fall away; that we might dissipate ambiguities and make level the way by which a loyal soul, aided by grace, might end by discovering in what way he could please God or might find the truth again.

Mercier felt, in other words, that the union of the churches could have only one meaning, namely, the sincere reconciliation of Christian hearts, a living union realized between the disciples of Christ. He saw no possibility but for good in the honest exchange of thoughts and the generous gesture of love which would bring together hearts that had been separated and defiant. Though the world grew old, the Church was constantly renewing itself, who could tell by what means?

Both the delegates and their actions were entirely unofficial. Ecclesiastical authorities on both sides of the Channel assumed no responsibility for them, but none the less approved them, and followed them with deep interest. In 1924, Pope Benedict referred in unfortunate words to the British participants as "the strayed souls who were seeking out their different way to truth." This did not arrest the Englishmen, however, for they loved Mercier, and knew his mentality. When Pius XI ascended the throne, he proclaimed his hope that the great work of his papacy might be the return to the Church of Rome of the Christian brothers who had left it. Mercier felt, too, that even the attempt at union would be a double service to England and her people. It would help them in fighting the growing indifference and irreligion within the Church of England, which seemed to him to be running rapidly toward atheism and anarchy, and also he felt that he might bring to his friends through their talks genuine spiritual assistance. To those who feared that Mercier might possibly yield in his Catholic faith, he replied, "Neither I nor my friends have ever for a moment thought of sacrificing, at any cost, for a senseless desire for union, a single article of the Catholic, apostolic, Roman faith." To the very end of his life he was earnest in the purpose and active in the cause. On the very bed of death, two days before he died, he dictated a letter on the subject, and in almost his last breath he nominated van Roey to succeed him in the work.

During these last years Mercier made several trips to Rome. In 1922 he went for the election of the new Pope. He liked to break his trip by stopping at Milan with his friend, Cardinal Ratti, the Librarian of the Ambrosian Library. Mercier telegraphed ahead announcing that he was coming, and received the following answer:

My departure already arranged Tuesday morning. Archbishop's palace at your disposal. My secretary at station. Please wire hour of your arrival.

CARDINAL RATTI.

Now Ratti means in Italian quick or agile, and Cardinal Ratti had chosen as his motto: *Raptini transit* (he passes

247

rapidly as the eagle), and placed on his ecclesiastical arms a white eagle. Thus when Mercier met Ratti in Rome, and listened to his expressions of regret at not seeing him in Milan, Mercier could not help replying smilingly,

"Raptini transit."

Mercier's rank as the oldest member of the Sacred College accorded him the privilege of giving the absolution during the last service for the departed Pope. The Cardinals then proceeded to the election of a new Pope, which they do, not in their capacities as Bishops of the various countries, but as titular Bishops of Roman parishes. It is thus solely as members of the Roman clergy that they choose the one to fill the position of Archbishop of Rome. If he is a Bishop and accepts the election, he becomes at once the head of the Church.

Mercier had planned to return to Milan with his friend Ratti, and make up for his lost visit with him. But again his visit was not realized, for Ratti remained in the Vatican as Pope Pius XI.

The next year, in October, 1924, Mercier went to Rome to be present at the opening of the Holy Gate during Holy Year. It was a disappointing visit, for illness prevented him from speaking in Naples and other cities as he had planned. He spent his time chiefly in working for the sanctification of his own Belgian clergy.

His last visit was in the spring of 1925, the year before his death. Pius XI received him in the Vatican with the same intimacy as that with which Cardinal Ratti had received him in Milan. The Pope even begged him to be seated during audiences, but Mercier refused. Sick and old as he was, he said in a letter to a friend, "I was so happy to remain on my knees before the Vicar of Jesus Christ." Part of the visit was spent in the canonization of M. Vianney, the Curé of Ars, who had died on the very day Pius X became Pope. The decree authenticating the French country priest's miracles, as well as the advice to the clergy to take his life as an example of holiness, was quickly followed by the Curé's beatification. His extraordinary career had fascinated Mercier from his earliest youth. He had questioned many of those who had returned comforted or healed from the little village church of Ars, and confirmed the report that he spent sometimes as much as sixteen hours a day in the confessional, and that many invalids and cripples returned healed through the intercession of the Curé. Thus Mercier was only too ready to aid and participate in his canonization.

"I have known joy and I have known suffering during the course of my life, but I have never been unhappy."
                                   —CARDINAL MERCIER.

CHAPTER XIV

LAST YEARS

THE people of the Low Countries have for centuries delighted in every form of civic spectacle. Here at least the colorful days of the Renaissance are not entirely gone. Whenever they can find excuse the people hold gay street pageants in which sumptuously adorned effigies of the Virgin are borne in triumphal cars, saints emerge from the secluded gloom of the churches into the sunlight and festivity of the street. Malines was, during Cardinal Mercier's episcopate, the scene of several such celebrations in which he himself played an important part.

The first was a reunion of the Catholics in 1909. To this reunion came not only the living but the dead in the form of the effigies and reliquaries of saints. Before the giant altar erected in the square facing the *Palais du Grand Conseil*, lay thirty-six of Belgium's saints in their glittering shrines. St. Rombaut, whose reliquary had twice been sold to buy off Malines' destruction, St. Fenillien, St. Trudon,

Ste. Ermeline, St. Perpete, St. Albert, Ste. Lydwine, St. Ghislain, and many others, were all there bearing mute testimony to the vitality of the Catholic Church in Belgium. Tens of thousands of living devotees streamed into the cathedral city from all parts of the kingdom. High aloft Jef Denyn pealed his bells, while below in the square and the streets forty thousand adherents of the Great Mother Church sang the *Te Deum*.

Another important meeting was the Provincial Council of Malines, which Mercier convoked in the spring of 1920. There had been three meetings in the sixteenth and seventeenth centuries the purpose of which had been to make the ecclesiastic discipline of Belgium conform to the canon laws decreed by the Council of Trent in 1545–65. The fourth Council called by Mercier met for a similar reason. Pius X had drawn up a new Codex which was promulgated by his successor, Benedict XV, in 1918. It thus became necessary once more for the Belgian Church to bring its diocesan statutes to conform to the new ecclesiastical legislation. Mercier handled the problem of drafting with great efficiency. He had his auxiliary bishops, Legraive and De Wachter, to assist him, and for help in theological questions he had one of his Vicar-Generals, van Roey. The first session in the spring was secret, and in the Archbishop's palace. It was to discuss such matters as: The Rudiments of Faith; The Rudiments of Christian Morality; Religious Services, Liturgy and Faith; Pastoral Science, sermons, work, parish organization, etc. After the work had been laid out and assigned to its various drafting committees and heads, the Bishops disbanded until the fall. When they met, this time in St. Rombaut, they read the new decrees, *Acta et Decreta*, which gave increased unity to the Belgian Church.

No one equalled Mercier in dignity on such occasions. Dessain remarked that Mercier *was* the law. So marked was his dignity that Berard, the former French Minister at Brussels, when asked what quality distinguished Mercier from ordinary men, answered, "Dignity. And I believe this was created in him by his equilibrium and inner harmony and the co-ordination of those great qualities which go to make a perfect whole."

Great was the celebration held in Malines on Mercier's jubilee, in 1924. Once more the Cathedral City celebrated as of old a *Joyeuse Entrée* for the Lords of Malines. The month of Mary, 1924, was just half a century after Mercier's ordination as a priest by the Nuncio on April 4, 1874. While the national celebration belonged to Malines and to the Catholics, the Belgian nation as a whole entered into the festivities that honored its hero. Other towns such as Brussels, Louvain, and Braine l'Alleud held their own celebrations. Delegations turned up at the Archbishop's palace over and over again from many parts of the country. The celebration in Malines, however, exceeded all the others. It was an arduous day for the white-haired Cardinal who felt the infirmities of age creeping upon him. After welcoming the Royal family and the many dignitaries, Mercier held the church ceremony. Then came the open air celebration with many speeches including his own, and finally the long dinner in the refectory of the Lower Seminary which was sure to have many more speeches. And even after this there was to be no rest, for on the next day there was to be the Diocesan synod.

The Church ceremony was marked by great color, beauty, and solemnity. St. Rombaut's columns had been wrapped in scarlet, and the transepts were banked with hortensias. The Queen had picked fresh forget-me-nots for her Cardinal from her Laeken garden. This courtesy touched him deeply. When she herself arrived, he welcomed her on the threshold of his Church, saying,

"Madam, only Your Majesty is capable of showing such delicate attention."

Pius XI had issued an order, authorizing the Cardinal to give the Papal Benediction with plenary indulgence that day. The magnificent singing by the *Schola Cantorum* contributed greatly to the beauty of the occasion.

After the *Te Deum* came the open-air ceremony. It was held in the Cathedral square where the Knights of the Golden Fleece used to meet. It was crowded with hundreds of priests and students, "the preferred of his heart," white and black and brown and blue friars and nuns. To give it color there was the gorgeous Nuncio, Monseigneur Micara, purple Bishops, the gold and khaki of King Albert and his staff. The scaffolding was bright with bunting and banners and spring flowers. And on the platform stood Mercier in his brilliant Cardinal's hat of red and gold, wearing on his breast the crosses of the orders of Leopold and the Legion of Honor. Trumpets blared and cannon thundered. Even St. Salvator was booming, which was a rare thing, for it was used only on great occasions.[1] But on this occasion it was indeed fitting, for in Belgium a Prince of the Church has the traditional right to the honors ac-

---

[1] One of the great bells of St. Rombaut.

corded to a Prince of the Blood. And the Pope had honored him with a tribute by letter, saying:

You have rendered the Church of God signal services. Two characteristic traits mark your whole career, a vigorous and tireless application to the knowledge of, and to the protection of unadulterated truth, and an ardor in pastoral zeal. To increase the influence of Christian wisdom and to assist in spiritual endeavor throughout the whole of the vast diocese, such have in truth been the objects of your efforts.

The speech that Mercier made that day held the crowds spellbound. He told them the secret of his attainment:

In view of my age and that intimacy of the heart which unites us at this moment, you may allow me to betray a secret. Like every one else, I have known joy and I have known suffering during the course of my life, but I have never been unhappy. Whether in the years of peace or in the years of war, whether in poverty or prosperity, whether in failure or in success, never have I ceased to feel, deep down in my heart, a sense of tranquillity, confidence, and peace. And as I want you all to be happy, I must tell you the secret of Christian serenity. It lies in giving yourself confidently to the goodness of the Lord.

My intention, my constant desire, my profound aspiration has always been to rise, and to help those to rise, with whom I might have any influence.

He stood before them, a living example of what a well-directed life could accomplish. Both intellectually and spiritually his attainments had been supreme. He had given a modern articulation to Thomistic philosophy under one Pope, and had been master of spiritual life under three others. His great force had been in his knowledge of self and his self-control. Like his hero, St. Paul, he had thought no evil, and had hoped all things. It must have given him the greatest satisfaction to look back over his life at this point.

Among his greatest pleasures on that day must have been the heartfelt attention of the Royal family.

Mercier was devoted to King Albert. He had appreciated and co-operated with Leopold II, and when the new King had come to the throne he continued to uphold the royal house. Much as he had admired Leopold, his love for Albert went far deeper. Perhaps that was partly because he remembered him as a golden-curled lad bending over the books in the cheerless throne-room at Malines. But it was chiefly because of Albert's splendid character as a man. His physical characteristics showed the quality of the man within. Tall and lithe, wearing a simple uniform, with gray-blue eyes and a clear complexion, he would stand out in any crowd. He appeared in splendid health, and looked on the whole younger than his gray hair and wrinkled forehead showed him to be. His body stood up wonderfully through all the strain it was subjected to. His thoughtful expression showed the habits of mental concentration. And often on his face would play a cordial but reserved smile. He always gave his best efforts to whatever he did. Loyalty and rectitude governed his actions both as man and ruler. With a solicitude born of his patriotism, Mercier had watched the Prince mature, and it had filled the priest's heart with joy to see how unsparingly the Builder had taken of His best clay to fashion the sovereign of Belgium.

Albert was a real ruler of the constitutional monarchy, for he proved to be the most respectful and devoted servant of his nation's institutions. He was a perfect democrat, for he always listened to the will of the people. For Mercier the King and the country were synonymous. There seemed to be a gentleman's agreement between Albert and his people. On their side the people had promised to obey his orders and listen to his advice. On his side the King had solemnly sworn to respect, maintain, and defend the liberties and franchises of the people. Both sides knew there would be no faltering. Mercier knew that Albert in his deep human sympathy was heartily in accord with all the endeavors of Mercier to help the laboring classes. Both King and Cardinal followed with the most lively interest the attempts of the workers to better their condition.

Mercier knew better than other observers what the King would do when the war was declared. Quietly and courageously Albert had assumed the military leadership of the little country, even though none knew better than he what a forlorn hope it was to attempt to withstand the German hordes. To him it simply meant Duty which he had never shirked. His courageous action suggests William the Silent's observation, "It is not necessary to hope in order to undertake, nor to succeed in order to persevere." When Mercier heard what the King had replied to the German ultimatum, he fell on his knees and thanked God for the words He had placed in the hero's mouth.[2] He considered

---

[2] It is interesting to note the irony of fate in the disposal of the kingdoms of Albert and Wilhelm. In the last audience with which an earlier Chancellor was honored, the Kaiser said,

"Albert shall keep his Belgium, since he too is King by Divine Right —though, of course, he will have to toe the line there. I imagine our future relationships as rather that of the Egyptian Khedive to the King of England."

"That was the last pronouncement on politics," says von Bülow, "I heard from the lips of Wilhelm II."

And now the King of Belgium sits securer on his throne and more firmly

Albert a divine instrument for the salvation of the country, for four years later he said:

After God, Albert, King of the Belgians, is the author of the great moral victory which is being proclaimed throughout the world. His words of steel, clear and trenchant as a sword, opened the way for the nation towards the ideal of sacrifice. His example, to which was added the charming simplicity and compassionate charity of the Queen, sustained our soldiers' morale until the end—a primordial requisite for military success.

Belgian in heart and soul, Belgian by education, blessed with qualities of observation, of practical sense, of tact, of delicacy and activity, which we flatter ourselves in believing are distinctive qualities of our race, carrying even in his looks the visible characteristics of our national temperament, the King is Belgian in the full sense of the word, and it is for this reason that the whole nation's soul is so spontaneously drawn to that of its royal compatriot.

The Cardinal noticed how on delicate occasions the King had proved himself champion of the country's parliamentary institutions as against the errors of certain deputies, and how his exquisite goodness and tact had brought the approval of the entire people. Many times he offered his ministers in hours of political crises the best of his experience and well thought-out conclusions.

Mercier noticed the King's ease of conversation, his interest in intellectual matters, his ability to put all at their ease and inspire their confidence. And he observed that in doing this, Albert never lost his own prestige. He would welcome any one, Belgian or foreign, who might enlighten

established in the love of his countrymen than any other ruler whether or not by Divine Right of Vox Populi, while Wilhelm II hides ignominiously, ignored and forgotten in the very shadow of Albert's kingdom.

257

him on subjects in which he was interested. Diplomats, statesmen, business and professional men, financiers and explorers, and above all scientists, he received with sympathy and eagerness. And all left astonished at his understanding of widely varied subjects. Whether he had addressed them in French or Flemish or their own foreign tongue, whatever it might be, they felt how concise was his expression, like a scholar's.

Mercier loved King Albert because of his virtues. He appreciated his hardworking, painstaking temperament, anxious for every beneficial reform and passionate for progress. His scientific tastes and interest in practical and theoretical questions appealed to Mercier. He understood the King's modesty and shyness. The two men had in their different ways taken each other's measure and then clasped hands. Mercier paid Albert a great tribute when he said that the King had reached the summit of the moral ladder. And also when he preached:

Albert the First is a man of duty. He is what is meant by men of integrity when they say, "He is an honest fellow." However great a soldier and head of the State he may be, it is not by his greatness that King Albert has captivated the hearts of his subjects, but rather by all they have in common, by his simplicity, uprightness, and his unaffected goodness.

"Lord, guard our King, Albert, keep him safe and sound, Hear us, when we pray for him today. Saviour, assist him to stand, upright, strong with Thy strength Midst the aureole of Thy sublime name."

Mercier was very fond of the Queen and the children as

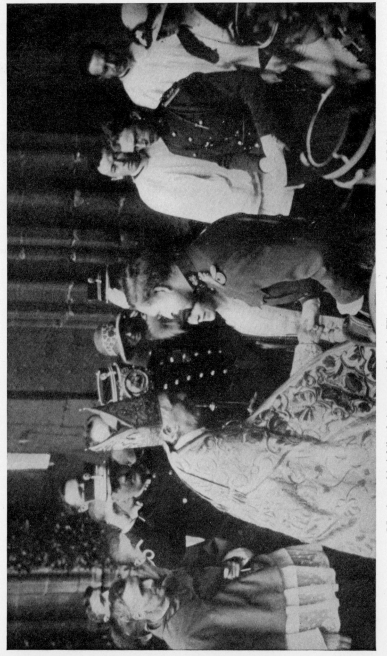

Mercier at his jubilee being greeted by the King and Queen in his cathedral at Malines

well as of Albert. The Princes were to Mercier as his own children. A frequent companion of both the Queen and the Cardinal said that Mercier always broke into a smile when he caught sight of her, so kindly and sympathetic was she always.

Later on, in Louvain, the students held their own celebration for him. So enthusiastic were they that they unharnessed the horses of his carriage so that they might pull him themselves through the cheering crowds. His words to his old pupils were as always memorable:

The universities are the levers of the intellectual world. A nation may possess an élite class of seekers, which impartially, with no thought for the immediate economic, moral, or religiously useful results, makes use of its penetrating intellectual vision. It may further do so with that serene patience which has been called the basis of genius, and submit the results of the new ideas which it has reached, to the light of documentation, observation, and experimentation. The mere fact of possessing such a class, capable of such action, raises the level of all classes of the nation.

His Belgian friends were anxious to express their affection during this jubilee year in some more concrete way than a sum of money for him to give to his favorite charities. They suggested the erection of a statue of him. But this was distasteful to him, for, as he expressed it, monuments are for the dead, and he did not wish to be excluded yet from the living. What he finally used the money for was to aid the building of a boys' school on the outskirts of Braine l'Alleud. It was afterwards named the Collège Cardinal Mercier, and in its chapel was placed the Virgin Mediatrix from the Cardinal's palace.

The pauses of relaxation which he allowed himself when he felt the need to be imperative usually took the form of a few days at a time at "l'Hermite," which he and his brother Léon had converted into a modest *pied-à-terre* for the purpose, and whenever he felt the need of a few days there, he would try, so long as it was possible, to get his brother to go with him. It was originally a workman's cottage, standing with one foot in the cobbled Alsemberg road, up the hill and across the fields, some five kilometres from Braine l'Alleud. Its white stuccoed walls and stepped gables showed far about above the tiled farm roofs, and sweeps of grain and meadowlands, dotted with sleepy cows and nibbling sheep. So it remained unchanged save for a slight addition which Mercier made to it after he became Archbishop. On the first floor was the generous living and dining room with old and faded furnishings, including portraits of the Mercier family of seventy-five years ago, painted in their time by the budding artist, Paul-Léon. A tortuous staircase led to the study on the second floor, with Léon's desk, which after his brother's death, served the Cardinal for all his work, and a smaller table inscribed, *Sit sapientia merces*, the whole littered with books and papers, the mark of a student's work room. On the wall hung a Renaissance painting of St. Jerome, the Monk of the Desert, kneeling with hand on a skull. One more flight of stairs, and the Cardinal reached his own tiny bedroom next to the chapel, which he could conveniently visit at all hours of night and day. He preferred it to the village churches, with which he had no more to do than to officiate now and then at confirmation or some such occasion. If they missed him, his family knew that they would find him at his altar.

LAST YEARS

The family was, of course, that of his brother Léon, whom of all men Désiré-Joseph loved best. His life was that of a busy physician in Brussels, of some importance in intellectual circles, but more so for his unsparing devotion to his free medical service to the poor. It was a genuine and rare fraternal affection from the time they were tiny little fellows together at Braine l'Alleud, and it had increased with the years. When Léon was threatened with appendicitis, Désiré-Joseph dropped his pen, the sentence half finished, rushed to the railroad station, and finally to Léon's house, where he prayed and the children tiptoed till the doctor felt better. Such haste was not evident when Désiré-Joseph, years later, heard of his own election to the Archbishopric. Then he finished his sentence before he started for his train. After the doctor's death in his brother's arms, the family circle at l'Hermite consisted only of his sister, Jeanne Mercier, Léon's widow Anna, her three boys, Joseph, Charles, and Paul, and the servants, Julie and Ernest Glibert.

Like most great men, the Cardinal was reserved concerning the things which meant most to him. Though his friends were legion, his intimates were few, but they did include his sister-in-law, and his nephews, Paul, Charles, and Joseph. As the years went by, Mercier was to lean more and more on the mother and Joseph, and to rely on them for sympathy and help. Anna, an exquisite, fragile, little bit of Sèvres china, but oh, with such a wise head and closed lips, and Joseph, a cheerful servant of the Lord and lover of boys, merited, both of them, and to its full extent, the confidence of the great man. And they helped him in his work, with his letters and speeches, correcting and editing. During the war when it was so essential for Mercier to be well informed as to German press opinions of his activities, it was, strange to say, the sweet little, modest lady at l'Hermite who read and summarized and blue-pencilled the important dailies spirited out of Germany, often through the intermediary of Abbé van den Helst. Von der Lancken, time and again, was astonished at his opponent's knowledge of German newspaper criticism. And it was the same timid, reliable sister-in-law who helped him pass on that pastoral letter to Holland, from where it was to stir the world outside.

With Spartan fortitude, coupled with what we still prize as a "New England conscience," Mercier felt that those who should carry out his own most dangerous tasks during the German occupation, must be those who were nearest and dearest to him. If any one was to be sacrificed, it must be his own flesh and blood. So he entrusted Joseph, then a student at the Upper Seminary of Malines, with the task of thwarting the German agents and aiding with the perilous distribution of *Patriotism and Endurance* to many of the churches throughout the diocese, before the enemy could confiscate and destroy it. And during the later war days, the Abbé Joseph became the Archbishop's *"homme-de-confiance."* Legraive, Van Vrancken, Van den Helst, and others of his ecclesiastical family, upon whom he relied, had all been imprisoned, some of them surely because they were believed most serviceable to their master; so he turned to his nephew with much of what was most dangerous. When all peril was past and there were no more letters or messages to send, the Abbé Joseph learned that his uncle had appointed him his literary executor. In his lifetime, he had given him the motto: *"Recta sapere."*

While he was Cardinal, Mercier would rarely have a chance to let Julie and Ernest know when he might descend upon them at l'Hermite. If he had time to warn them in advance, they would scurry around the neighborhood and beg milk and butter and eggs from the kind farmers who even in war and prohibition days always somehow produced the modest amounts their own Cardinal might want.

"Get a little more than I need!" said he to Ernest, "for there are always the needy and starving who come to the house, and with whom I should like to share."

Every one was strictly forbidden to call at l'Hermite, for this was his sanctuary, and he saw very little of those living around him. Here he wished to be alone so as to be able to think and write undisturbed. Franz generally accompanied his master, but even the Nuncio and bishops came motoring up the hill only when they felt that what was on their minds could not possibly await the Cardinal's return in another twenty-four hours. But if an humble neighbor called for some good reason and happened to run across him, the Cardinal was courtesy itself, never indicating that his thoughts were elsewhere.

The motor accident which almost cost his life necessitated a two months' stay at l'Hermite, and the little family circle felt this was the only reason some of the Cardinal's most important literary work was ever completed. On the ride from Malines, a man had suddenly appeared in front of the car. He proved to be demented. The chauffeur instinctively did what his master would have ordered; he swerved the car into a tree rather than injure the crazy man. The car upset and Mercier escaped by a miracle, with the loss of a number of his teeth, but he had a serious shake-up. The good Lord had still some work for him to do.

He enjoyed every moment of each l'Hermite visit, during which he could do exactly as he pleased. Here he could be a boy again, as he remained to the end. Both his father and grandfather had been practical jokers, and no one loved better than the Cardinal any prank or intended mystification in the bosom of his family. Though the nephews held him in the greatest respect and veneration, always calling him *"Parrain,"* and he remained their father confessor throughout his life, yet he enjoyed it hugely if little Joseph sneaked the buttered slice of bread away from his plate when he happened to launch into a topic so vehemently that he became oblivious to the thief by his side. He was merriest at meal times, seeming then to have thrown off all serious thoughts and cares. As soon as the bell sounded, his ungainly feet would come clattering down the staircase from the library, and if he had done a good morning's work and his ideas had flowed freely, he would rub his hands with glee.

"Ça a marché bien aujourd'hui," he said.

He had no false pride; for that he was too honest. He knew very well when he had made a good speech or written something really worth while. His faith had developed happiness within him, beyond the natural gaiety with which he was born. He used to say, *"La belle humeur des braves gens est un hommage à la bonté du Créateur."* One day, in the midst of the little Hermite circle, he read to it an account in the evening newspaper of a speech made that day in the Chamber of Deputies dealing with "Liberty in Teaching." "How well that is put, isn't it?" he said. Then he continued reading. A smile broadened on his face. Finally he put the paper down and burst out laughing. He had, to his surprise, discovered at the end of the article that the deputy had merely quoted Monseigneur Mercier.

One of the days when he unexpectedly turned up at l'Hermite so as to write in peace, the little garden was filled with a group of Joseph's boisterous boy scouts. For just a second the saintly face fell. Joseph offered to gather in the boys immediately and go elsewhere.

"No, Joseph," he replied, "what is philosophy compared to the ring of happy voices?" "*Ça va, les enfants!*"

The main routine of the day was much the same as at Malines. He arose at half past five, meditated for an hour on his knees at his *Prie Dieu* and then said Mass. Leaving the chapel, he would joke for a few minutes with the family, after which they would all have their coffee and a "*tartine*," and wait for the postman to come bicycling along and stop to ring the doorbell. As soon as he had disposed of the letters, Mercier would generally start on his tramp, pencil and pad in hands. Stalking the avenue of small, bushy pines skirting the garden, he walked on along the lanes and into the woodland. He often stopped and stood preoccupied in his thinking. He looked out over the immense plains of Waterloo. He jotted down an idea to be worked out later, or wrote part of what he had in mind. As he walked along, he was so lost in thought that he all but ignored the friendly smile or kneeling figure of some humble neighbor. At times, he would take the path across the fields, straight towards the Croquet lands and the farm of *Tout-li-faut*, where had lived his great-great-grandfather Jean-Joseph, and then, just before reaching them, turn aside to enter the forest of his friend, Baron Snoy, and seating himself on a log or on the grass, he would pause in his work to watch the inquisitive squirrels chattering around him. If the Baron saw the Cardinal first, he had the delicacy to retrace his steps so as not to disturb his great guest.

"*À mes séminaristes*" was written here, "this humble work in which I have placed the most intimate parts of my soul." It was addressed to those who were his first solicitude and for whom he had, until his dying day, the greatest sentiment and affection, begging them to imitate Saint Charles Borromée, Saint Francis de Sales, and Saint Vincent de Paul, so that they might understand them. Through the lectures which the book united, Mercier trusted that his Seminarists might obtain a clearer view of what the Church, their Mother, was, and how to live like Christians, and also that they might learn to preach less "*morale*" and more the love of Jesus Christ.[3]

Here also he wrote "*La vie Intérieure*," a characteristic expression of his spirituality which animated the vast knowl-

---

[3] Mercier did not merely wish to lecture and spiritually advise his seminarians, but to participate in their recreation. One day, he suggested a visit to the Congo Museum at Tervueren on the outskirts of Brussels, followed by a call at his own l'Hermite. The authorities at Tervueren were informed, and well-disposed Louvain butchers and bakers and candlestick-makers lent their lorries to take all the boys. In the midst of the procession of trucks, bumping along the cobble-stoned highway, a red *barrette* was seen bobbing up and down above the crowd.

There was considerable excitement among the museum authorities at the thought of the great Cardinal's visit. Dignified and beribboned curator and staff were waiting, silk hats in hand, on the steps, when a cloud of dust in the Louvain highway announced the arrival of the guests.

The Cardinal, who certainly had travelled "*en camarade*," scrambled down from the truck, mid the cheers of his young friends, straightened his stray locks, brushed the dust off his soutane, and then, with his incomparable smile, held out his hand to the astounded dignitaries.

edge he had acquired from his own experience of the interior rhythm of life. Nothing, he felt, could give his priests a better mastery over self than personal sanctification, for he believed that "they that wait upon the Lord should renew their strength." So throughout these pages, Mercier preached to them to be a living hymn to the glory of God. The book was really the fruit of long and intimate communion with his Master, and its object was to unite the souls of his priests also to Him. He wished to raise to its true position of prestige the diocesan clergy (whose members were sometimes obstinate as well as pious!) throughout the entire Catholic Church.

The morning's writing or thinking over, Mercier would return to the house. Then, in the middle of the day at l'Hermite, he sat down to soup, meat, and vegetables, and fruit in season, all washed down with water, and then he would resume until half past five, when he made a visit to the Blessed Sacrament, recited the Breviary, and counted his beads. For supper he had milk and a "*biscotte*." If Julie ever tried to smuggle in a piece of pastry, he refused to eat it. No coaxing availed! Nor did her remonstrances over his threadbare underclothes, which he never would throw away, and would renew only when further mending and washing proved impossible. Once in a while, when his mind needed rest, he might drop into the kitchen for a long chat with Ernest and Julie.

There was always time in his busy life for sympathy and encouragement. There was a birthday—or Ernest's father had died. He never forgot. Then there were the poor and sick of the neighborhood to whom Ernest and Julie were sent with alms. Mercier might find time for a little reading of philosophy or even some excellent novel which a friend had sent. Finally he conducted chapel and retired about ten o'clock.

The love for nature which he had shown as a little boy increased as he grew older. The countryside in and around l'Hermite touched something deep down in him, quieted his anxieties and stimulated his mental powers. He responded sensitively to its moods, how sensitively is evident in this which he wrote one wintry morning:

Our souls seem to meet under the great gray sky, flecked here and there with blue, in the melancholy silence of the passing winter, beside a brook with the last thaw upon its bosom, by a fountain, still choked by the withered grass, in the fir-tree thickets, of such impressive solitude, only animated by the brief and intermittent whisper of the wind through their needles.

Nothing could have been more modest and primitive than this life which the Prince of the Church dreamed of as earthly bliss. It would not have satisfied an American mechanic. No earthly goods encumbered Mercier. Of this he was aware. He knew years back, when he made his will, that he would give away in life anything he might acquire. So he had written:

I have not much to leave. I am possessed of no private means and the little I have earned by the exercise of my functions and by my publications, I have always endeavored to use in good works, living only from day to day. The few, small savings which may be found at my death should be employed in meeting any arrears of my household and the expenses of my funeral, and anything over, used for char-

+ Samedi Saint 1905

Au nom du Père et du Fils et du Saint Esprit. Ainsi soit-il

Ceci est mon testament.

« Le bon Pasteur donne sa vie pour ses brebis ». En union
avec notre Divin Sauveur, qui a donné sa vie pour le salut du
monde, je vous prie, aujourd'hui, mon Dieu, l'humble offrande
de ma vie. J'accepte maintenant, en pleine conscience, l'arrêt
de mort que votre Justice a porté sur moi, je m'y soumets
en vue de réparer le mal que j'ai commis dans le cours de ma vie
et avec l'espoir que mon sacrifice sera utile au troupeau
dont vous avez daigné me confier la garde.

Recevez donc mon âme, ô mon Dieu, je la remets en vos
mains, in manus tuas, Domine, commendo spiritum meum.
Enlevez-moi la vie quand vous le voudrez et de la manière que

First page of Mercier's last will

itable purposes and educational institutions. I bequeath to my nephews, my equity in the country property known as "l'Hermite," As regards everything else, they know that they must earn their means of livelihood by their own toil.

Mercier emphasized many times that this life is only a preparation for death, which is the greatest and the crowning achievement. One need not despise life in looking upon death as something beautiful, for, "So long as the grain of corn dies not in the earth, there can be no hope of life and fruitfulness."

In the last years of his life, the Cardinal's activities and restless energy seemed to increase, as if he had a premonition that he should soon have to lay down his work. His own words describe most aptly his attitude of selfless devotion to that work:

Certainly a powerful personality cannot reveal itself fully without riding roughshod over humdrum habits, without endangering even estimable claims of secondary importance. Any far-reaching course of action demands some violence at the start, for humanity as a whole is not roused, without a shock, from its drowsiness or its dreams.

In the fall of 1925 the Catholic University of Paris was to celebrate its fiftieth anniversary. This celebration might also have been looked upon as the anniversary of the establishment of higher education in France. Mercier was asked to deliver the address. There was a double reason for him to accept since it concerned both France and education, both of which he dearly loved. The Catholic world of France, headed by Cardinals Lucon, Dubois, and Touchet, were waiting to receive him at the Trocadero. Mercier's speech was to be his last. In his rich, powerful language he spoke of the illustrious names of the university and of the glory of higher education. Then he expressed his love and admiration for France.

In the name of the Bishops of Belgium, I bring to the Bishops of France, whose energy and unselfishness we honor, and in the name of all my countrymen, I bring to the France we love, the homage of our abiding admiration and affection. Seven years separate us from the armistice. In that time, how many of our hopes have been disappointed! And yet, there is a vision that still stands clear and sharp before our eyes: The alliance of our two peoples for the triumph of righteousness, our memory of the heroism of your soldiers, the thought that you gave fifteen hundred thousand of your children that justice might prevail over violence and honor over bad faith! This vision, this memory, this thought are and will remain the cement that binds our two peoples together in union—that union which makes for strength.[4]

Mercier's faith in the French is shown in the following quotation:

I need to tell you the truth, as I see it, and as I feel it in the very depths of my soul: Among all the peoples of the world, the most attractive, the most beautiful, the greatest, owing to the lustre of its thought and the precision and charm of its language, owing to the smiling valor of its soldiers, its chivalrous character, the enthusiasm of its apostleship, the fruitfulness of its Christian heroism, that people is —your own, the French people.

It could not fail to please Mercier when he was eagerly welcomed to the illustrious society of scholars known as the *Institut de France*. The greatness of the French Republic

---

4 The Belgian motto is: *"L'Union Fait la Force."*

was assembled under Mazarin's dome when Émile Boutroux said:

With a precision and brilliance of which history offers at best one or two examples, Cardinal Mercier upheld those things sublime above all: Right, Truth, Justice, and Virtue. He upheld them to such a degree that they of themselves withstood an enemy which had for its motto: "Force before Right." And they did so with no aid except that of their own virtue and by divine grace operating through them.

Cardinal Mercier, armed alone with his righteousness, through sheer purity of heart and evangelical charity, brought Force to its knees.

Mercier once asked Marshal Foch what contributed to his success, whether he relied solely on his own military genius, or whether he sought help elsewhere.

"Your Eminence," answered Foch, "I studied my problems as carefully as lay in my power, I conferred with those whose opinions I respected the most, then after I had completed my plans for battle, I said my prayers, in a church if it were possible, and I left the rest to God."

Mercier smiled and replied,

"I knew it! You went for help to Him who alone could give it."

As his years advanced, Mercier prayed more and more. The traditional garrulousness of old age took, with him, the form of increased communion with God. Prayer gave him a sense of the enlargement of life beyond the narrow horizons of the individual self, increasing his love and sympathy for others.

> He prayeth best, who loveth best
> All things, both great and small.[5]

[5] Coleridge: "The Ancient Mariner."

Prayer seemed the very essence of his religion. It seemed to release all of his tremendous store of energy and give him an immense elation and freedom. You could see his beatification in his face as he arose from prayer. His self-surrender had been so complete that it had become self-immolation. No matter how disturbed he was when he went to his *Prie-Dieu*, he was confident and calm when he left, possessing a complete inner security and repose. All around him whispered peace; the goodness and beauty of existence enfolded him.

William James, whom Mercier had admired and quoted, says:

Men of saintliness agree. They have arrived at an unshakable conviction, not based on influence, but on immediate experience, that God is a spirit with whom the human spirit can hold intercourse—that they can see him everywhere in nature and feel him within them as the very life of their life. . . . There is an organic affinity between joyousness and tenderness, and their companionship in the saintly life need in no way occasion surprise.

There came also with his age an increase in faith, "that substance of things hoped for and evidence of things unseen." And with the increasing of his tenderness and faith he lost none of the strength which had characterized him throughout his life. He also possessed grandeur. He saw and did things in a large way. So great was his vision that he never understood petty quibbling and mediocrity. All his acts were marked by daring and leadership. He always looked down on the timid. Perhaps he sometimes went a little too far beyond his rightful authority. But on the whole it was his virtue rather than a defect. His pupil, the Abbé Jacques Leclercq, said, speaking of his success in action:

He had all that is needed in action: Daring in initiative, feeling for the right opportunity, pliancy in the use of means, calculation in striking, patience in abiding his time, and promptness when the time had arrived.

"I have glorified Thee on Earth: I have finished the work which Thou gavest me to do."—JOHN xvii, 4.

CHAPTER XV

THE END

"I̲N his old age," said Dessain, "he bore fatigue which even the young would have had difficulty to support. Some days when I was all tired out, the Cardinal continued like an athlete, proving that the soul really supports the body."

Finally, however, the delicate machinery began to give way. Varicose veins made his legs swell and necessitated his holding them up a great deal. Though his chest and stomach were troublesome, he cancelled no lecture or necessary function, nor did his jesting good humor abate. His speeches at the University of Nijmegen, at Bishop Heylen's jubilee, at the University of Paris and at the King and Queen's silver wedding, had all been *tours-de-force*, but Mercier had gone through with them, and no one had noticed his pain. In the summer and fall of 1925, he confided, however, to his most intimate friends that he seemed incapable of nourishing himself or of getting any good out of such food as he took. The doctors whom he consulted found that he had for several years been suffering from cancer. In that supreme simplification of mental attitude brought about by the near perspective of death and the hereafter, Mercier met his surgeons' serious faces with a decision to work at top speed. He prayed harder than ever, and his changed manner of conducting the Mass was perceptible to those who stood nearest him. He planned work which, even if he had been well, he could not have accomplished, and made more engagements than he could possibly keep. Though he made Death ridiculous by his scorn, the enemy was fast approaching.

Mercier depended increasingly upon Francis Dessain, the head of the Episcopal secretariat. Half mystic and half athlete, Belgian priest and Irish gentleman, with deep-set, intelligent eyes, gaunt like his master, lawyer turned Abbé, he became more and more Mercier's constant companion, confidant, and friend.

Suddenly one morning, early in November, Mercier told his servant to telephone Dessain to come to the palace and join him in a trip to his beloved l'Hermite and the Braine l'Alleud country. The secretary's heart stood still. He knew what it meant. His master realized the end was near, and he wished to visit for a last time the haunts he loved most, and say good-bye to them all. A long hour in the motor which had been given him by his American friends brought them to the familiar hillsides, dotted with farms, the poplars and hawthorn hedges blowing in the autumn wind and the Holsteins turning their backs to it. First the churchmen visited the flourishing new *Collège Cardinal Mercier*. Then they went on to Virginal, the Convent where his sisters had spent their lives, and from there to the splendid new church of St. Étienne, at Braine l'Alleud, with its Romanesque nave, that had replaced the one where the altar boy had knelt behind good Father Olivier. Still on, to the little churchyard where slept his parents, his brother Léon, who had died in his arms, and all three of the sisters who had entered the church. Ah, yes! New flowers had sprung up in their stead. Two of the boys, sons of Léon, with whom he had so often joked, had, thank God, been consecrated. On their father's grave, he had cut: "*Surrexit Christus Spes Mea.*"

Last of all he went to l'Hermite—his little luxury, his great happiness. Ernest and Julie were at the door as the motor drew up. He walked painfully about the rooms. It was very hard for him to climb the steep stairs to the chapel by his little bedroom under the gable of the top story. How much of the intellectual work nearest his heart he had done in the little home, and how many of his prayers made there God had answered! On the study table, he placed a little photograph of himself, his arms extended in blessing. There—now he would always be among them, giving them his benediction, and Anna and the boys would all know what he had meant when they saw the photograph! Then, tired and spent, he journeyed back to Malines, back for the last time to his beloved St. Rombaut.

After the X-ray examination, early in December, he said to Dessain, "Yes, Francis, tonight I have something to offer the Holy Virgin. It is something quite out of the ordinary, thus to receive one's death sentence."

The surgeons felt they must operate at once, to which the patient merely replied, "In God's good keeping."

Three days before he went to the hospital, he motored to the Malines Seminary where scholars and masters instinctively felt an overhanging tragedy as the Cardinal mounted the platform. He told them simply of the state of his health —so simply he might have been recounting any other trivial occurrence in the day's work, and finally that he had decided to be operated on at once. He had absolute confidence in God and in the skilful surgeons to whom he was turning. He placed himself in God's hand. He finished with his paternal blessing, and told them that instead of saying "good-bye" he was merely bidding them *"au-revoir"*; yet many of his young hearers felt as if they had lost their best friend.

His poor body was of little consequence to him. Physical or moral fear he had never known, but there were tasks un-done—many things to complete which were near his heart, and above all, the sanctification of his clergy, the care of his seminarists, the unity of the church, and the pronouncement of the dogma of Mary Mediatrix. It was particularly hard to leave the "Conversations" unfinished. Perhaps he might see Halifax once more. He must, in all cases, write a last letter to Davidson at Lambeth.

During the grief of the war, Mercier had constantly turned in his prayers to Mary, the Lady of Sorrows. He had felt he must do all that lay in his power to claim for her the honor of being the universal mediatrix of grace. He had, while preaching a retreat to his clergy, begged them pray Divine Providence in the matter. He had also, when in Rome, shortly before the war, fervently pleaded this cause with the Cardinal Prefect of Rites, who heartily concurred with Mercier, and so did the Congregation. The diocese of Malines, the various Belgian religious congregations, the theological faculty of Louvain and the bishops of Belgium, had all begged the Holy Father to recognize dogmatically the universal mediation of the Virgin. Mercier had, in fact, brought up all his troops. The Pope had appointed three theological commissions to study the matter, one in Belgium, another in Spain, and a third in Rome, instructing each to make a thorough investigation of the doctrine of the Mediation of Mary and its definability. Ten Cardinals and three hundred Bishops and Archbishops had responded that they would support the dogma as also that of canonization for Louis Grignon de Monfort, who had first advocated it.

When Christ, by His sacrifice upon the Cross, had offered Himself as an atonement for our sins, and thus became our Mediator with God, the Blessed Mother had collaborated with her son, the Saviour in his mediatory work. Mercier believed that the Saviour had granted His Mother the right to be the sole Mediatrix between Him and humanity, and that no gift of God arrived on earth without Mary's intervening with her Son, though Christ assuredly was the only Mediator. But, argued Mercier, as Christ and Mary are inseparable, He associated His Blessed Mother in that Mediation.

"One does not," said Mercier, "separate the Mother from the Child."

He and Pope Benedict had had considerable sympathetic correspondence and discussion on the subject, and Mercier had made a tremendous effort in the matter during his last visit to Rome, only a few months before. To his deep disappointment, the final steps were deferred, and no definite pronouncement was made. All he had accomplished was to have granted to the dioceses of Belgium and those that might ask for them, a proper office and Mass of Our Lady, under the

THE END

title of Mediatrix of All Graces. His old friend, Cardinal
Vico, had written him that the Pope wished him to select the
Blessed Virgin's fête day, and so he did, May 31st, the
last one of Her month and the first before the month of
the Sacred Heart. But the fact that Her mediatory power
was undetermined was, now that his work was probably over,
more than ever a poignant regret. He had, alas, been unable to carry to a successful termination the laying of an
honor at the feet of the Blessed Virgin, as he had so ardently
wished.

Mercier had always had a tremendous belief in the powers
of the Carmelite Sister, the little "Therèse of the Infant
Jesus." He knew that God in His infinite wisdom would do
with him as He found best, yet he felt he might write to
Therèse's older Sister, Agnes,[1] the following letter:

The doctors have told me today that I have an ulcer in the
stomach. I bless God with all my soul that he has permitted
me to make him this offering by the hands of my Holy
Mother, Our Lady of Seven Sorrows, and I recite my *Magnificat* with happiness.

Ever since I have been suffering, I have never felt I had the
right to beg to be cured. I leave my fate in God's hands,
and only ask one thing of Him: to draw such glory as is possible from my humble person, at whatever price it may cost.
Nevertheless, on the 15th of November, when I was giving
a greeting to the Carmelites at Brussels, in honor of your
dear little sister, it suddenly came into my mind as I was
crossing the threshold of the Church, to appeal to her. When
I reached my *Prie-Dieu*, I wondered if I might beg for my
recovery (I did not then know how ill I was, but merely suspected it), but I did not dare to do so. I made a conditional
request which resolved itself into an act of surrender.

[1] Prioress of the Carmelite Convent of Lisieu.

I am in the midst of my work, which I am indeed anxious to pursue for the glory of God and for my dear clergy. But is it not better to make the personal sacrifice, and to serve the interests of the divine glory? God needs none of us.

I believe I am thus right in retaining my attitude of surrender. I do not believe I depart from it, in begging you to question your little sister as to what is best and to ask you to be my spokesman with her.

In writing shortly afterwards to one of her Hainaut friends, the Prioress said:

Yes, I am asked on all sides to beg for the recovery of the saintly Cardinal Mercier, and I am sorry to see that our Thérèse does not heal him. . . . Heaven probably claims him, and there is hidden mercy in this cruel trial of Belgium and her priests, who always know that what the good Lord desires and permits, is what is best for the soul. It is this thought which consoles.

SISTER AGNES.

To a friend, Mercier wrote:

My friends urge me to ask God for a cure. I shall not do so. . . . And yet, you know, there are great problems that lie near my heart. Had it been God's will, I should have chosen to live a few years longer to devote myself to these important matters. As it is, I go away with a sense of leaving things half done.

So Mercier thought, despite the fact that no one in our age and generation had done things, great and small, more thoroughly or well.

He wrote Lord Halifax, full of courage, saying the doctors had first thought a complete rest was all that was needed. A surgical operation was, however, inevitable, though it involved no danger. He hoped, he said, that the "Conversations" might be continued in January and then to be able to resume all his former activities.

It was really only the flesh that was weak; his spirit was as strong as ever. He had, in fact, possessed the rare faculty of preserving his youthful qualities of spirit in his riper years. He had kept his spring with his autumn, and until the end, the freshness of his boundless optimism.

He returned from l'Hermite with unbelievable fortitude, to those around him, to all manner of pastoral work, dictating, writing, calling, consulting, and receiving visitors. The last visit he made before leaving for the operation in Brussels was to pray in his beloved St. Rombaut. He had always, in returning to Malines from his endless trips, scanned the horizon for the first glimpse of its tower. Would he ever do so again? The dusk was falling when he entered its nave. This time, he went to the altar of Our Lady of Miracles to prostrate himself before its black Virgin. He had suggested receiving the last sacraments, but was advised that the time had not yet come. He must practise the patience which had proved such a useful curb to his iron will. A brave good-bye to his palace, and then he and Dessain and Brother Hubert entered the motor. The time on the road to Brussels was well spent, in their all saying their beads together.

In the rue des Cendres in Brussels stands an inconspicuous house. The Duke of Richmond gave a boisterous dinner and dance in it on a June evening before he galloped down the road to the Guards, who had no dinner while waiting on the soggy fields of Waterloo. The blond curls of Lady de Roos had never looked lovelier, and Wellington had come in "grand gala" to sip his port. The ball room is still there in the selfsame house, but the gay costumes and sparkling wines have been replaced by tired nuns washing down their bread and cheese with water. For the house is now a spick-and-span modern hospital, tended as is often the custom in Catholic countries by *Sœurs Hospitalières*, who glide noiselessly through its corridors in their white flannel garb.

The surgeons had diagnosed the case right, but the cancer was of so malignant a character that upon seeing the havoc, they decided no operation would help. He who had fed so many would have to starve to death. Devoted and gentle Sister Julienne, with Sister Caroline to help, took her place near the Cardinal, instead of vicars-general, canons, and priests. The door was closed on church and world, the patient was to see no one and speak to no one.

Though far from his own palace, he proved, however, that he was still the master. The anesthetic had barely worn off before he ordered the flowers taken to the chapel and the wards, and forbade the Sisters to remain beside him while others were in need. The command was so stern and insistent that they glided silently out of the room to await his bell whenever he might want them.

Soon his door was opened to admit the many, for so he ordered. The great Catholics came to kneel for a last time beside him and receive the blessing that could not fail to sanctify.

His friend, Carton-de-Wiart, told the sufferer how sorry he was for his pain. With noble scorn, which even now never left him, the Cardinal answered:

"Physical pain is such a petty thing."

THE END

The first soldier of Yser with his Queen beside him, knelt by the iron cot for the benediction.

"If only Leopold arrives in time," she sobbed, thinking of the son who was returning from the Congo and whom the sufferer had done so much to make a man of.

The Queen, knowing full well how short a time was left Mercier, remonstrated with him for not taking better care of himself. He replied that he had no illusions as to his real condition.

"You have no right to say that, Your Eminence," said the Queen. "You know very well, that the shining light you radiate is indispensable to us."

"Far less than Your Majesty's gracious smile," replied the Cardinal.

The many callers left the room only when the air became too exhausted for the one remaining, hardworking lung. But in spite of all, the sufferer never complained. He ate next to nothing. Every little comfort had to be suggested by Sister Julienne or Sister Caroline or the faithful Brother Hubert, who would not leave and slept in the adjoining room. All the dying man asked for was the recitation of such prayers as he selected. The churchmen suggested he might have Mass said in his bedroom, but even that he refused until special permission was granted and Rome wired its assent. Then a little altar was improvised at the foot of his bed, with the crucifix of Père Chévriet which he had treasured so long, and on the wall, where he could constantly gaze at it, was hung a painting of the Christ.

As a last act of thoughtfulness towards one of them, he instructed his secretary to wire to Rome begging that a prelacy be given to von Olmen, who had for forty years been secretary of the Archbishopric. Of course it was granted forthwith. Always something for some one else!

He rallied all his mental force, dictated a last pastoral letter, and also a long, touching, and pathetic farewell to his clergy, begging them to make the Mass, which he himself had always loved to celebrate, the central act of each day. In the long, lonely hours of the night, he constantly thought of them and prayed for them.

He spoke to those around him about what was nearest his heart. "Tell my seminarists," he said, "I love them all, I love them so much, do tell them how much I have loved them. . . . Tell them that I am thinking of them continuously, they are always before me, for they are the apple of my eye. Yes, I belong to them now and forever."

How much time he had spent with those boys! Lecturing, telling them about his Roman trips, taking a bite with them —loving them.

A pall of sadness hung over Brussels. Believers and non-believers alike felt oppressed. The rich, who belonged to "*le beau monde*," stopped in their seeking of pleasure and left their opera boxes empty. The poor, who belonged to the slums, stopped their drudgery for bread, and filled the churches. Their knees warmed the pavements before the altars of the invalid's beloved Maria Mediatrix. She would intercede with Her Son and help the great Cardinal home. He had guided so many a bewildered aged one safely to his journey's end. Now, the Blessed Virgin would, in Her turn, take the good Cardinal's hand. He had said that affliction was a two-edged sword, wounding the rebellious, but sanctifying him who was willing to endure. He had believed in the victory of good over evil, and his life and its experiences had proved he was right. If it be true, as Montaigne says, that philosophy is learning how to die, then the Cardinal had indeed become a great philosopher. It was very quiet in the palace at Malines. Belgium was hushed in prayer. A little more work to do, a last great effort of his iron will, and then: "Thy will be done." He had fought the good fight, had run his course, and had been true to the faith!

The agony increased. Slowly the Reaper was gaining. Mercier flung back the defiance: "I am content, very content. I thank the good Lord for having permitted me to follow Him, at least part of the way towards Calvary and to have suffered on the Cross. Suffering—that is the complete apostleship."

Abbé Joseph Mercier celebrated Mass daily, though the weary sufferer could no longer partake of communion.

They wired Portal and Halifax, for it would give Mercier much happiness if there were any chance of their coming. Portal hurried from Paris, also sending word to Lord Halifax that their friend could hold no more "Conversations," but would like to have him come to a last communion by his hospital cot. In spite of his eighty-four years Halifax did not hesitate but hurried immediately across the Channel.

The fog of January 21 was slowly closing in around the houses in the Brussels valley. The wet evergreens glistened under the lights of the garden to the sleepy eyes of the nurse. The cushions of the patient's fingers moved slowly forth and back over his crucifix.

"The English Lord is coming today," he whispered. So it must be a busy day with much for him and Francis to do, and he would need all his strength. Not one of the many papers littering chairs and tables in the little room must be disturbed, nor must he lose strength by being washed. Probably it would be his last great effort. Francis would offer Mass instead of Joseph, for it was the fête of St. Agnes.

The travellers who had hurried to Mercier's bedside knelt with the few friends and sisters as Dessain raised the Host, and all, Catholics and Protestant alike, joined in the prayers. The Blessing, The Last Gospel, "Hail, Mary," "Hail, Holy Queen," prayers by Dessain. As the little group arose, a sweet smile broke over the quivering lips. He opened wide the bony arms, and drew his English friend to his heart. For a long while, Mercier rested his tired head on the other's shoulder. Then he slipped his pastoral ring off his finger.

"You see this ring," he whispered. "It is engraved with the names of Saint Désiré and Saint Joseph, my patron Saints, and Saint Rombaut, the patron saint of our cathedral. It was given to me by my family when I was appointed a bishop. Well, if I am to die, I ask you to accept it as a gift."[2]

But to work—There were vital matters to be discussed, for efforts towards church unity must not cease.

He would send Thomas Davidson a last letter of thanks for all his understanding. So he dictated:

Brussels, January 21, 1926

Your Grace,

In the midst of the trial which it has been God's good pleasure to send me during these recent weeks, I cannot voice the satisfaction and the consolation I have experienced at

[2] Lord Halifax, now ninety-two years old, still wears the ring in a chain around his neck.

receiving a visit from our revered friend, Lord Halifax. He has told me of the constant desire for union which you harbor. I am happy to have that assurance. It is a source of strength to me in this present hour.

Ut unum sint is the supreme desire of the Master. It is the desire of the Pope, it is mine, it is also yours. May it be realized in its fullness.

The tokens of sympathy which Your Grace has been kind enough to send me have touched me deeply. I thank you for them with all my heart, and I beg Your Grace to accept the expression of my most worshipful devotion.

D. J. CARDINAL MERCIER

Archbishop of Malines.

Beads of sweat broke out on the immense white brow, now doubly curved by the deep hollows on either side.

"We shall soon meet again," he said to Lord Halifax. They both knew it must be soon, and where there would be no conversations needed to bring about one fold and one Shepherd.

The end was near. His house was in order. The Queen's prayer had been answered, for, though few could be admitted now, the Prince arrived in time for the gentle blessing. On the 22d of January, the patient asked:

"What day is it?"

"It is Friday, Your Eminence."

"What time is it?"

"It is not three o'clock yet."

"Call my family at once," said the sick man, "and my vicars-general, and have the prayers for the dying recited."

So they sent for those nearest his heart who were not already there, his brother Léon's widow, and his second nephew, the Nuncio, his old secretary, Canon Vrancken, his faithful servants, Virginie and Franz, and Oswald, the chauffeur, his confessor, Father Van den Steene, and Sisters Caroline and Julienne who had tended him night and day, and Mgr. Legraive who had anointed him a fortnight ago and now read the prayers for the dying.

It was the 23d of January, 1926. They were praying in the Archbishop's city. The women of the *Beguinage* were on their knees, their wrinkled old faces under the white caps turned to heaven in supplication. The seminarists had forgotten their youth and pranks and knelt before the crucifix. There was no play in the courtyards, and the shrill voices were hushed. They pleaded in St. Rombaut's, in St. Catherine's, in St. Peter's and St. Paul's and in the church of the two St. Johns. They prayed in Our Lady's Church Beyond the Dyle, where the good Father Oliviers had comforted the Cardinal when he was a boy. They asked for the repose of their faithful Shepherd. They prayed all over Belgium, as men do when afflicted. The peasants knelt on the frozen black of their fields.

In the little hospital room the patient was assailed by a terrible thirst. He thought of his Saviour.

"*Sitio! Sitio!*" he sighed.

His thoughts cleared.

"Yes, I thirst," he whispered, "to lead souls unto thee, O Lord!"

He wished that the last Mass he was to celebrate should be that in honor of Mary the Mediatrix, with the *Magnificat* and the *De Profundis*.

Round about the bed knelt those he loved the most. Some of them wept. So did many in the dense, silent crowd in the

288

rue des Cendres outside, a quiet backwater in the crowded, bustling portion of the City. *In Paradisum deducant te angeli,*[3] thought the good sisters.

His confessor, Father Van den Steene, was reading prayers and psalms aloud. He hesitated for a moment, broken by his emotion, when he came to the final liberation.

"Proficiscere," murmured the dying man.

"Proficiscere, anima Christiana," "Return to God, O Christian soul!" repeated the priest.

"Now there is nothing more to be done, except to wait," said the Cardinal.

The glazing eyes clung to the crucifix.

"Offer your life for the Church," said the Confessor. The Cardinal nodded.

"Offer your life for your country and the welfare of your people," said the Confessor. The Cardinal inclined his head.

The Nuncio whispered something in the ear of the priest.

"Offer your life for the reunion of all the Christian Churches." The Cardinal nodded his head thrice.

The Abbé Joseph placed the crucifix on his breast.

He had joined his Master.

The tiny feeble tinkle of the hospital bell sounded. It was followed at once by the deep guttural clang of St. Gudule's bourdon, further up the hill, and then by the bells of all the sister churches of the country.

Joseph Désiré Mercier had stated in his will that such money as he might leave should defray his funeral expenses. But the amount was pitiably small.

He had also during his life written to Vandervelde, the

[3] "May the angels escort you to Paradise."

Minister of Justice, and said how dearly he would love to rest in his cathedral despite his knowledge that burial there was no longer permitted, by law. Thrice during the history of the little kingdom had the State itself found it fitting to bury an illustrious son.[4] Albert, King of the Belgians, decreed that Désiré Joseph, Cardinal Mercier should be buried by the nation whose name he had covered with glory. Catholics, Liberals, and Socialists, representatives of the people, rose in the Chamber to ordain that the Law of the Land be set aside and that Désiré Joseph, Cardinal Mercier be laid to rest in the Church which his piety had made a place of pilgrimage for Christians.

In the dusk of the gray winter morning, clad in mitre and cape, the Cardinal left his palace and city to enter for the last time the city of the King. As he slowly passed south through Brabant, the peasants laid down their hoes, crossed themselves, and knelt in their labor. All that was gallant in Gaul met him at the city gate.

Behind Désiré Joseph, Cardinal Mercier walked his King and his Prince, the first Marshal of France, and the chivalrous de Castelnau. On each side, the poilus lowered the tricolor of Belgium while their bands played Chopin's march. The Government had decreed "the cannon to boom and the music of the regiments to play." The *Defensor Civitatis* proceeded slowly. Today, as always, when the people knew he was coming, they blocked his path. They thought of the war which had melted rancors and dissipated rivalries and jealousy. They thought of the disillusionment. Now they had returned to their petty quarrels, Flemish and Walloon, cler-

[4] Rogier, Lambermont, and Leman.

Mercier's cathedral, Malines (thirteenth century), where he was buried

THE END

ical and anti-church, socialist and conservative squabbles. How short-lived was understanding! How much they had seen, Liège's resistance, Antwerp's fall, the Yser's last rampart of blood and mud—the massacres and pillage and debasing slavery, all wrought by the Hun—but amid it all, they had also seen the glorious, shining figure that now was passing. Ashes to ashes and dust to dust.

Past where Charles, the Emperor, had laid down his kingdoms so as better to prepare for the one he coveted. Past where the skulking, rickety Philip repaid the valiant Egmont for St. Quentins by severing his head. Up the steep hill to the Gothic temple, where slept the Dukes of Brabant and Burgundy, under whose vaults Philip had ordered Requiem Masses celebrated for his great father and his English Mary, and where Louis of France unfurled his *fleurs-de-lys* after the victory of Fontenoy. Désiré Joseph Mercier, Cardinal-priest of the Holy Roman Church, of the title of St. Peter's of the Chains, by the grace of God and the holy, apostolic See, Archbishop of Malines and Primate of Belgium, rested under the twin-towered majesty of Ste. Gudule to accept the last homage of Belgium and her allies.

The great French churchman and academician[5] brought the sister country's last thanks.

He raised the world up above himself. He showed to it the things eternal, which are not discussed, which are adored or denied, but before which all men tremble, as did the prophets to whom the word of God was revealed.

He was not to see the day he prophesied under these very vaults, ten years before; yet his prophecy was to come true.

[5] Mgr. Baudrillart.

291

The sound of voices singing the *Dies Irae* and *In Para-disium* floated through the portals of the church to the multitudes outside. Then the funeral procession journeyed back to his own church. On his way, the well-known Cardinal and the unknown soldier beside the "July Column" saluted each other in death. The soldier of King Albert and the Soldier of Christ were now marching shoulder to shoulder.

A long and illustrious line had sat on the Archbishop's throne since Granvelle, Emperor Charles's minister, first to ascend to that dignity. On January 29, 1926, Désiré Joseph Mercier, sixteenth in succession, was laid to rest under it.

St. Rombaut's carillon rang out the joy of his Christianity.

"He had lived and accomplished the task that Destiny gave him, and now he passed beneath the earth, no common shade."

APPENDIX

Some interesting sidelights on Cardinal Mercier's American tour are to be found in the shrewd and often keen and witty comments of Franz, the Flemish valet who accompanied the Cardinal. His diary, hitherto unpublished, shows that he had his eyes wide open. His terse summaries of events have a value of their own, but they also give occasionally an intimate glimpse of Mercier's character and habits and of the respect and devotion which he inspired in every one. The most interesting bits of the diary are here presented:

"The Ritz Hotel in Paris almost made my eyes pop out of my head. We went to church to pray the next morning at five o'clock. I do not question that His Eminence makes the best possible use of his time; nevertheless, it seems to me, we might have done something else in this particular city."

"The French photographers bother the life out of us. His Eminence merits being left in peace."

"I had as travelling companions to Brest, a widow and her two little girls. As the girls were restless, their mother gave them an edifying mass book to read. When the little girls asked if they should kneel while reading on the train, I told the mother that being His Eminence's valet, I knew all about such things and His Eminence had told me that while travelling we sometimes would find it impossible to conform to home rules. I made a mistake, for later the little girls kicked my shins, while the widow read her paper."

"We crossed a country full of beautiful churches, and had lovely pancakes for lunch."

"Everybody saluted us most respectfully before we hoisted anchor at Brest."

"The American soldiers aboard are very noisy. Those who are taking French wives home with them are the most subdued, for the sensible French girls have found the hidden liquor and thrown it overboard when their husbands were on deck. . . ."

"We are having frightful storms. I have not taken my clothes off for four nights and days. Seasickness is one of the worst diseases known to civilized man. The American doctor has assured me I have suffered more than any one he has ever seen. It does not help that soldiers come to look at me and joke and offer me cigars. It only makes me sicker. It is frightful that I cannot get to His Eminence to help him. Why did we ever leave the comfortable hall of the Archbishop's palace? I think of 'Molenberg' and the old saying, 'an old cart in the fog is better than a good ship at sea.' God protect us."

"I'm in New York. A boat all covered with Belgian and American flags has come out to meet and welcome us."

"There are military bands and many committees. Silk hats must be cheap in this Wonderland. We followed one of the Committees to the Archbishop's palace, to the sweet strains of the Belgian and American national airs. I am very grieved that I so often have to stay with the baggage, when I might be employing my time more usefully."

"People constantly speak to me in French, proving that it is nonsense to tell me this is not a cultivated race, despite its being so far from Belgium."

"Wonder of wonders! The Archbishop of New York has a man who serves at the table who is a real *Luxembourgois*, and the cook is French. It is *'rigolo'* in the servants' hall. Mgr. Hayes lives in what I must call a terrestrial paradise."

"Before going to sleep, I must jot down that I have eaten a milk soup with fish in it. They say it is nourishing, though it tastes badly. They say it is not made of snails."

"More surprises— The door opens and in walks Sister Marie, from the Louvain Convent. I have promised to have His Eminence bless her. Of course I can arrange it when I undress him tonight."

APPENDIX

"We have a travelling habitation in which a pious railroad director or head stationman (though with very little gold lace) is going to roll us around America. I have never imagined such an installation. Sleeping rooms, smoking room, cardroom, bathroom, kitchen, and reading room. Everything just as good as in a château, and three negroes—the cook could lick the tar out of the best whites."

"We are now on board this rolling paradise, going at a terrible pace through vast prairies and forest, and once in a while I see cattle not half as fat as at home."

"The buildings are sometimes so tall that those who live in the attics need surely never fear floods."

"We are in Baltimore,[1] which I think is a lucky place, for the potatoes in the fields round about are in flower, while at home we are still eating last year's."

"It is so hot now that we sleep with open windows. That is not dangerous in this country, but it is dangerous to look at some of the women, for these proud daughters of Eve wear so little clothing."

"There are more motors in America than persons in Belgium, and women drive them too, at a terrible speed, with as little concern as if they were rolling hoops. These astonishing women drive their cars as well as the best of peasants drive their farm carts at home."

"Here at Mgr. Gibbons', we have black servants who have to work, and white ones who only make believe they do. They all eat a great deal, and meat everyday, except of course, on Fridays. We have three sisters who look after bedrooms. Two black servants are dressed as finely as the King's servants at home."

"If you are shaved, it costs you, if you please, eight francs. You could buy a beautifully smelling piece of soap for that price at home."

[1] When asked which city he preferred, New York or Baltimore, Mercier replied, diplomatically: "They are as alike as two tumblers both filled with the same beverage, only one is larger than the other."

APPENDIX

"We have returned to New York where we are going to stay this time. His Eminence was very glad to hear from me that there are two million Catholics and the Governor and Burgomaster have been elected because they are of the Faith."

"You would not know us, for though His Eminence and I remain as virtuous as Mother Superiors, we are accompanied by twelve *Sergents-de-ville*. Everybody is pushed aside by them. One of them took me to the zoo, and they all took His Eminence to the Cathedral, which is closer to the Archbishop's Palace than St. Rombaut is to ours."

"There is much luxury in New York. I have been told masons and carpenters roll to work in their autos, but perhaps they were merely stuffing me."

"Now we have gone back south again to Virginia. Mr. Ryan has been very kind to us. He has a friend who has sixteen servants and fifteen automobiles, and makes his own ice and electricity, or directs it when he has no guests and the servants wish to work."

"Today we are in Philadelphia. Almost all the citizens are Catholics. They have given His Eminence much money, for they are much more generous than in any European city."

"Whenever our train passes, there are pious people to salute us. Some of them almost fall under the train in order to be blessed. In Blackstone they live in wooden houses so as not to be too hot."

"At Springfield, there were immense crowds, and twelve Catholic churches. The population is about as it would have been in the earliest days of Christianity."

"Boston is a very big city, surrounded by beautiful *châteaux*, all built on a mountain chain surrounding the City. The King and the Cardinal were received in American fashion. The Cardinal wore his best clothes at a nearby University town."

"Now we are travelling again. Bengalese candles have been lit in the stations. The bands have played the *Brabançonne*,

296

and we have been deeply moved. I am sorry that where we visited I saw the servants cleaning the house on Sunday."

"We are on the way to Canada, and one of our faithful negroes has told a friend who has told me in French that both workmen and millionaires travel, sitting on cushions. Just think of it. I have even seen washstands and bureaus being transported by automobiles, to say nothing of the meanest curé or village abbé. I have met a Fleming, and I was mighty glad. A boulevard leads to his farm instead of a dirt-filled country lane. He sells more beans in the fall than are on the *Grande Place* of Malines from the Assumption to Christmas."

"Niagara is one of the marvels of the world. Its vapor wet us in two minutes. The river has two branches, each as big as the Escaut."

"We are on the road to Cleveland, surrounded by vineyards, and the poor people must eat the grapes, for they dare not drink their juice. Drinking water with meals certainly is harmful to their digestion."

"Mr. Ford has shown us his factories in a place called Detroit. They are larger than Witte Peeter's factories. The workmen earn tremendous salaries. I am sure they could all, if frugal and saving, retire and buy nice little country properties or lucrative '*estaminets.*' Everybody is rich, but His Eminence has warned me not to think so much of money, but to say my prayers oftener. Even when I do, I can't help thinking what I would do if I earned ten dollars or three hundred and fifty francs a day."

"St. Louis is a bad place. I hope we will never come back, for though it is the end of October, rivers of perspiration run down our faces. You cannot wear your underclothes as long as you should, and it is hard to keep His Eminence's lace looking neatly starched. I arrive at Mass as wet as if I had been in bathing."

"We are in the Columbia,[2] and the press printed every word

2 *I.e.,* District of Columbia.

we said two and a half hours after we had spoken. What do you think of that? President Wilson is sick."

"Most of the people in Pittsburgh are negroes and irreligious. There are many oil wells."

"We are once more on the way to Canada. There are mountains around us, and François is sewing on His Eminence's cape. We were waked up at midnight by people shouting, 'Long live Cardinal Mercier.' "

"Here it is winter. The cities and villages have the names of saints. I am glad to say there are many cathedrals in Quebec and even its river has the name of its patron saint. Thank God, the people speak French so I can speak to every one once more."

"We are again at sea, surrounded by birds fed by generous passengers. I have also told His Eminence there are two whales and an iceberg."

The observant and humble writer of these diary extracts, who dogged his master's footsteps so faithfully for nineteen years, was asked whether he had not other vivid recollections of the Cardinal. He responded with the following homely recital:

"During the first days of my service in 1907, I was struck by the Cardinal's great goodness and love towards us all. His serious and austere life did not prevent him from always having a smile on his lips. Once when I asked him how he could always be so pleasant and cheerful, he replied, 'When one is in God's service, then whatever happens, nothing affects you.' Once when he had been working very hard for several days, I begged him to rest. He only answered, 'There will be plenty of time for that in eternity.' "

"I once remarked on the kindly reception he had given a most ungrateful person. His Eminence answered very seriously, 'Franz, when you were living with your father and mother and your brothers and sisters were at times sick, were they not treated with more loving care than you who were well? Well, I am the father of all and act as did your parents.' "

APPENDIX

"When the war broke out, His Eminence shook my hand sadly, saying, 'Franz, do your duty as a soldier, and I will do mine as a priest.' When he heard of our home being burned, he went to comfort my parents. He was a father to me during my nineteen years of service."

"On leaving Rome, I asked His Eminence whether I should not buy some food for the journey home. His Eminence replied, 'The heat will dry it up, we will buy it en route.' I tried to purchase some in Milan, but did not succeed. When we reached Paris, I again asked whether I might not purchase food, for I felt frightfully empty. His Eminence answered laughingly, 'It is scarcely worth while, we are almost at home,' and so we continued starving until we reached Malines."

"And another time, the Cardinal said to me, 'Never mention a fault you may see in your neighbor, for the same neighbor may see a larger fault in you. We constantly demand perfection in our neighbors, while we are ignorant of our own faults. If every one said what he thought, there would be no more friends. . . .'"

" 'Treat him whom you believe to be your enemy with greater love than any one else. He will soon become your friend.' "

APPENDIX

FAMILY TREE

OF DÉSIRÉ FÉLICIEN FRANÇOIS JOSEPH MERCIER

Arms: Azur, with a chevron, or, on which three roses, argent.

Pierre Mercier—1663
owner of the farm of Williamsbrauz, near Nivelles
m. Marie Resjean

Nicholas—1701	Guillaume	Jean
	Entered a monastery	b. 1648-1693
m. Jeanne Du Vieusart		
(and had seven children)		

Guillaume Joseph Mercier (3rd son of Nicholas)
b. 1684-1732
m. (1712) Barbe Marguerite Dorothée Dernanet
moved to the farm of Basse-Court, Braine l'Alleud
(and had seven children)

Jean Joseph Mercier
b. 1718 at Braine l'Alleud–1776
lived on the farm of Tout-li-faut
m. Dame Anne Catherine Gobbe, b. 1717–1759
(and had seven children)

François Joseph Mercier
b. 1774 at Braine l'Alleud—1790
Cultivated the farm of Basse-Court, Braine l'Alleud
m. Dame Marie Françoise Tumerille of Ophaim-Bois-Seigneur

François Joseph Mercier
b. Jan. 24, 1771   d. July 18, 1841
m. Dame Marie Therese Hulet, b. Jan. 22, 1773   d. June 18, 1851

Paul Léon Hubert Mercier
b. July 19, 1808, at Braine l'Alleud   d. Sept. 11, 1858
m. Dame Marie Barbe Croquet, b. Aug. 27, 1815   d. Feb. 2, 1882

Estelle	Emerence	Clara	Léontine	*Désiré Félicien*
(Sœur Marguerite)	(Sœur Salesia)	(Mère Marie-	b. 1850	*François Joseph*
b. 1843	b. 1845	Madeleine)		Cardinal, Archbishop
		b. 1848		of Malines
				b. Nov. 22, 1851, at
Jeanne	Elise	Léon		Braine l'Alleud
b. 1853	b. 1856	Lucien Adolph		d. Jan. 23, 1926,
		b. 1857		at Brussels

300

APPENDIX

TRANSLATION OF THE FIRST PAGE OF DRAFT OF MGR. MERCIER'S ORIGINAL SCHEME FOR THE INSTITUT SUPÉRIEUR DE PHILOSOPHIE AS FORWARDED BY HIM TO POPE LEO XIII

Louvain, July 27, 1889.

Very Holy Father:

Acting upon the orders which I have had the honor of receiving from Your Holiness, I have attempted to give in the following pages the antecedents, the object, the organization and the conditions governing the execution and future stability of the Higher School of Philosophy which Your Holiness proposes to found at Louvain.

The supreme authority of the Vicar of Jesus Christ as well as the high confidence with which He has deigned to honor me imposes upon me the duty of speaking with all frankness and I obey Him most heartily.

I shall start by making a brief historical account of the project which is now to be executed.

1. The *History* of the project. In September, 1882, the Holy Father took the initiative in founding a chair of Higher Philosophy at the University of Louvain. He declared formally that He wished it to be "His Institution," and deigned from the outset to charge the occupant to study the means whereby the teaching of the philosophy of St. Thomas might be developed as far as possible.

In 1885, I was ordered to Rome, and during the audiences which I had the signal honor of being given, His Holiness decided to increase my courses of instruction and found a complete Institute to be placed under His august patronage.

I was instructed to inform the Lord Bishops of His Holiness' project and to invite them on His behalf to seek the means to put it into effect. The absorbing duties of the Belgian episcopate hindered them from taking the matter up actively prior to the reunion which was held in Malines in July 1887. At this reunion, the Belgian episcopate expressed unanimously its desire to carry out the intentions of the Holy Father, but was forced to add its regrets that owing to lack of funds it could not do so immediately. I was instructed to bring to Rome the resolutions of my superiors and in their name to solicit the financial support of the Holy Father. His Holiness led them to believe that this might also be expected and at the General Audience given the Belgians in April, 1888, He recommended particularly to Catholic generosity . . .

301

APPENDIX

REFERENCES

Ageorges, Joseph: *Le Cardinal Mercier.* 1927.

L'Annuaire de l'Université de Louvain, 1920–6, 1927–9.

Batifol, Pierre: "La lettre du Cardinal Mercier et la conscience catholique" (*Le Correspondent,* 1915).

Baudrillart, Mgr.: *Éloge Funèbre du Cardinal Mercier.* 1926.

Berger-Creplet: *Une figure mondial. Le Cardinal Mercier intime.* 1928.

Biervliet, A.: *Le Cardinal Mercier. Souvenirs Intimes.*

Blondel, Georges: *Le Cardinal Mercier.*

Bonnefon, Jean de: *Le Cardinal Mercier.* 1919.

Cammaerts, E.: "Cardinal Mercier in Occupied Belgium" (*Fortnightly Review*).

Catholic Encyclopedia.

Charles, Pierre: "Mercier, L'Écrivain Spirituel" (*La Revue Neo-Scolastique de Philosophie,* May, 1926).

Coffey, Rev. P.: Cardinal Mercier. 1926.

Davignon, Henri: "Le Cardinal Mercier et la Guerre" (*La Revue Hebdomadaire*) Jan. 30, 1915.

Dessain, F.: Souvenirs (*Revue du Collège Cardinal Mercier,* June, 1932).

Dubly, Henry Louis: *The Life of Cardinal Mercier.* 1928.

Gibson, Hugh: *A Journal from our Legation in Brussels.* 1917.

Goyau, Georges: *Cardinal Mercier.* 1926.

Haflants: *Le Cardinal Mercier.* 1919.

Harry, Gerard: "Le Cardinal Mercier" (*Annales Politique et Littéraire*).

Herscher, Mgr.: *Le Cardinal Mercier.*

Jehan d'Ivray: *Le Cardinal Mercier.*

Joannes, G.: *Cardinal Mercier.*

Jonghe de, Chanoine P.: *Le Cardinal Mercier.* 1926.

Kirsky, Wilhelm: *Der Kardinal Mercier und Wir.* 1926.

Ladeuze, Mgr.: *Inauguration du Monument de Mercier à l'Institut Supérieur de Philosophie.* May, 1931.

Lancken-Wakenitz, Baron Oscar v. d.: *"Meine dreissig Dienstjahre."* 1931.

Laveille, Mgr. A.: *Cardinal Mercier.* 1926.

Lechartier, G.: "S. E. le Cardinal Mercier et son Œuvre" (*Le Correspondent,* 1915).

Leclercq, L'Abbé Jacques: *La grande figure du Cardinal Mercier.*

Lenzlinger, Dr. jur. Joseph: *Kardinal Mercier.*

Levy, Raphael Georges: *Le Cardinal Mercier. L'Académie de Sciences Morales et Politiques.* 1926.

APPENDIX

Marès, Roland de: "Le Cardinal Mercier" (*Revue de Paris,* 1926).

Massart, Jean: *The secret press in Belgium.*

Mercier, Cardinal: *À Mes Seminaristes.* 1908.

—— *The Origins of Contemporary Psychology.* 1918.

—— *Œuvres Pastorales,* I–VII. 1906–1928.

—— *La Vie Intérieure.* 1919.

—— *Les Conversations de Malines.*

Mercier, Charles: "La Vie du Cardinal Mercier" (*La Revue Universelle*).

Le Cardinal Mercier, 1851–1926. Edition Lucien Desmet-Vertenueil. 1927.

Milot, A.: "La mort du Cardinal Mercier" (*Revue Générale,* Feb., 1926).

Noël, Chanoine Léon: "Le Cardinal Mercier et l'Esprit de son œuvre philosophique" (*Le Flambeau,* March, 1926).

Noël, Mgr. Léon: In *Histoire de la Belgique Contemporaine,* 1830–1914, Vol. III, 1930.

—— "L'Œuvre Philosophique du Cardinal Mercier" (*Bulletin*).

Preville, de R. P.: *Le Cardinal Mercier.* 1926.

Ramaekers, G.: *Le Grand Cardinal Belge.* 1926.

Revue Néo-Scolastique: Feb. and May, 1926.

Roupain, Eugene: *Un caractère—Le Cardinal Mercier.*

Roux: *Mercier.* 1915.

Rutten, Père O. P.: "Le Cardinal Mercier" in *Études religieuses* No. 141.

Schyrgens, Mgr.: "Mercier" (*Revue Catholique des Idées et des Faits,* 1926).

Seeholtzer, Dr. jur. H.: *Kardinal Mercier.* 1925.

Stillemans, Rev. Joseph F.: *Cardinal Mercier, Pastoral Letters and Allocutions.*

Velge, Henri: *Le Collégiale des Saints Michel et Gudule de Bruxelles.*

Vermeersch: "À la pieuse mémoire du Cardinal Mercier" (*Nouvelle Revue Théologique*).

Vervoort, C.: *Kardinaal Mercier.*

La Vie Diocésane, 1924–5–6.

Waha, Baron de: *Memorial du Cardinal Mercier.*

Weltschinger, Henry: *Le Cardinal Mercier.*

de Wulf, Maurice: *History of Mediæval Philosophy.*

—— *Notice sur le Cardinal Mercier.* 1927.

—— "Le Cardinal Mercier, philosophe et initiateur." (*La Revue Néo-Scolastique de Philosophie*), May, 1926.

INDEX

Abbé Joseph, literary executor, 262
Abbeloos, Mgr., 58, 62; becomes rector, 53; dismissed, 60
Adrian, of Utrecht, 20
Adrien, brother of Madame Barbe, 3; called *the Saint of Oregon*, 4
Æterni Patris, encyclical by Leo XIII, 27 f.
Albert, King of the Belgians, 129, 131, 138, 177, 214, 224, 253, 290, quoted, 150; fine qualities of, 255 f.
Albertus Magnus, 26
Ambrose, St., 203
American Relief, 182
Anthones, Coadjutor Bishop, president of the Seminary, 19
Aquinas, St. Thomas, 21, 26, 41, 49, 55, 75, 203; quoted, 45, 131; his philosophy, 26 f.; statue of, 64; recognized everywhere, 82; three elementary requirements for waging a righteous war, 131
Aristotle, 26, 32, 38, 41
Augustine, St., 48, 70, 203; *De Veræ Vitæ Cognitione Libellus*, 38; *Singularitate Clericorum*, 38
Aurelius, Marcus, quoted, 101

Balmes, Spanish philosopher, 32
Barbe, Madame, mother of Mercier, 4, 6, 7, 8; saintship of, 3; moves to shabby quarters, 4; difficulties of, 8; portrait of, 103
Basil, Catholic Father, 203
Battifol, Mgr., 243
Bautin, traditionalist, 30
Beaconsfield, flattery of, 18
Becker, de, 86
Beeser, de, Canon, headmaster, 14
Beethoven, 124
Belgian clergy, fighting spirit of, 112 f.; higher education of, 115 f.
Belgians, a national union of, 113; deportation of, 178
Belgium, 8, 24; political history of, 95 f.; its internal dissensions, 96 f.; problem of schools, 97; language question, 97; political history of, 111 f.; Catholic church in, 116 f.; isolated in

World War, 129; a unified country, 130; temporary government of Germans, 139
Beneden, Van, biologist, 49
Benedict XV, Pope, 135, 251; quoted, 186; summons Mercier to Rome, 158; protests, 181; aids Mercier, 185; his unfortunate words, 246
Berard, French Minister at Brussels, quoted, 252
Bétancourt, M. de, quoted, 73
Bethmann-Hollweg, von, quoted, 130
Bissing, von, 184, 185, 187; Governor-General, 139; acts regarding Mercier, 150; refrains from punishment of Mercier, 162; prepares for Independence Day, 168; publishes decrees, 183
Boerenbond, organization of, 115
Bossuet, 70, 104, 233, 240; his *Meditations on the Gospel*, 127
Botticelli, *Annunciation*, 103
Bourne, Cardinal, 244
Boutroux, Emile, tribute to Mercier, 271
Bradford, Gamaliel, quoted, 45
Braine l'Alleud, town of, 2, 11, 21, 32, 87, 252, 259, 260, 261, 275
British, opinion on church unity, 244
Bruges, 83
Brussels, 1, 24, 252
Bülow, Prince von, War Chancellor of German Empire, 130

Cæsar, quoted, 128
Cajetan, Church Father, 203
Call to Reunion, A, by Lord Halifax, 243
Cambrai, region of, 1, 2
Canon law, 13
Cartuyvels, Mgr., friend of Mercier, 201
Catholic Association of St. Francis Xavier, the, a boys' club, 11
Catholic Institute of Paris, 82
Catholic Unity, Mercier's letter, 243
Catholics, 97, 155, 240; not dominant party in Belgium, 84 f.; on good terms with Liberals, 113 f.
Cattani, Mgr., Papal Nuncio, 21
Cauvenbergh, Van, vicar-general, 103
Cauwelaert, van, advised by Mercier, 43

INDEX

Cercle d'Étude, name given to discussion group, 44
Ceretti, Cardinal, 186
Charcot, at *Salpetrière* in Paris, 34
Charles, of Hapsburg, 20
Chartreux, Denis le, manuscripts by, 38
Château du Castegier, 2, 4
Cherubino, musician, 124
Chesterton, G. K., quoted, 166
Chislehurst, residence of Napoleon, minor, 18
Chrysostom, John, Church Father, 203
Church of England, 242, 247
Church unity, difficulties, 243 f.
Cicero, *Officia,* 38
Ciencia tomista, founded, 82
College of Bishops, 53, 56
Collège Cardinal Mercier, 259, 275
Collinet, Monsieur, professor of Comparative Literature, 57
Commune in Paris, 18
Congregation of Studies, 56, 57, 60, 158
Congress of Vienna, 98
Council of Bishops, 57
Council of Trent, 127, 251; quoted, 12
Cours de Philosophie, 80
Criteriologie, 69, 80
Crooy, Mgr., Bishop of Tournai, 156
Croquet, character of, 3

Damien, Father, 210
Darwin, *The Descent of Man,* 18, 32
Davidson, Thomas Randall, Archbishop of Canterbury, 243
De Veræ Vitæ Cognitione Libellus by St. Augustine, 38
Denyn, Jef, greatest of *carillonneurs,* 89, 105, 251
Deploige, M., pupil of Mercier, 42, 65, 66; in sociology, 55
Députation Permanente, 13
Descartes, philosopher, 27, 56
Descent of Man, The, by Darwin, 18
Deschamps, Cardinal, 22
Desiré, see Mercier
Dessain, Francis, Mercier's secretary, 137, 146, 200, 215, 217, 220, 252, 275, 276, 286; quoted, 107, 274
Dionysus, Mercier's study of, 203
Dordolot, of the Abbeloos faction, 86

Edmond, the old janitor, quoted, 66
Edouard, Cousin, 6
Elise, sister of Mercier, 4
Elocution in the lower school, 13
Emerson, Ralph Waldo, 111

Ephrem, Père, statue of Mercier by, 63
Epistles of St. Paul, learned by Mercier, 19
Eucken, Rudolf, recognizes work of Mercier, 82
Evrard, Monsignor, 86, 151

Faber, Father, writings of, cause stir in London, 69
Falkenhausen, Baron von, becomes Governor-General of Belgium, 188, 190, 194
Ferdinand, General-Oberst Moritz, 140
Fête Nationale, 6
Fichte, Mercier's knowledge of, 32, 192
Forêt de Soignes explored by Mercier and his brother Léon, 7
Francis, St., 76, 108
Francis de Sales, St., likeness, 94; his *Introduction to a Devout Life,* 127
Francis Xavier, St., 210
Francqui, Emile, president of the *Comité,* 177, 190
Franz, Mercier's faithful valet, 107, 109, 136, 214, 263; extracts from diary, 293-299

Gasparri, Cardinal, 243
Gasquet, Cardinal, 244
Gehuchten, Van, professor of neurology, 49
Geography, studied by Mercier, 13
German Empire, proclaimed, 18
Germans and the World War, 128 f.; efforts to discover printing-press, 169 f.; orders for deportation of Belgians, 175 f.; overture to Belgian Government, 189
Ghent, Bishop of, 83
Gibbons, Cardinal, 213; visit of Mercier, 220
Gibson, Hugh, Secretary of the American Legation, 135, 181
Gioberti, philosopher, 30
Giraud, Victor, quoted, 136
Gladstone, reforms of, 18
Goltz, von der, General, Governor-General, 139
Goossens, Cardinal, death of, 83
Gore, Bishop, the Dean of Wells, 243
Gounod, musician, his music forbidden, 124
Grand, le, M., quoted, 123
Grand Séminaire, 8, 19; Mercier enters, 17
Gregorian Chant, 13, 124

306

INDEX

Gregory the Great, 203
Gudule, Ste., Cathedral of Brussels, 170

Halifax, Lord, English nobleman, 280, 285; interested in church union, 241; visits the Pope, 242; his *A Call to Reunion*, 243
Hartmann, von, Cardinal, quoted, 141
Harvard University confers degree on Mercier, 218
Haydn, his music forbidden, 124
Hebbelynck, the new rector, 60
Hegel, antagonism to, 192
Heineman, Leopold, incident related by, 166
Helleputte, Monsieur, plans for buildings, 61
Hemnen, Abbé, meeting with Mercier, 243
Henry IV, façade of the time of, 14
Hermite, l', Mercier's retreat, 275; Mercier's last visit to, 276
Herry, Gerard, quoted in *Annales Politiques et Littéraires*, 47
Hertling, von, Chancellor, 185
Heupgen, Georges, quoted, 237 f.
Heylen, van, Mgr., bishop of Namur, 86
History, studied by Mercier, 13
Hoover, Herbert, 153, 206; quoted, 183; his plan for feeding Belgian children, 152; opinion of von der Lancken and Germans, 195; his instructions, 196
Hout, van der, Abbé, editor, 169
Huene, von, General, military governor, 139
Humanists, Fifteenth-century, 28
Huxley, drawn away from science, 18, 32

Ibsen, his message, 18
Ignatius, St., 210
Imitation of Christ, by Thomas à Kempis, 127
Institute, scheme of Mercier's, 52; becomes integral part of University, 54; produces many books, 82; at Rome, 82; at Cologne, 82; at Innsbruck, 82
Institutiones Philosophiæ, by Father Tongiorgi, 16
Introduction to a Devout Life, by St. Francis de Sales, 127
Iron Chancellor, his dream, 18

James, William, quoted, 272; *Varieties of Religious Experience*, 70
Janson, Paul, associate of Mercier on temperance, 231

Janssen, speaking likeness of Mercier, 63, 190
Jeanne, sister of Mercier, 4
Jerome, St., 210; spiritual companion of Mercier, 203
Jesuits, friction with University of Louvain, 24
Johnson, Doctor, compared to Mercier, 163
Joyeuse Entrée, of Wencelsas, Duke of Brabant, 35

Kant, Mercier's antagonism to, 25, 32, 192
Kempis, Thomas à, manuscripts by, 38; his *Imitation of Christ*, 127
Kidd, Doctor, of Keble College, 243

La Force, M., teacher of Mercier, 12
La Libre Belgique, sheet published during German occupation, 168
La Mennais, traditionalist philosopher, 30
Ladeuze, Mgr., quoted, 67
Laforet, Rector Magnificus, of University of Louvain, 29
Lalaings, castle of the, 14
Lambeth, council at, 242
Lancken, von der, aide of German Governor-General, 142, 155, 173, 174, 182, 188, 189, 192, 195, 262; quoted, 191 f., 194; character of, 147; calls on Mercier, 148
Latin, Mercier's defense in the best, 4, 16; in the lower school, 13; Latin scholarship advocated, 56
Lebbe, Abbé, meets Dessain in Rome, 200
Leclercq, Abbé Jacques, quoted, 273
Legraive, vicar-general, 103; bishop, 251
Leibnitz, in Latin language, 56, 240
Leman, General, defender of the fort of Loncin, 153
Leo XIII (*see* Pecci), 56, 61, 233, 241; quoted, 178; appearance of, 24; friend of Leopold I, 24; turns to Middle Ages, 25; affected by low spiritual tone, 25; finds his answer in Aquinas, 26; encyclical entitled *Æterni Patris*, 27 f.; founds academy, 29; brings forth edition of St. Thomas Aquinas, 29; proceeds with practical measures, 29; founds chair at University of Louvain, 30; questions Mercier, 33; insists on a return to

INDEX

America, 220; reaches London, 222; returns home, 222; catholicity of his interests, 223; some of his efforts, 224; his pastoral letters on Belgian life, 225; his speeches, 226; address, *The Poetic Genius of Dante*, 226; respect for Dante, 227; his culture is French, 230; on relations of the sexes, 230; on patriotism, 230; and the temperance movement, 231; practical social work, 232; founds the *Association de la Jeunesse Catholique*, 232; organizes the *Union Internationale d'Études Sociales*, 232; on Socialism, 233; on Capitalism, 234 f.; on Socialism, 235 f.; on the working classes, 236 f.; sponsor of church unity, 240; Cardinal, enlisted in cause of church unity, 243; his letter, *Catholic Unity*, 243; goes to Rome for election of Pope, 247; goes to Rome for opening of Holy Gate, 248; assists in canonization of M. Vianney, 249; convokes Council of Malines, 251; jubilee, in 1924, 252 f.; love for King Albert, 255; prayer for King Albert, 258; affection of students for, 259; his retreat, *l'Hermite*, 260; the support of Léon's family, 261; his motor accident, 263; his day's work at l'Hermite, 265 f.; his love for nature, 268; his last speech, 270; questions Foch, 271; prayer the essence of his religion, 272; his physical suffering, 274; King and Queen receive his last blessing, 283; his last pastoral letter, 284; his last letter, 286; his last Mass, 288; death of, 289; his funeral, 290 f.

Mercier, François-Joseph, called affectionately, *Le Vieux Maire*, father of Désiré, 2

Mérode, Cléo de, the blandishments of, 18

Meunier, 63, 102; called upon by Mercier, 47

Micara, Monseigneur, 253

Milan, University of, influence of Institute upon, 82

Milton, John, quoted, 45

Mittendorf, Mgr., Chief Catholic Chaplain for German armies, 152

Monsieur le Baron, park of, 7

Montague, shrine of Our Lady of, 66

Montalembert, Mercier's enthusiasm for, 19

Montmartre, the streets of, 18

Moretus, Count, friend of Mercier, 136

Mozart, his music forbidden, 124

Namur, bishop of, 83, 128

Napoleon, time of, 20

Napoleon, minor, at Chislehurst, 18

Navez, the painter, 2

Newman, Cardinal, 24, 25, 69, 241; quoted, 29; *Idea of a University*, 29

Newton, corresponded in Latin, 56

Nietzsche, professor of classical philology, 18

Noël, Monseigneur, successor to Mercier, 77; quoted, 80

Nys, in cosmology, 55, 58, 65

Officia, by Cicero, 38

Oliviers, Father, teacher of Mercier, 4, 5, 6, 21, 276; appointed Vicar of Our-Lady-Beyond-the-Dyle in the Cathedral City of Malines, 7; finds lodging for Désiré, 9

Ontologie, 69, 80

Oregon trail, the, 3

Origins of Contemporary Psychology, by Mercier and Mgr. Pelzer, 70

Our Lady, shrine of, 66

Oxford Movement, 241

Papal Nuncio, 24

Paul, St., 70, 203, 254

Paul Henry, professor of chemistry, 49

Paul-Léon, a puzzle to his father, 2; marries Barbe Croquet, 3; death of, 4

Pecci (*see* Leo XIII), sent to Brussels as Papal Nuncio, 24; elected to Papal throne, as Leo XIII, 24

Pelzer, Mgr., collaborator with Mercier in *Origins of Contemporary Psychology*, 70

Pensionnaire, 13

Perosi, choirmaster, 123, 133

Petit Séminaire, buildings of, 8, 14, 17

Piaeraerts, Father, 53; headmaster, 11; teacher of Mercier, 12; rector of Louvain, 31, 51

Philosophy, in the upper school, 13; two years to be completed, 14; had lost its authority, 25; a systemized reality, 41

Pius X, approves Mercier, 76; death of, 131

Pius XI, 233, 243, 246, 248, 251, 253; quoted, 254

Plato, 26, 32, 119

Poincaré, quoted, 200

310

INDEX

Pompiers, drill of the, 6
Pope, election of Cardinal della Chiesa, Benedict XV, 133
Pope's College, dormitory at Louvain, 20
Portal Abbé, Catholic priest, 240, 241, 242, 285
Princeton University confers degree on Mercier, 218
Prisco, master of Thomism, 33
Psychologie, work of Mercier, 80

Queen of Belgium, 129; Mercier's affection for, 258 f.; receives Mercier's last blessing, 283

Ratti (*see* Pius XI), 247; chosen Pope, 248
Rampolla, Cardinal, 241
Revue Catholique des Idées et des Faits, 39
Revue Néo-Scolastique, 69, 79, 82
Rhetoric, in lower school, 13
Rivista di Filosofia neoscolastica, founded, 82
Robert, M., teacher of Mercier, 12
Roey, van, Vicar General, 103, 243, 251
Rombaut, St., 10, 89, 99, 123, 137, 161, 174, 190, 219, 250, 252, 276; College of, 8; curriculum of, 14
Rosmini, the antilogism of, 30
Rougon-Macquart, Les, by Zola, 18
Rousseau, du, Father, Mercier's headmaster, 14, 20, 22, 64
Rutten, Father, 136, 137; leader of Christian Socialist party, 232
Ryan, Mgr., head of Thurles Seminary, 73
Rydam, Demoiselles, home of, where Mercier lived as student, 9

Sacred College, 248
Saint-Simon, artist, picture of Fénelon, 202
Salpetrière, the work of, 45
Satolli, Cardinal, 60
Schelling, Mercier's antagonism for, 192
Scheuremanns, companion of Mercier, 9
Scheut missionaries, 64
Scholasticism, The New, founded, 82
Scholastik, founded, 82
Schopenhauer, Mercier's knowledge of, 32
Sciences, natural, in lower school, 13
Séminaire, aim of, 13

Séminaire Léon XIII, dormitory of the Institute's ecclesiastical students, 65
Simeon, Mercier's uncle, 6
Simons, Canon, 87; quoted, 59, 71; letter to, 70
Singularitate Clericorum, by St. Augustine, 38
Silesia, sister of Mercier, 4
Socrates, 32
Spencer, Herbert, 32; declaration of, 18; read by Mercier, 69
Stempel, von, Captain, adjutant, 149
Sureté Publique, the agents of, 35

Tacitus, Mercier's knowledge of, 10
Talamo, Mgr., master of Thomism, 33
Theology, in the schools, 13, 14
Thiery, M., in experimental psychology, 55, 61, 62, 65, 66, 72, 125
Thirty-third Moira, Wellesley's regiment, 1
Tocqueville, quoted, 95
Tongiorgi, Father, his *Institutiones Philosophiæ*, 16
Tournai, Bishop of, 83
Trent, Council of, decree of the, 12
Trooz, van, friend of Mercier, 86
Tyndall, John, his work studied by Mercier, 69

Vanutelli, Cardinal, 21
Varieties of Religious Experience, by William James, 70
Vatican Library, 70
Vaughan, read by Mercier, 69
Vercesi, Dom Ernest, friend of Mercier, 134
Verdun, battle of, 176
Vico, Cardinal, 85, 89, 134
Victoria, Queen, 17
Villalobar, Marquis de, Spanish Minister, 150, 181; suggests organization of committee, 182
Vischering, Clemens August Droste zu, Archbishop of Cologne, 162
Vrancken, Canon, Mercier's secretary, 132, 137

Wachter, de, vicar-general, 103, 251
Waffelaert, Mgr., candidate for cardinal, 86
Warny, printer, imprisoned by Germans, 71, 146
Waterloo, time of, 2, 7, 265
Weddingen, van (Mgr.), suggested as benefactor, 31

311

INDEX

Wellesley, Arthur, young Irish colonel, 1

Wergersky, Colonel, Kreischef of Malines, 151

Whitlock, Brand, American Minister to Belgium, 181, 213

Whittier, J. G., quoted, 91

William of Orange, 113

Wilson, President Woodrow, visits Mercier, 213; Mercier visits, 221

Wiseman, Cardinal, Catholic hierarchy in person of, 241

Wooters, canvases by, 102

Wulf, Maurice de, professor of history of mediæval philosophy, 55, 65, 71, 72, 73, 77; quoted, 72, 197, 210

Zigliara, master of Thomism, 33

Zola, 19; *Les Rougon-Macquart*, 18; his doses of crime, 18